D1614917

Debating Scotland

Debating Scotland

Issues of Independence and Union
in the 2014 Referendum

Edited by
Michael Keating

OXFORD
UNIVERSITY PRESS

OXFORD
UNIVERSITY PRESS

Great Clarendon Street, Oxford, OX2 6DP,
United Kingdom

Oxford University Press is a department of the University of Oxford.
It furthers the University's objective of excellence in research, scholarship,
and education by publishing worldwide. Oxford is a registered trade mark of
Oxford University Press in the UK and in certain other countries

First Edition published in 2017

Impression: 1

Published in the United States of America by Oxford University Press
198 Madison Avenue, New York, NY 10016, United States of America

British Library Cataloguing in Publication Data
Data available

Library of Congress Control Number: 2016946196

ISBN 978-0-19-878981-9

Printed in Great Britain by
Clays Ltd, St Ives plc

Preface

Referendums on independence are rare events in advanced, stable democracies. Only the Quebec referendums of 1980 and 1995 are truly comparable with Scotland's experience in 2014. Yet Scotland is far from being the only place in Europe, let alone the world, where demands for national self-determination have resurfaced in the early twenty-first century—Catalonia, the Basque Country, and Flanders are prominent examples. Scotland's experience provides us with an opportunity to examine the dynamics of self-determination in an intense form. The referendum campaign also furnishes an example of a society discussing its future in an uncertain world, as the debate widened from narrowly constitutional issues into questions about the economy, welfare, and citizenship.

We were privileged to observe these debates from close up in a major project funded by the Economic and Social Research Council (grant ES/L003325/1). Our Centre on Constitutional Change is a consortium of eight universities and research institutes, covering the disciplines of economics, politics, law, and social policy. Between 2012 and 2015 we conducted analyses of the economic, political, social, and legal implications of a Yes and a No vote and tracked the evolution of public opinion. We worked with both the Scottish and UK governments on their analysis papers, while remaining strictly neutral on the main independence vs union question. We were present in print, broadcast, and social media and organized and spoke at dozens of public events across Scotland and beyond. It is these experiences that form the material for this book.

We do not aim to explain the referendum result, although our other publications do analyse the vote. The objective here is, rather, to analyse the issues at stake and the arguments made by both sides. We are acutely aware of the ways in which policy analysis and political arguments were intertwined in the two campaigns and this is a recurrent feature of the chapters that follow. Few of the contentious issues were definitively resolved during the campaign and the constitutional issue was not closed by the 55 per cent to 45 per cent victory of No. Scotland remains a small European nation bound to its neighbours in a complex mesh of interdependence and the big challenges of sustainable growth, social cohesion, and equity remain. This will be the subject of our next major publication.

Michael Keating

Aberdeen and Edinburgh
December 2015

Contents

Contents

Contents

List of Figures

List of Tables

List of Contributors

David Bell is Professor of Economics at the University of Stirling

Coree Brown Swan is PhD candidate at the University of Edinburgh

Liam Delaney is Professor of Politics at the University of Stirling

David Eiser is Research Fellow at the University of Stirling

Colin Fleming is Research Fellow in the Centre on Constitutional Change

Malcolm Harvey is Research Fellow at the University of Aberdeen

Ailsa Henderson is Professor of Politics at the University of Edinburgh

Michael Keating is Professor of Politics at the University of Aberdeen, part-time Professor at the University of Edinburgh, and Director of the Centre on Constitutional Change

Patrizio Lecca is Research Fellow at the University of Strathclyde

Robert Liñeira is Research Fellow at the University of Edinburgh

Nicola McEwen is Professor of Territorial Politics at the University of Edinburgh and Associate Director of the Centre on Constitutional Change

Peter G. McGregor is Emeritus Professor of Politics at the University of Strathclyde

Bettina Petersohn is Lecturer in Politics at the University of Swansea

J. Kim Swales is Emeritus Professor of Politics at the University of Strathclyde

Stephen Tierney is Professor of Law at the University of Edinburgh

1

The Scottish Independence Debate

Michael Keating and Nicola McEwen

On 18 September 2014, Scotland held a referendum on the question: *Should Scotland be an independent country?* This is a most unusual event in modern politics.

In the late nineteenth century, Europe witnessed an 'awakening of the nations' as national movements emerged across the continent, challenging the consolidating states and the great empires. Following the First World War, the collapse of the Ottoman, German, Russian, and Habsburg empires gave birth to many new states. Even the British Empire lost the greater part of Ireland. Since the Second World War, many former colonies have gained independence. At the end of the twentieth century, the collapse of the Soviet Union and Yugoslavia produced yet more small states. None of these, however, quite compares with the case of Scotland, which belongs to a different group of cases: mature, democratic states (rather than empires), in which there is no manifest oppression. Other examples are found in Catalonia, Quebec, Flanders, and, perhaps, Northern Italy. These cases have long puzzled political scientists, who tended to regard national integration as a one-way process and secessionist movements as a sign of delayed modernization, or of real or imagined oppression.

The only one of these that had staged a formal independence referendum prior to 2014 is Quebec, which did so in 1980 and 1995, the latter being only narrowly defeated; but in that case the Canadian Government, while participating in the campaign, did not accept the referendum as binding. In 2014 the Catalan Government, unable for constitutional reasons to hold an official referendum, staged an unofficial 'consultation', but the conditions and the low turnout rendered it purely symbolic. Scotland, then, stands out as a unique case of an agreed referendum on an agreed question and a long period of intensive debate. Not surprisingly, it has attracted a lot of international

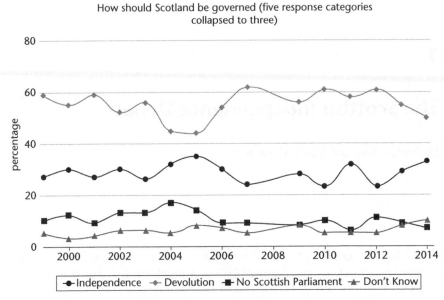

How should Scotland be governed (five response categories collapsed to three)

Figure 1.1. How should Scotland be governed, 1999–2014
Source: Scottish Social Attitudes Survey

interest as a way of debating the future of a nation and of resolving a self-determination claim in a peaceful and democratic manner.

One explanation for why there was a referendum in Scotland is down to short-term political tactics and happenstance. In 2007 the Scottish National Party (SNP) won a plurality of seats at the third elections to the Scottish Parliament, which had been established in 1999. The minority SNP government was perceived to have managed the country well and was re-elected with an absolute majority in 2011. This was not because of their policy of independence, since support for independence was actually falling slightly both in 2007 and in 2011 (see Figure 1.1). Having promised a referendum, they were obliged to deliver, hoping against the odds to win. Their unionist opponents, having opposed a referendum to that point, changed tack in the belief that they could call the nationalists' bluff, score an easy victory, and see off the idea of independence for a long time.

Such an explanation, however, is superficial and ignores longer-term trends in Scottish politics. A rival explanation is the 'slippery slope' argument, frequently deployed in the debates about Scottish devolution from the 1970s onwards. This holds that, by granting Scotland its own Parliament, the United Kingdom was unwittingly promoting its own disintegration since such a parliament would never be content with mere devolution. The institutional dynamics would inevitably propel it towards full independence, and Scottish

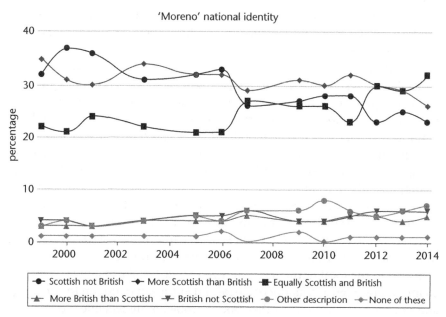

Figure 1.2. National identity in Scotland, 1999–2014
Source: Scottish Social Attitudes Survey

nationalists would always claim that more powers were needed and blame Westminster for policy failures. There is evidence for such a dynamic in the case of Belgium, where successive state reforms empower institutions, which in turn demand more; but it has never been demonstrated as a general rule. Devolution in other instances has been stabilizing, reinforcing the legitimacy of the state. There is evidence that this happened in Scotland after 1999. The (almost) annual Scottish Social Attitudes Surveys revealed that devolution failed to generate increased popular support for independence. Although being Scottish remained their primary attachment, Scots became more, rather than less, inclined to see themselves as British as well (see Figure 1.2).

We see the Scottish case, rather, as an instance of something more profound: the transformation of statehood itself in a changing domestic and international context. The twentieth-century nation-state represented an aspiration to construct a form of sovereign political order within fixed territorial boundaries. Within these boundaries, there would be a national society, a national economy, a system of authoritative government, a system of popular representation, and a sense of social solidarity. The nation would provide legitimacy for political order and affective solidarity. The state would provide the institutions for public policy. In what was known as the 'Keynesian welfare state', governments would undertake macroeconomic management and secure growth and full employment while providing social security through public services and welfare programmes. As well as a space for affective solidarity, the nation-state would furnish a space for a mutually beneficial social compromise between capital and labour.

Of course, this was never more than an ideal-type and many states contained fault-lines inherited from the past (Rokkan, 1999), but it did provide a strong rationale for national unity and centralization in the post-war period. Since the 1970s, however, the formula has come under a lot of strain. International free trade and capital mobility have reduced the capacity of states in macroeconomic management. Welfare compromises have been undermined as capital is more mobile than labour and can opt out by relocating. Social change has altered family and household structures and, along with job insecurity, posed new social risks and challenged the old welfare model. The rise of free-market ideology has questioned the desirability of government intervention in economic and welfare matters. In a process of spatial rescaling, some functions have migrated to the supranational level while others have relocated to the local or the regional (Keating, 2013). For example, economic change is now seen as a matter of global and European trends on the one hand and local conditions on the other. Social problems are redefined to take into account the local and regional context. Identities are reconfiguring as local identities are rediscovered (or created). Government is being restructured as new levels emerge above, below, and across the existing states. The most dramatic example is that of the European Union, which has in some ways helped the nation-state to survive (Milward, 2000) but in other respects has reduced its autonomy.

This has transformed understandings of statehood and independence. If states no longer command the levers of economic and social policy, then self-government may not be simply a matter of statehood but of governing capacity in a complex and interdependent world. The focus of debate might shift away from legal and constitutional issues towards substantive policy questions and how they can best be addressed. The new, interdependent world, and particularly the evolution of the European Union, may favour small states, which can sustain self-government while still retaining access to a large market. The cost of independence is thus lowered. On the other hand, small states are vulnerable and need to surrender some of their independence to enjoy the shelter of supranational bodies (Baldersheim and Keating, 2015).

Many scholars have argued that sovereignty itself has been transformed so as no longer to be unitary and attached only to nation-states. In a post-sovereign order, there may be multiple sources of sovereignty and different sovereign orders co-existing (MacCormick, 1999; Keating, 2001; Tierney, 2004). These understandings themselves may resonate with historic traditions in those societies where the principle of sovereignty was never definitively resolved; these include Scotland, where the meaning of the union settlement of 1707 has remained contested (MacCormick, 1999).

Scotland as a Political Community

Scotland is one of the clearest examples in Europe of a 'stateless nation'. Its national status has hardly ever been contested (unlike, say, Catalonia) in spite of it not being an independent state since the Union of 1707. Yet the meaning and salience of nationality have changed over the years, sometimes being primarily historical, at other times cultural or intensely political. The Union was a compromise, which left intact much of Scottish civil society, including the famous 'trinity' of law, education, and church, while merging the parliament with that of England.[1] While there was a fashion among some people in the nineteenth century to refer to North Britain, the identity of Scotland never disappeared, even as its political distinctiveness may have diminished.

The development of the modern state in Scotland from the late nineteenth century followed two rather different trends. On the one hand, there was an assimilation to a wider British state in fields such as economic policy, taxation, and (especially after 1945) welfare. On the other hand, there was some differentiation for Scotland, most clearly visible in the traditional reserves of law and education but also in the organization of new public services. The establishment of the Scottish Office in 1885 started a trend to administrative devolution in which the delivery of services, if not the basic policy lines, was increasingly organized differently in Scotland (Mitchell, 2014). In the course of the twentieth century, political behaviour in Scotland and England seemed to converge as the two-party Labour/Conservative pattern of competition was generalized. Yet, as this system has weakened we have become more aware that some of the convergence was only superficial. It has often been remarked that the only party to gain a majority of Scottish votes in the twentieth century was the Conservatives, but in reality this was the Scottish Unionist Party, a rather different social coalition from the Conservatives in England. Labour later came to dominate Scottish politics, but by combining British centre-left welfare and class politics with a role as a brokerage party, bringing resources to Scotland. Its peak was in 1966 when it gained 49.8 per cent of the Scottish vote.

Since then, Scottish voting behaviour has progressively diverged from that in England, and the main UK parties, while experiencing ups and downs, have

---

[1] Wales was legally absorbed into England in the sixteenth century, while retaining its national identity.

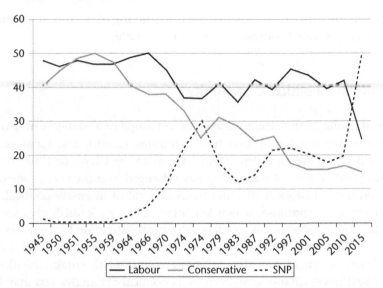

Figure 1.3. Percentage share of the vote in Scotland, General Elections, 1945–2015
Source: House of Commons Library and own compilation

progressively lost support, culminating spectacularly in the 2015 General Election, when the three unionist parties gained just one seat each, with the SNP almost exactly equalling previous Conservative and Labour highs, with 50 per cent of the popular vote (see Figure 1.3).

It is tempting to attribute this to some underlying divergence in social structures or attitudes, but that would be highly misleading. Over the same period, Scotland's social and economic structures have become more like those in the rest of the United Kingdom (Paterson, Bechhofer, and McCrone, 2004), while GDP per capita has converged. Scottish social attitudes do not differ markedly from those in England and, on matters of social liberalism, seem to have converged (Rosie and Bond, 2007). There is a slight but persistent tendency for Scotland to be to the left on issues of social equality and redistribution, but even in these matters the outliers may not be the Scots but people in the south of England (whose numbers weight the British averages) (Rosie and Bond, 2007). Rising support for nationalism in Scotland is thus an example of what Dion (1991), in the Quebec context, called de Tocqueville's paradox—where political divergence coincides with cultural convergence. Scotland has been reconstituted as a political community, the frame of reference for appraisal of political issues and political competition. It is in fact common for modern nationalisms to base their appeal not on particularism but on universal values, with the nation as the appropriate place to realize them.

Political Traditions in Scotland

Since the Union, and particularly since the advent of mass politics in the late nineteenth century, Scotland has had three political traditions with regard to the national question. The winning one, until the end of the twentieth century, has been unionism. Unlike its continental counterparts, British unionism has never been assimilationist (Kidd, 2008). On the contrary, it has accepted and even celebrated national diversity, including symbolic recognition of the home nations, but has sought to empty it of constitutional or political implications. As Colls (2002) put it, unionists never allowed the wires of nationality and statehood to be crossed. Indeed, unionists like A. V. Dicey (1912; Dicey and Rait, 1920) argued that home rule should not be extended to Ireland or Scotland precisely because they are nations so that their institutions would inevitably make claims to sovereignty; municipal self-government was another matter. During the twentieth century, another element was added in the form of 'welfare unionism' associated with the Labour Party, which argued that social solidarity should be state-wide and based on sharing (McEwen, 2006).

The second tradition is that of home rule or devolution. First formulated with regard to Ireland by the Liberal Party of W. E. Gladstone, home rule aimed to transform the United Kingdom into a family of self-governing nations combining local parliaments with an overarching one at Westminster. This has long been the preferred option in Scottish public opinion, but for over a hundred years was resisted by unionists in both Conservative and Labour parties (although both did contain home rule wings). Only at the very end of the twentieth century did the Gladstonian vision prevail, albeit without England.

The third tradition is that of independence, which did not become a serious option until the 1970s. It did, however, always remain a presence in the background of Scottish politics and reminded unionists of the contingency of the union settlement and the need to work continually to renew it. In the last thirty years, independence has become a major issue and recently even the main fault line in Scottish politics.

The boundaries between these three options have always been rather fluid. Unionists might change their tune if they felt that Scottish interests were not being served. Home rule proposals in the nineteenth and early twentieth centuries were usually placed in the context of the Empire or Commonwealth and, since the 1980s have been accompanied by support for European integration, avoiding the connotations of 'separatism'.

Devolution to Scotland in 1999 appeared to have simplified matters since, overnight, nearly all unionists accepted the new dispensation. Nationalists, previously divided between those often identified as 'gradualists' (who wanted incremental change) and 'fundamentalists' (who wanted nothing short of immediate independence) united on the next stage of the journey. Home rulers, defending reformed union, even started describing themselves as 'unionists'. It was not long, however, before the middle option re-emerged in the form of calls for further home rule or 'devo max'. This term is notoriously imprecise but most versions include three key items. The first is a post-sovereigntist conception of authority, in which Westminster supremacy is challenged. Second is control of most taxation powers. Third is Scottish control over large areas of welfare policy. In the most advanced version, Westminster would retain control of defence and foreign policy, and Holyrood would control everything else, although in a modern state the lines between foreign and domestic policy are difficult to draw, especially where the European Union is concerned.

Towards the Referendum

Recent decades, then, have witnessed, not a radical shift from a unitary conception of the United Kingdom towards a separatist agenda, but rather a realignment of these linked fields. Support for independence, when it was first measured in the late 1960s and 1970s, usually ran at around 20 per cent (Ipsos Mori, 2015). There was a step change during the late 1980s and 1990s, as Scotland was for eighteen years governed by a party, the Conservatives, with only minority and steadily declining support in Scotland until its defeat in 1997, when it lost all its remaining Scottish seats. Over the same period, support for independence increased to around 30 per cent, and sometimes a little more. Devolution in 1999 was partly intended to contain rising support for independence, and independence support did seem to stagnate. Surveys measuring constitutional preferences among the options of independence, devolution, or no Scottish Parliament, found that independence support ranged from 24 to 35 per cent between 1999 and 2014, with the lowest level of support recorded at the time of the SNP's first election victory in 2007 (What Scotland Thinks, 2014). However, the setting up of a Scottish Parliament and a Scottish Government created a platform and an opportunity for the pro-independence party to advance its goals, and provided a more realistic pathway to independence than had been thinkable when the SNP was confined to the political margins. On the other hand, the success of the nationalist party in governing Scotland under devolution suggested that Scottish aspirations to self-government could be met without independence.

The surprise success of the SNP in gaining an absolute majority of seats at the Scottish Parliament elections of 2011 pushed the issue to the fore. Until 2000 the historic policy of the SNP had been that winning a majority of the Scottish seats at Westminster would constitute a mandate for independence. They then changed tack to support a referendum whenever they could muster a majority in the Scottish Parliament to hold one. Conservatives, Labour, and Liberal Democrats insisted, after the SNP had formed a minority government in 2007, that there was no demand for a referendum and that it would be unconstitutional. The 2011 events, however, forced their hand and they accepted the referendum challenge. This in itself was a historic move, since it gave official recognition to what had long been accepted, even by Margaret Thatcher (1993) and John Major (1993), that Scotland could, if it really wanted, secede (although Thatcher said this in the context of insisting that it could not have devolution). This stands in marked contrast to Spanish governments, which have insisted that independence referendums cannot take place under any circumstances. The issue of constitutionality was dealt with briskly in the UK by passing a 'Section 30' order temporarily giving the Scottish Parliament the right to stage a referendum.

The Edinburgh Agreement, however, explicitly ruled out a 'third way' or 'devo max' option by stipulating that there should only be one question and that it should be about independence. The unionist parties were insistent on this point, anticipating an easy win. Nationalists were more inclined to accept a second question, calculating that it would make them look more reasonable and give them a second prize should the independence option fail, but they did not insist on it (Salmond, 2015).

Since the 'devo max' option was never elaborated into a real proposal, it is not possible to judge how much support it would have gained. It might just be that, faced with a binary choice, people will seek a middle ground, which by definition always exists. On the other hand, there is evidence that many voters favoured something like full domestic autonomy, especially control over taxes and welfare, but were not interested in the traditional trappings of sovereignty or in Scottish control of foreign and defence policy. Both sides in the referendum campaign were aware of this and sought to position themselves close to this middle ground. So the SNP presented a rather attenuated form of independence, described by some as 'independence lite', which it set out in the Scottish Government's (2013f) White Paper, published in November 2013. For their part, the unionist parties all had commissions working on more powers for Scotland and, in the last week of the campaign, issued a 'vow' to come up with proposals, with an agreement by St Andrew's Day (30 November) 2014 and draft legislation by Burns Night (25 January) 2015.

The Rules

Both Scottish and UK governments agreed that the referendum rules would be based on the principles of the Political Parties, Elections and Referendums Act 2000 (PPERA). The Edinburgh Agreement set the broad parameters, but otherwise ceded to the Scottish Government the precise wording of the referendum question, the details of the franchise (which extended the vote to 16- and 17-year-olds), the precise date of the referendum and the rules and limits on campaign financing. These were subject to the regulatory oversight of the UK Electoral Commission (specifically its Scottish arm). Responsibility for the conduct of the referendum, including vote counting and the declaration of results, was given to the Electoral Management Board, a body set up in 2011 to coordinate the administration of Scottish local government elections.

A key role of the Electoral Commission was to test the intelligibility of the referendum question, which was originally formulated as: *Do you agree that Scotland should be an independent country? YES/NO.* This was tested for clarity and impartiality alongside three other formulations with very minor modifications to the initial framing of the question, including the eventual question which replaced 'Do you agree that...' with 'Should'.[2] The most contested aspect of the question—what it means to be 'an independent country'—was not challenged. Indeed, the Electoral Commission (2013: 15) noted that participants in its research demonstrated an unusually high and consistent understanding of what they were being asked, noting 'Almost everyone had a clear understanding that "independent country" meant Scotland being separate from the rest of the UK'. The terminology of 'separation' is politically loaded in the Scottish context and only ever used in debate by opponents of independence. Much of the debate nonetheless centred around contested meanings of independence and union, and the Electoral Commission itself acknowledged that 'the precise definition of the word "independent" in the proposed question will not be known before the referendum takes place' (2013: 15).

The Protagonists

The regulations followed PPERA in requiring that lead organizations be designated for each side. Yes Scotland included the SNP and the Greens, while Better Together united the Conservatives, Labour, and Liberal Democrats.

---

[2] The two other formulations tested by the Electoral Commission were: 'Do you want Scotland to be an independent country? YES/NO' and 'Should Scotland become an independent country? YES/NO'.

Table 1.1. Referendum campaign spending

Campaign group	Spending limit	Actual spend
Better Together (designated lead NO campaign)	£1,500,000	£1,422,602
Yes Scotland (designated lead YES campaign)	£1,500,000	£1,420,800
Scottish National Party	£1,344,000	£1,298,567
Labour Party	£831,000	£732,482
Conservative & Unionist Party	£399,000	£356,191
Liberal Democrats	£204,000	£187,585
Scottish Green Party	£150,000	£13,734
Other registered campaigners	£150,000	£64,896

Source: adapted from Electoral Commission, 2015: 12

During the regulated referendum period (30 May–18 September 2014), the designated Yes and No campaigns each had a spending limit of £1.5 million. Political parties could spend within limits based on their share of the popular vote in the 2011 Scottish elections. Other bodies spending in the campaign were obliged to register with the Electoral Commission. In total, forty-two campaigners or campaigning organizations officially registered with the commission—twenty-one for Yes and twenty-one for No. As Table 1.1 shows, spending was fairly evenly split between Yes and No campaigners.

In the absence of public funding for campaigners and political parties, both sides had to rely on donations. Just under 60 per cent of all donations made to non-party campaigners were in support of No, including a £1 million donation to Better Together from Harry Potter author J. K. Rowling. But for a fortuitous lottery jackpot in 2011, which saw an Ayrshire couple win €185 million from the EuroMillions lottery, the balance of spending may have been tilted more heavily towards the No. The lucky winners donated £1 million to Yes Scotland and over £3 million to the Scottish National Party, which in turn was, by far, Yes Scotland's biggest organizational donor.

Resources go beyond money. Each campaign had the institutional support of government. The Scottish Government set out in a series of policy documents and on its website what independence would entail. The centrepiece was the White Paper, *Scotland's Future* (Scottish Government, 2013f), which set out what it claimed would be an eighteen-month transition to independence, what the accession to independence would mean for the powers and responsibilities of the Scottish Parliament and government, and what an SNP-led government would prioritize if it were to win the first post-independence election. A summary was sent to every household, with copies of all 887 pages available on request and online. The UK Government, for its part, led a *Scotland Analysis* programme, publishing a series of papers proclaiming to provide an evidence base to inform the debate, though all accentuated the risks of independence.

The role of the civil service proved controversial. Before the SNP first came into office in 2007, some questions had been posed as to how far civil servants in Scotland—who remain part of the UK home civil service—could carry out a policy which could lead to the break-up of the United Kingdom. In the event, the convention held that civil servants carry out the policy of the government of the day. There was further criticism of their role in drawing up the independence White Paper, although once again this work conformed to the normal practice of implementing the government's programme. A more precise criticism was that the White Paper contained substantive policy commitments for an independent SNP government, and so could be seen as analogous to a manifesto. The engagement of the UK civil service appears to have been more direct and politically focused (Pike, 2015) than that of their Scottish counterparts, which was easier to do as the issue was not contested within Whitehall or between the main Westminster parties. In a controversial intervention and breach of normal protocol, the Permanent Secretary to the Treasury, Sir Nicholas McPherson, published his advice to the UK Government that a currency union should not be countenanced. In a later speech at King's College, London, McPherson revealed that his stance was not limited to the technical issue of the pound sterling, but that he and his officials saw their role as being to support the unionist cause generally: 'Her Majesty's Treasury is by its nature a unionist institution. The clue is in the name' (Macpherson, 2015). A subsequent inquiry by the House of Commons Public Administration select committee was critical of what it regarded as breaches of civil service impartiality during the referendum campaign on both sides (House of Commons Public Administration Committee, 2015).[3]

The political parties channelled their support through the official campaigns. The Scottish National Party and the Scottish Green Party worked together within Yes Scotland, the latter helping to nurture the impression that the campaign was bigger and broader than the SNP. While these two parties provided most of the staff of Yes Scotland, its chief executive, Blair Jenkins, a former Head of News and Current Affairs at both Scottish Television and BBC Scotland, was at pains to stress his independence from party politics. The campaign's chairman, Dennis Canavan, was a former Labour MP and independent MSP. Yes Scotland set out to spawn a grassroots campaign, nurturing local networks and generating a coalition of political, cultural, community, and sectoral groups in support of a Yes vote. The most prominent of these, including the Radical Independence Campaign, Women for Independence, and National Collective, were themselves keen to stress their independence from both the SNP and the formal Yes Scotland campaign, which they achieved without

---

[3] There was a hidden agenda here as some members were keen to head off moves to involve Treasury officials in a future referendum on the European Union.

creating any significant tension or division. Many of these groups have continued since the referendum and are a sign of one of its consequences—the creation of a civil society movement in favour of Scottish independence.

The Scottish Labour Party made what would become a fateful decision to join forces with the Conservatives and Liberal Democrats, then partners in the UK Government, under the banner of Better Together. Labour provided Better Together with many of its key staff members, among them Alistair Darling, a well-respected Labour MP and a minister in the Labour governments throughout the party's three consecutive terms, latterly as Chancellor of the Exchequer for three years. Blair McDougall, a long-time Labour staffer and activist, became Better Together's Chief Executive. The Labour Party also tried to run its own campaign, United with Labour, but this lacked a strong figurehead and was heavily overshadowed by Better Together. The dominant role played by the Conservative-led UK Government in steering and supporting that campaign made it difficult for the Labour Party to champion a distinctive and positive case for Union. The party's electoral fate since the referendum, which included losing forty out of the forty-one Westminster constituency seats it had held comfortably for many years, is, in part at least, the price it paid.

Notable for their relative absence from either campaign were the trade unions. The Scottish Trades Union Congress (STUC) and several of the larger trade unions (UNISON, T&G) had played a key role in the campaign for a Scottish Parliament, including through membership of, or affiliation to, the Scottish Constitutional Convention. The STUC had been one of the architects of the 1989 Claim of Right for Scotland: a declaration of Scottish popular sovereignty in the face of the then Conservative government's refusal to concede devolution. They shared in the prevalent vision of Scottish home rule as key to Scotland's social and economic well-being, and a tool to resist unwelcome policies of Conservative governments. In the independence referendum, and despite the affiliation that most unions maintain with the Labour Party, the trade unions and the STUC mainly held a formal neutral position, with a few exceptions on either side. The shopworkers union USDAW, the general union GMB, the Communication Workers Union (CWU), Community, the train drivers union ASLEF, and the National Union of Mineworkers signed a joint statement supporting a No vote (though some CWU branches came out for Yes). The National Union of Rail, Maritime and Transport Workers (RMT) declared its support for the Yes campaign after a ballot of its members, along with several branches of the CWU and the Prison Officers Association. Individual leading trade unionists, including the General Secretary of the STUC, appeared to express more sympathy for the Yes campaign (*Daily Record*, 20 February 2014), while less formal groupings of trade unionists emerged mainly as part of the grassroots Yes campaign.

The business community were overwhelmingly against independence (Bell, Delaney, and McGoldrick, 2014; Mackay, 2014), but their organizations tended to stay out of the debate. The Confederation of British Industry (CBI) caused itself considerable embarrassment by seeking to register as a No supporter, before realizing that it contained members like the BBC and universities, which are politically neutral. The situation was saved only when it was discovered that it had not registered properly in any case. The Institute of Directors, by contrast, remained neutral because its members were not united. At the very end of the campaign, a group of leading businesses, under pressure from the UK Government and No campaign, did come out decisively for No. On the Yes side, Business for Scotland represented a smaller sector of the business community.

The referendum dominated the news agenda for the two years leading to September 2014. Among the print media, only the *Sunday Herald* openly supported independence. The remainder were openly in support of the union or tried to remain neutral. Amid declining newspaper readership, social media played a key role, and here the numbers stacked firmly in favour of the Yes campaign. The neutral #indyref hashtag was used by 5.4 million tweets in the year prior to the referendum, with 2.3 million of those in the last thirty days of the campaign, many helping to motivate and mobilize the grassroots Yes campaign. That same thirty-day period saw around 232,000 uses of the hashtags #bettertogether and #nothanks, while more than three times as many used #YesScotland or #VoteYes (Cellan-Jones, 2014). The biggest reach, however, remains with broadcast media, with both the BBC and Scottish Television staging debates featuring leading figures in both campaigns. Sixty per cent of respondents to one poll claimed to have watched one or more of the leaders' debates during the campaign, while 52 per cent watched a TV programme about the referendum, not including the news (TNS-BMRB, 2014). In spite of being bound by rules of impartiality, the broadcasters faced accusations of biased reporting, especially from Yes supporters. No complaints of partiality were upheld by the BBC Trust, but the Audience Council Scotland, which advises the Trust, reported concerns that BBC network (UK-wide) broadcasts came too late in the campaign and were less well-informed than BBC Scotland (BBC Trust, 2015).

Experts and Evidence

As explained below, the two sides supported essentially the same values and visions of society, but each insisted that its own constitutional formula would realize them better. This opened the way for a strong focus on evidence, which accumulated massively by the end of the campaign. The UK Government produced a series of sixteen Scotland Analysis papers, covering issues from economic policy and currency to welfare, energy, and international and constitutional issues. University academics[4] produced analyses across a wide range of issues. Think tanks intervened, with the Institute for Fiscal Studies (IFS) being prominent. The Future of the UK and Scotland Programme, a major initiative of the Economic and Social Research Council (ESRC), produced an online book in collaboration with the David Hume Institute and the Hunter Foundation (Jeffery and Perman, 2014). It provided academics' responses to sixteen questions, and was downloaded some 120,000 times in the run-up to the vote. It does appear that, by the end of the campaign, people felt somewhat better informed although there was still a great deal of misunderstanding (see Chapter 10). On the other hand, serious questions must be asked about the nature of this evidence.

First, there was an unclear line between analysis and political advocacy. The UK Government's analyses were clearly intended to find evidence in support of a No vote and indeed they did not find a single argument for independence. The Scottish Government produced much less analysis due to its limited resources, but this tended to dismiss objections to independence and argue that all would be well.

Second, the debate was about what might happen in the future under either independence or union, and this is inherently unknowable. Social scientists can construct scenarios and produce models of what any given policy changes might lead to. These, however, are often based on the *ceteris paribus* principle, seeking to explore the effect of a change on the assumption that other matters remain constant. The more changes that are taking place, the more variables are introduced into the analysis and the greater the difficulties of prediction. Independence would have been a big change, with multiple effects, many of which are unknowable and dependent on behaviour that is impossible to predict. The difficulties of prediction were amplified by the lack of other real cases of a comparable country transitioning to independence.

Third, notwithstanding the important work of academics, much of the evidence used in campaigns was commissioned by the two sides or explicitly intended to support one campaign or another. As a result, there was a failure to explore the counterfactuals or realistic alternative scenarios. So estimates about the resources of an independent Scotland for public expenditure were often compared with those of continuing the present funding formula (Barnett), which was itself under strain. Independence supporters often assumed that, after independence, other things would stay the same and actors would behave according to rational self-interest to help stabilize the new state. They also made some bold assumptions about oil prices and the ability of an independent Scotland to increase its economic growth rate. The IFS analyses were generally seen as being impartial but they were based upon

---

[4] Including our own ESRC Centre on Constitutional Change, and the broader ESRC Future of the UK and Scotland programme.

assumptions about future economic and expenditure trends without always acknowledging their inherent uncertainty.

Finally, it was sometimes difficult to see at whom the evidence was aimed. The Treasury-led analyses tended to be very long, rather technical, and not easily readable. The papers did not have the status of impartial scientific analysis, given the brief the civil servants had, but nor were they digestible by the general public. The Scottish Government's (2013f) White Paper, by contrast, was intended for public consumption, in spite of its 887 pages, much to the frustration of those looking for the technical and detailed analysis.

The Issues

A striking feature of the long referendum campaign is that it did not, by and large, pitch radically different visions of Scotland's future against each other. It was, rather, a competition over what political scientists call valence issues, in which the goal is largely agreed but parties compete on how best to get there. We have already noted that Scots are only slightly to the left of England on most policy issues; they are also internally divided. On the other hand, four of the five parties represented in the Scottish Parliament belonged within the social democratic spectrum while the centre-right was represented only by a shrunken Conservative Party. There were a few voices on the right, such as Michael Fry's *Wealthy Nation* calling for a radical downsizing of the state and a neoliberal vision of independence. The Radical Independence Campaign came from the opposite side of the spectrum. Labour and the SNP were, however, almost indistinguishable on most economic and social policies, divided clearly only on the constitution. Referendum debates were thus dominated by how best to secure the post-war welfare settlement. Even on the constitutional issue, both sides sought to occupy the middle ground, with some similarities between the SNP's diluted form of independence with a maximalist form of home rule within the Union.

Where valence issues are at stake, parties will usually seek to claim ownership of them and to define them on their own terms. This was a central feature of the referendum campaign, where each camp strove to define the agenda for the debate, emphasizing themes on which it had the advantage and framing the issues in its own way.

Identity: Scottishness, Britishness, and Union

Independence movements are often seen as concerned with identity, the idea being that identification with the state or with the stateless nation will drive voting behaviour. There is evidence of this in the Scottish case (Chapter 10), but the issue is very complicated. It is widely accepted by social scientists that identities are socially constructed and malleable (for the Scottish case, see McCrone and Bechhofer, 2015; Reicher and Hopkins, 2001). Rather than being an independent factor or variable, identity is often the dependent variable, the product rather than the cause of political mobilization. In some societies, identity has been constructed on an exclusive basis, so that citizens are under pressure to identify with one pole or another, especially at times of tension. Scottish identity, however, is something that is available both to unionists and to nationalists. There is an association between feeling strongly Scottish and voting for independence, but it has always been rather loose (Bechhofer and McCrone, 2009). Most Scots feel both Scottish and British, even if the Scottish identity appeared to grow from the 1970s. According to the Scottish Social Attitudes Survey, however, the number of people identifying themselves as exclusively Scottish had fallen since the advent of devolution in 1999[5] (see Figure 1.2). It appears that a sense of alienation from Britain had peaked under the Conservative governments of the 1980s and 1990s. Nor does Scottish identity correspond to a social divide within Scotland, in the way that happens in Northern Ireland.

This does not mean that identity was irrelevant in the campaign but that it was available to both sides, to reconstruct and press into the service of union or independence. The Yes side drew on longstanding myths of Scottish egalitarianism often summed up in the legend of the 'lad o'pairts'.[6] This had been an important trope for Radical and Labour home rulers from the late nineteenth century and was linked with the Presbyterian ethos and Scotland's early lead in mass education. Scotland's historic hostility to the Conservative Party, except for a period in the mid-twentieth century, was another element.

In response to the rise of Scottish nationalism (as well as multicultural challenges), successive UK governments have sought to promote a culture of 'Britishness'. The idea has been that, while Scottish, Welsh, or English identities are legitimate forms of expression, they are partial and subordinate to a higher and shared sense of belonging. For Conservatives, Britishness is rooted in a historical narrative, whether the glories of empire or the Whig story of progress. For Labour, the emphasis is on shared welfare and solidarity. Both parties stress the qualities of freedom, democracy, and fair play. These are universal values and Labour in particular has often promoted them against nationalism, but in practice they are being used to promote a specifically *British* national identity.

[5] Based on the Linz–Moreno question, which asks people if they feel only Scottish; more Scottish than British; equally Scottish and British; more British than Scottish; only British.

[6] The ordinary youth who rises in the world due to free education and opportunity.

There is something ironic in the new Britishness agenda since in the past it has consisted precisely in not having an explicit national ideology. Britishness, rather, has been construed differently in different parts of the state; this is the genius of traditional unionism. The effort to construct it as a single thing, over and above the constituent parts, always risks destroying its roots. Modern Scottish nationalists like Alex Salmond, moreover, have not sought to deny the British component of Scotland's social make-up but say that it is not inconsistent with voting for independence. This, combined with their programme of attenuated independence, even allowed the nationalists to appropriate the very language of union. Salmond famously declared that Scotland currently belonged to six unions: the political; the monarchical; the monetary; the defence; the European; and the social. After independence, it would leave the political union but retain the other five. This was disputed by the No side, who insisted that monetary union was out of the question and membership of the European Union and the defence union (NATO) would be very difficult. There was a lack of clarity about what 'social union' meant, since it could cover anything from continuing family ties to common policies for welfare, but it was a reassuring phrase.

Identity appeals in the Scottish campaign did not, therefore, take the form of a stark division between 'us and them' as in some other cases. It was more a matter of each side seeking to reconstruct the nation of Scotland or Britain with substantive social values, where the relevant values were largely the same in both camps. It is for this reason that so much attention was focused on social and economic policy and the likely effects on each constitutional option.

The Economy

The Scottish case can be seen neither as a 'revolt of the poor', a reaction to relative underdevelopment, nor a 'revolt of the rich' found in wealthy territories complaining about having to support their poorer compatriots. Scottish economic output per capita is close to the UK average. Yet, the economic question was prominent during the campaign. The SNP had long presented the small independent states of northern Europe as exemplars, at one time calling them the 'arc of prosperity'. After the collapse of Ireland and Iceland, the comparison was reduced to the continental Nordic states. They drew on a strand of literature purporting to show that small states in the modern world are more successful economically (Skilling, 2012) although the evidence is actually mixed (Keating and Harvey, 2014). There was less detailed analysis of exactly which small states did well and why, or of the internal changes that Scotland would need to undertake to match the Nordic model. The No side insisted on the benefits of being in a large state and the Treasury analysis papers stressed the costs of independence, including the 'border effect', transition costs, and the high cost of borrowing. Part of the SNP's (and thereby Scottish Government's) strategy was to cut corporation tax in order to attract investment, which looked to be at odds with its commitment to higher levels of welfare and was repudiated by other elements on the Yes side, including the Greens and left-wing social movements.

The Yes side insisted that Scotland could pay for its own services, as it had long been a net contributor to UK public finances. The No side, supported by much academic opinion and think tanks like the IFS, disputed the figures and argued that an independent Scotland would depend on fluctuating oil revenues, which were declining in the long term. The unionist parties then promised that, in the event of a No vote, the Barnett Formula would safeguard public spending levels in Scotland. This helped promote a backlash in England and Wales, as it seemed to prove their complaint that Scotland gets more than its fair share. The Scottish Labour Party (2014) even claimed, erroneously, that Barnett distributes expenditure across the UK on the basis of need—underwriting the social union.

The flurry of claims and statistics on both sides created a great deal of confusion, but the issue tended to work to the benefit of No, if only because it raised levels of risk and uncertainty. On the other hand, a strong emphasis on the dire economic consequences of independence could come across as threatening and unduly negative, implicitly suggesting that Scots were incapable of managing their own affairs. It also risked identifying No with big business; the association was reinforced at the end of the campaign when, faced with polls showing Yes to be ahead, there was an orchestrated intervention by big firms, banks, and even some supermarkets warning of calamitous consequences should there be a Yes vote.

Welfare

Welfare is one of the themes around which Scottish political identity had been reconstructed since the 1980s, as a contrast to what was seen as a neoliberal Westminster. The theme recurred in response to the Conservative–Liberal Democrat coalition's welfare reforms after 2010. The SNP contains numerous strands, including a social democratic and a pro-business one, but since the 1990s the former has tended to dominate. The emphasis on welfare has allowed the pro-independence coalition to extend itself towards the left, taking in many social movements and some minor parties who are much more radical than the SNP, without necessarily fracturing the coalition itself. The narrative of Scotland as a caring country has allowed nationalism to penetrate lower income groups while at the same time avoiding anti-English rhetoric since Yes supporters were also able to pose as opponents of austerity across the UK and Europe more generally. This strategy was pursued with great vigour during the subsequent 2015 General Election campaign.

The No side's response to this was necessarily led by the Labour Party, which played on the theme of the 'sharing union', based on the notion of solidarity as a component of Britishness and on the UK's greater resource pool. The argument was articulated most forcefully by Gordon Brown whose book was one of the major intellectual contributions to unionism (Brown, 2014a). On the other hand, Labour was constantly at risk of over-reaching itself by insisting that public services like health and education should be provided on the same basis everywhere, when, since devolution, they have been devolved and are organized in a distinct way in Scotland, with much less emphasis on marketization and contracting out.

The Yes side, and particularly the SNP, were under pressure to explain how they would pay for a higher level of welfare and how this squared with the SNP's promise to cut corporation taxes and air passenger duties. This issue was pursued by the No side, but it was a more natural fit for the Conservatives and risked portraying Labour as opposed to the social democratic project as a whole. It added to Labour's embarrassment by its association with the Conservatives in the Better Together campaign, which looked as though it was defending the Westminster government.

The External Dimension

Small, independent states in the modern world require an external support system to provide security, access to markets and protection against unilateral behaviour by larger powers. The European Union is critical here and the SNP have been in favour of membership since the late 1980s. By the time of the referendum, this was a central plank of the independence platform. As the No campaign was also largely pro-European, Europe itself was not an issue; the debate rather concentrated on whether and how Scotland could become a member of the EU and on what terms. Since there is no precedent, nor any provision within the EU Treaties, there was no legal answer, but this issue was used to suggest either assurance or risk, from the two sides respectively.

Membership of NATO and defence policy were more difficult. Until 2012 the SNP had been opposed to NATO membership, reflecting pacifist traditions in the party and strong opposition to nuclear weapons. The change in policy was highly controversial, passed only narrowly at the party conference, and resulted in the defection of two MSPs, the most serious breach in party unity since the SNP had arrived in government. At the same time, the SNP reaffirmed its opposition to the stationing of the UK nuclear deterrent in Scotland

and promised to remove it after independence. The No side argued that this was not compatible with NATO membership, while the SNP pointed to other NATO states which did not host nuclear weapons. Leftist independence supporters continued to oppose both NATO and nuclear weapons. Overall, however, defence and foreign affairs did not feature strongly in the campaign.

Risk and Uncertainty

Since the proposal for independence was unprecedented and the evidence so contested, there was a great deal of uncertainty about the likely outcome of either a Yes or a No vote. This gave the No side an inbuilt advantage, as it did not need to prove that independence would be damaging, just to suggest that it was a risky proposition. They identified this as a potential asset at a very early stage (Pike, 2015) and pressed it at every opportunity, as all the chapters show. The Yes side sought to counter this by pointing to the risks inherent in continuing union, including being dragged out of the European Union, continued Conservative rule at Westminster and further austerity. This had some traction but was less effective since it was rather speculative. The No side heightened perceptions of risk by refusing, as they put it, to 'pre-negotiate'. Having accepted in the Edinburgh Agreement that they would respect a Yes vote, the unionist parties thus declined to give any detail on how they would react and what the terms of independence might be. The one exception concerned the pound, where they made a joint statement that a currency union would not be on offer. Yes, for its part, insisted that self-interest would force the UK Government, as well as international actors such as other states, the EU and NATO, to behave rationally and to cooperate in Scotland's transition to independence. Again, this was less convincing.

The desire to minimize the risk and uncertainty of their own respective options explains the conservative tone of many of the arguments on both sides. One might expect independence supporters to promote a very different vision of Scotland and, while groups like the Radical Independence Campaign and Common Weal did so, Yes Scotland and the SNP were more inclined to offer reassurance. There was a reluctance to talk about taxation or what resisting austerity might entail. Assurance was offered on keeping the pound, although this would seriously curtail the effective independence of Scotland, and alternatives to sterling were kept off the agenda, to the frustration of the Greens. The 'Nordic model' of social democracy was mentioned regularly but never spelled out. So the independence prospectus at times appeared to offer a continuation of the status quo, only in an independent state.

Modern understandings of social and economic behaviour emphasize that people do not generally weigh up evidence on both sides of an argument and decide on the basis of long-term implications. Rather, they take cognitive short cuts (Kahneman, 2011). They may reduce complex issues to familiar choices; they think in the short term; and they are more sensitive to possible losses than to potential gains. They also judge messages according to how far they already trust the messenger. Both campaigns were aware of this and sought to move the debate onto familiar terrain of their choosing. This explains the No side's emphasis on potential economic losses, even though this made them look negative. It also explains why, in the latter stages, the Yes side chose to focus on threats to the NHS, even though this is already fully devolved to the Scottish Parliament.

The Chapters

Chapters 2 and 3 deal with economic issues. Patrizio Lecca, Peter McGregor, and Kim Swales note the degree of uncertainty surrounding the likely effects both of independence and of continuing union. There is no relevant precedent or comparative data. Much would depend on the settlement negotiated between an independent Scotland and the UK and international bodies, particularly on the crucial issue of monetary union. The future price and volume of North Sea oil is unpredictable. Economists disagreed among themselves and likely outcomes varied according to the assumptions that were made, as shown by the issue of borders. With much of the material coming from the two camps or people sympathetic to them, it was sometimes difficult to distinguish analysis from advocacy. Rather than engaging in static analysis of likely outcomes, we can gain more insight using the findings of behavioural economics, which uses more realistic models of behaviour. The evidence suggests that voters were acutely sensitive to risk and uncertainty and the two sides sought to play on this. Hence the No side emphasized issues like borrowing costs and the potential crisis in public finances. The Yes side raised fears about continued austerity and the future of the National Health Service, even though the latter is already fully devolved. This meant that the two sides were often talking past each other. In a future referendum campaign, it would be useful to have a more impartial source of data and analysis.

David Bell and David Eiser, examining public finances and taxation, also stress uncertainty. They look at debates about whether an independent Scotland's public finances would be sustainable; how to allocate public debt between Scotland and the rest of the UK (rUK); North Sea oil and its importance to the Scottish finances; the role of taxation in stimulating the Scottish economy; and how pensions would be managed in an independent Scotland. While independence is a long-term proposition, much of the debate focused on short-term current issues and as the campaign developed, the Yes side increasingly emphasized the UK Coalition government's austerity policies. Both campaigns tried to quantify the gains from their preferred option, with Yes claiming that Scots would be £1,000 a year better off while No claimed that they would lose £1,400, both based on contestable assumptions. There was less emphasis on what precise policies would ensure these outcomes. There were particularly intense debates on an independent Scotland's public finances. The debt inherited by the new state would depend on what principles were used to allocate it, on which there was no agreement. The No campaign added to the costs of independence the cost of policies to which the SNP was committed. These were not, of course, costs of independence as such, but the SNP had opened itself to this criticism by including them in the White Paper. Another issue was the costs of pensions, given Scotland's ageing population, while there were arguments about the future yield of oil taxes. Equally significant are the issues that did not feature, including the costs of universal services (to which Scotland has been committed); the market for government debt; and whether cutting corporation taxes as the SNP (but not other Yes campaigners) proposed really does increase economic growth. Bell and Eiser echo Lecca, McGregor, and Swales in pointing to the lack of hard data, the speculative nature of many projections, and the consequent focus on uncertainty itself as the key issue in the campaign.

The SNP proposal for an independent Scotland to use the pound sterling was a central issue in the debate, as both chapters 2 and 3 note. In Chapter 4, Coree Brown Swan and Bettina Petersohn consider how it played out during the campaign. While the SNP had previously supported an independent Scottish currency and later considered the euro, by 2014 they were firmly committed to keeping the pound in a currency union with the UK. Brown Swan and Petersohn see the two sides operating with different frames, the Yes side believing that they could withdraw from the political union but retain the currency union, with the No side disputing this. They review the knowledge claims made by either side, which drew on academic evidence about currency unions. They then examine the campaign tactics, with the No side issuing a rare categorical statement that currency union would not be available while the Yes side insisted that this was mere bluff. Matters were further complicated by the preference of some Yes supporters, including the Greens and the radical left, for a separate currency and by Yes Scotland's reluctance to spell out a Plan B in case a formal currency union was not available.

Nicola McEwen looks at the debate around welfare in Chapter 5. The fundamentals of the existing welfare settlement were not disputed by either side, but each attached it to a different vision of the relevant community of solidarity. Yes played on the idea of Scotland's egalitarian and welfare tradition, while No emphasized the role of the UK as a sharing union, which could pool risks and mobilize a larger resource base to deal with economic shocks. Once again, both sides sought to highlight the risks in the other's option. The Yes campaign stressed the dangers of further austerity and welfare cuts imposed from Westminster. Their opponents questioned whether an independent Scotland could afford to maintain the existing levels of services and entitlements, let alone the enhanced provision that the SNP proposed. There was also discussion about the practicalities of dividing a complex welfare state. The Scottish Government's expert group on welfare had suggested that Scotland and the UK could continue to share administration of some welfare programmes, at least for a transitional period. The UK Government's analysis paper questioned the viability and cost of this and whether it would be possible to run different policies through the same administrative apparatus.

Since the mid-1980s, the SNP has been pro-European, seeing the European Union as an external support system for an independent Scotland. While Europe is a divisive issue in England, both sides in the Scottish independence debate viewed it positively. As Michael Keating shows in Chapter 6, the main question was whether and how an independent Scotland could become a member. The Yes side argued that it could and proposed two possible routes. The No side's position was less clear. Unwilling to advocate Scotland's exclusion from the EU themselves (which could have looked like threatening) they suggested that unnamed member states might veto it. They also suggested that Scotland would have to leave and be readmitted—a difficult, costly, and painful process. This was another instance of playing on uncertainty and risk. The Yes side countered that, if it stayed in the UK, Scotland risked being dragged out of Europe by the weight of English votes in the EU referendum proposed by the Conservatives, but this was seen as a less imminent danger.

Defence and security issues are central to national sovereignty, but they played a relatively small role in the campaign, compared with economic and social questions. In Chapter 7, Colin Fleming argues that the two sides approached this question from different perspectives. The Yes side saw Scotland as a small state and derived their conclusions as to its role in the world and the consequent needs from that. Better Together took a large-state perspective based on the United Kingdom's position as a major power and permanent member of the United Nations Security Council. The SNP embraced collective security, having recently abandoned its opposition to NATO, and proposed that Scotland play its part in that. It also promised continued defence cooperation with the remaining United Kingdom but insisted on the withdrawal of the Trident nuclear weapons system and that Scotland would have a constitutional ban on nuclear arms on its territory and in its waters. The No side claimed that the anti-nuclear stance was inconsistent with NATO membership. The nuclear issue aside, this was another example of independence being presented as largely a continuation of existing collective defence arrangements, but the pro-independence left took a more radical position. Some on the unionist left were also unhappy about the apparent endorsement of nuclear weapons by Better Together. Once again, risk was at the centre of the argument, with the No side presenting independence as a security threat, while Yes insisted that an independent Scotland would not be drawn into reckless foreign ventures like the Iraq war.

An independent Scotland would have needed its own constitution, and Stephen Tierney reviews the debate around this in Chapter 8. The Scottish Government did make provision for an interim constitution, with a popular and inclusive process for drawing up a permanent one. Since this would only happen after independence, few details are available, but a number of key issues were nevertheless posed. One was the status of the constitution and whether it would be above the ordinary law. If so, that might have given judges the right to overrule parliament, so restricting the newly sovereign state. Another is whether social and economic rights would have featured, as they do in many modern constitutions. While the process of making the new constitution would be more inclusive, it was not clear what the role of politicians would be. Few of these issues had much resonance in the referendum debate, which was not an occasion for rehearsing different models of democracy. Had the Yes side won, however, they would have had to be addressed.

A recurrent theme of the pro-independence side was the advantages that small states have in the modern world. Transnational integration, collective security, and open markets have eroded the advantages of being big, while small states may enjoy greater adaptability and flexibility. In Chapter 9, Malcolm Harvey addresses the various strands of this argument. The SNP liked at one time to talk about the 'arc of prosperity' of small countries in northern Europe, but the collapse of the Irish and Icelandic economies in the financial crash undermined this portrayal. The focus then shifted to the Nordic countries with their successful economies and generous welfare states. Norway was held up for its wise use of oil resources. The No side countered with arguments about economies of scale and the costs of the Nordic welfare state. Neither side was able to take their argument to its full conclusion. The SNP (as opposed to the pro-independence left) would not face up to the tax implications of the Nordic model or its contradictions with some of their ideas about tax-cutting. On the No side, Labour had to be careful in criticizing the Nordic model too harshly, as that could easily be seen as attacking social democracy itself.

In Chapter 10, Robert Liñeira, Ailsa Hendeson, and Liam Delaney review the state of public opinion, drawing on surveys conducted before and after the referendum and a separate survey on the proposals of the Smith Commission, as part of our research project. In addition they draw evidence of longer-term trends from the Scottish Social Attitudes Survey. This allows them to chart change during the campaign and to link this to key issues in the debate. For some time, when people have been asked their preferences among the status quo, more devolution, and independence, a version of enhanced devolution was the most widely supported, especially after second preferences are taken into account. This to a large degree explains the strategy of both sides to conquer the centre ground. Socio-demographic factors like age, gender, and social class affect support for Yes and No, although during the campaign there was a shift towards Yes in all groups. Identity proves to be a strong indicator of referendum voting, as does being born in Scotland as opposed to elsewhere in the UK—although those born overseas are more like the Scots-born. They review voters' views on the claims made by both sides to show, for example that the number believing that Scotland would be able to keep the pound increased during the campaign to overtake those who thought it would not, but still did not amount to a majority. In this as in other issues, many people remained uncertain, a theme upon which the No side played heavily. It does appear that, were there to have been greater certainty about the outcome, the Yes side could have done better but not necessarily well enough to win.

Nicola McEwen and Michael Keating draw out some of the conclusions of our study in Chapter 11. They note the dominant themes of uncertainty and risk and how they played out. Neither side could claim a clear victory. The No side won the vote, but the unionist parties were devastated in the subsequent 2015 General Election. The referendum may have settled the independence issue in the short term but it did not resolve the constitutional question in Scotland. Immediately after the result, the unionist parties moved to fulfil their promise of further devolution, while the SNP consolidated its electoral position, leaving open the option of another referendum in the future. McEwen and Keating conclude by looking at the wider implications of the Scottish vote. It does set a precedent for a democratic way of resolving nationalities claims in modern Europe, but has not resolved the broader issue of how to accommodate national diversity in modern Europe.

2

The Economy

Patrizio Lecca, Peter G. McGregor, and J. Kim Swales

Introduction

The decision to secede from a political union and become an independent country has potentially important economic implications. Economic issues are often defined in quite a narrow way, as relating to outcome variables such as the real wage, the level of employment, the degree of income inequality, and the growth of GDP. However, we include here also some broad consideration of issues relating to the public provision of goods and services and also welfare transfers. Even if improving the performance of the country on such criteria is not the prime reason for seeking independence, the potential economic impact, good or bad, will necessarily be taken into account in the decision process. Authors such as Acemoglu and Robinson (2012) and those contributing to Helpman (2008) argue that the institutional structure is key to determining economic performance, so that this is potentially a very serious decision, especially given its virtual irreversibility. The Independence White Paper referred to it as a 'once in a generation opportunity' (Scottish Government, 2013f: i).

In this chapter we consider the economic debate around the independence referendum from two different viewpoints. First, we take the standard cost-benefit position generally adopted by the UK Government to appraise and evaluate public policy. We argue that the uniqueness of the decision, accompanied by the complexity and uncertainty that surrounded it, made such a framework impossible to operate in practice. We next consider an advocacy approach, which is what actually occurred. This is a potentially powerful way to present, scrutinize, and evaluate different views as to the likely outcomes following the structural and institutional changes that would accompany a positive or negative referendum vote. However, if a debate organized along these lines is to be effective, it needs to focus on long-term issues. We argue that in fact this process failed effectively to do this, concentrating on short-term current political issues in a very negative manner. While this might not be the best way to appraise the issues, it was an effective means of appealing to the voters, consistent with modern cognitive insights into decision-making.

Standard Economic Evaluation: Establishing the Counterfactual

The conventional economic argument relating to increased decentralization or devolution of powers, and by extension independence, primarily concerns the trade-off between economies of scale and specialization. With greater decentralization, it is possible to fashion policies that more closely align with the needs and preferences of the local economy and electorate (and the latter's desire for accountability). On the other hand, as part of a larger country the region benefits from the provision of national public goods more cheaply and also from pooling the risk of asymmetric economic shocks.

The HM Treasury (HM Government, 2013f) Green Book is a useful template to indicate how economists conventionally approach the appraisal of policy changes. The aim of this document is to outline appraisal and evaluation procedures that should be used to support policy scrutiny and implementation within the UK Government. In principle, the same criteria are relevant for the electorate in deciding on policy through a referendum, in so far as economic issues are involved. Essentially the Green Book adopts a cost-benefit or cost-effectiveness approach to appraisal (Boardman et al., 1996). This involves identifying the impacts of policy, then measuring the costs and benefits against a monetary scale. This requires the weighting of the positive and negative aspects of a policy to obtain an estimate of overall net impact. The process can be done with a high degree of sophistication, taking into account risk and uncertainty, optimism bias, distributional weights, and the choice of the most appropriate time discounting procedure.

In discussing this approach, we will here assume that the decision as to whether to favour independence depends solely on the costs and benefits to present residents in Scotland, as these were the only people allowed to vote in the referendum. Of course, independence might have negative or positive impacts on the rest of the UK and the rest of the world, and this can, in principle, be incorporated into the cost-benefit calculation, but only if their welfare is valued by Scottish voters.[1] In the case of the Scottish Independence

---

[1] Alesina and Spolaore (2005) show that in a highly stylized model without side payments from central to peripheral regions, in equilibrium democratically driven secession will produce suboptimally sized economies. This is because seceding citizens do not take into account the negative impact on those remaining.

referendum, the expected outcome of a No vote was, in some sense, the maintenance of the status quo, but this status quo itself was not well understood by Scottish voters. To begin with, though the facts were clear and in the public domain, the basic fiscal position of Scotland was widely misunderstood. In a Populus survey reported in the Financial Times on 7 June 2014, many months into the referendum campaign, 58 per cent of the Scots questioned thought that public spending per person was lower in Scotland than in the rest of the UK. In fact, official estimates suggest that it is around 10 per cent higher.

Similarly, there was a high degree of uncertainty concerning which public services are controlled by the Scottish Government and which by the UK Government. Scotland has a high level of devolved spending in Health, Education, Transport, the Police, and Industrial Development. These are primarily funded by the Barnett-formula based block grant coming from the UK central Government. Within that overall budget, the Scottish Government has complete discretion on the expenditure side in devolved policy areas. Nevertheless, for example, saving the National Health Service in Scotland, a responsibility already devolved, was often portrayed as being central to the independence case, an issue to which we will return.

However, the status quo issue is even trickier in that under the Scotland Act (2012) the future devolved powers to Scotland were due to change, even without independence. This would give higher levels of devolved revenue-raising power to the Scottish Government, matched by a corresponding reduction in the block-grant Barnett transfer. Of course, there could be further adjustments in the future in the level of devolved powers and also to the public financing arrangements. The Barnett formula has been the subject of extensive criticism (see, for example, House of Lords, 2009) as arbitrary, idiosyncratic and failing to reflect need.[2] However, it also delivers an outcome where the aggregate Scottish expenditure per head over devolved policy areas will be greater than for the same public services in the UK as a whole (Christie and Swales, 2010). Any change to the system of determining the block grant, through linking it to measured need, for example, is likely to be detrimental to Scotland, given that Scotland's per capita GDP and average household income are very close to the UK average.

A further complication was added when, days before the referendum vote, the unionist parties issued their 'vow' to provide extra powers (as explained in Chapter 1), meaning that the alternative to independence was changed.

---

[2] The Barnett formula gives Scotland, Wales, and Northern Ireland a population-based share of any increase or decrease in spending in England on services equivalent to those that are devolved. While it might have been expected, over time, to produce a convergence in spending levels, for a variety of reasons this has not happened, leaving Scotland's historically higher spending levels at least partly intact.

Standard Evaluation: Identifying the Alternative

There are numerous problems in estimating the economic consequences of independence. The first is that there is no real precedent for the secession of a large region within a highly developed modern economy. Scotland and England have been formally unified for over 300 years, and although Scotland has many independent institutions, the economies of the two nations are very closely integrated. This means that there are no comparable data for identifying the likely impact of independence using empirical (especially econometric) research. Economists specializing in a number of fields, including the economics of country size, fiscal federalism, international trade, and optimal currency areas, have an interest. However, there is no defined subdiscipline that would naturally specialize in studying such events. This means that there is no consensus about the trade-offs between possible costs and benefits which could have informed the debate, and the outcome is necessarily speculative. This is illustrated by the work that the UK Government did around economic issues. HM Treasury produced Research Reports on the following: Currency and Monetary Union, Financial Services and Banking, Business and Microeconomic Framework, Macroeconomic and Fiscal Performance, Science and Research, EU and International Issues, Borders and Citizenship, Energy, and Work and Pensions. Each was a substantial document but all relied on specific assumptions, which could be challenged by the other side.

A second issue is that the exact nature of the proposed settlement between Scotland and other key institutions was not determined before the vote took place. An independent Scottish Government would have had to renegotiate many agreements both with international and previously intra-UK bodies. The electorate would have needed to predict the nature of these agreements in order to be able to evaluate the post-independence position. This would in practice depend on the bargaining strength of the various parties, which in turn would depend at least partly on the implications for both sides of not reaching a bargain. In positions of imperfect information, it is in the interest of both sides to take prior bargaining positions that they might subsequently relinquish and also to attempt to misinform the other party.

Of major significance was the status of Scotland's EU membership (see Chapter 6) and whether Scotland would remain in a full monetary union with the rest of the UK, and therefore retain the pound and the services of the Bank of England, post-independence (see Chapter 4). An indication of the problems involved can be shown by considering the monetary union decision using a dynamic game in which there are three players: the Scottish electorate and the Scottish and UK governments. This is represented in Figure 2.1. In this figure each node is a decision point. At each end point there are pay-offs to the Scottish electorate and the UK Government. We assume for simplicity that the Scottish Government is trying to maximize the pay-off to the Scottish electorate.

The options are: to have a currency union with the UK as proposed by the Scottish Government; to adopt the pound sterling unilaterally (sterlingization); to have a separate Scottish currency; to adopt the euro.

At the first node, the Scottish electorate votes in the independence referendum. If the result is No, then the status quo is retained and the game ends. If the referendum decision is Yes, then the game moves to the node where the Scottish Government and the UK Government bargain over the conditions required to retain the monetary union. If they can agree, then we have monetary union and the game stops. However, on either side there might be no acceptable bargained outcome. This depends on the fall-back position, which is the outcome without an agreement. If there is no agreement the game moves to the third node where the Scottish Government continues to use Sterling but outside a formal monetary union (sterlingization), or joins the euro, or decides to issue its own (new) currency.

We will return to this question a little later, but the point we wish to make here is that from the perspective of economic theory, in order for the electorate to make a rational (optimum) choice at the first node it needs to be able to do two things. First, it needs to be able to rank both its own and also the UK Government's interests across all the possible outcomes. Second, in the standard analysis of the game, the determination of the optimal strategy requires the use of a process called backward induction (Gibbons, 1992). This involves knowledge and analytical powers outside those held by the median voter. Note that the position of the No campaign was that no monetary union agreement was economically viable, whilst the Yes campaign claimed that this was an empty threat and full monetary union would in practice accompany independence.

A third issue is that Scottish independence would affect how the economy operates in a necessarily uncertain future. Unless independence produces better outcomes than the union under all economic circumstances, this makes the relative ranking of independence as against remaining in the union uncertain. In principle this is not a problem for an economic evaluation. As long as it is possible to assign probabilities to all possible outcomes, and assess the costs and benefits of each, the expected value of the decision can be calculated. However, such a calculation might be extremely difficult in practice.

One particular issue was the oil price and consequent revenues. In an independent Scotland, oil revenues at the level prevailing around the referendum would be needed, initially at least, to maintain the relatively high per capita public expenditure unless other taxes were to increase. However, the oil price is extremely volatile, which would make the stabilization of the public finances more difficult. This issue of volatility is conceptually distinct from the expected evolution of oil revenues over the longer term—a hotly contested issue. Under the union, Scotland would be cushioned, to an extent, from asymmetric shocks through the automatic tax and revenue stabilizers funded from the rest of the UK, to which an independent Scotland would not have access. That is to say, short-run reductions in economic activity caused by events that solely, or predominantly, impact on Scotland can be partly offset by increased welfare spending that automatically increases as unemployment rises. The lack of these fiscal stabilizers is often seen as a problem for the effective operation of the euro single currency.

An additional problem is that within specific areas of the independence debate, there was frequently a lack of agreement even amongst supposedly disinterested economic experts. A prime example concerns the currency outcomes that could follow Scottish independence (explained in Chapter 4). Less than a fortnight before the referendum, the *Financial Times* asked six experts to rank the four currency options open to an independent Scottish Government. The options are those identified in the negotiation game discussed earlier and shown in Figure 2.1.

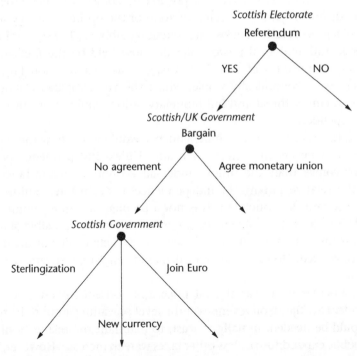

Figure 2.1. Extensive form representation of the monetary union decision

Table 2.1. The appraisal of the various currency options for an independent Scotland. Figures are valuations on a scale of 0–10, and the figures in brackets are the ranking of the option by the expert

	Julius	Bowman	Muscatelli	Yates	Armstrong	McDonald
Currency Union	10 (1)	5 (3)	10 (1)	10 (1)	3 (2=)	1 (2=)
Sterlingization	7 (2)	9 (1)	6 (3)	5 (3)	1 (4)	0 (4)
Own currency	5 (3)	7 (2)	8 (2)	7 (2)	6 (1)	9 (1)
Euro	1 (4)	2 (4)	2 (4)	3 (4)	3 (2=)	1 (2=)

Source: Financial Times, 5 September 2014

The experts were Dame DeAnne Julius, former member of the Monetary Policy Committee and Bank of England Court Director; Sam Bowman, Research Director of the Adam Smith Institute; Professor Anton Muscatelli; Professor Ronnie MacDonald; Tony Yates; and Angus Armstrong, Director of macroeconomics at the National Institute of Economic and Social Research and former HM Treasury official.

Their appraisal of the various possible outcomes from the perspective of the Scottish economy is given in Table 2.1. The figures give each expert's appraisal of the particular state on a scale of 0 to 10; figures in brackets give their ranking of that option, running from 1 to 4. This means that Tony Yates, for example, judges that the Currency Union is an optimal policy, giving it a value of 10 and ranked first, with sterlingization in some sense worth half of that, with a value 5 (and ranked third).

We are not concerned here with the detail of the results but rather their consistency. Remember that the electorate needs to be able to evaluate these outcomes for an independent Scotland, and also the outcomes from the perspective of the UK Government, to work out the possible result of negotiations over the currency post-independence. However, Table 2.1 indicates major differences amongst these valuations. No outcome gets a majority of number 1 rankings; only three of the six give a currency union with the rest of the UK as the highest ranked option. All the experts would value Scotland adopting its own currency as being preferable to joining the euro, but apart from that there is no unanimous agreement amongst their rankings of any other two options.

We are discussing here just one element of one aspect of the economic policy issue which was raised by the independence debate. This particular issue became a central concern in the debate and we return to it for other reasons, but there were similar differences amongst experts on many of the key issues. In many cases these problems of appraisal interact with one another. Take an example from an issue that played a surprisingly small part in the debate. This is the potential effect on Scottish trade, particularly with the rest of the UK.

A common aim of international economic policy in the period since the Second World War has been the reduction in trade barriers between countries. However, with independence a national border would be placed between Scotland and its largest trading partner. What would be the likely impacts of this? A small part of the international trade literature considers the impact of national borders on the level of trade. This analysis has primarily been conducted using North American data measuring trade between US states and Canadian provinces. When econometric techniques are used to model this interregional trade, the existence of a border has a large measured negative effect (McCallum, 1995; Anderson and van Wincoop, 2003). That is to say, the level of trade that the model predicts would occur between two regions located in different countries is much lower than would be predicted if states with the same characteristics (including the distance between them) were trading within their own country.[3] This effect is also revealed where countries have an open border and share a currency, such as between contiguous EU countries.

How should these findings be interpreted for the independence debate? First, there are no comparable data for the UK so that we do not have existing models of interregional trade, though we do have estimates of the level of Scottish trade with the rest of the UK and its composition.[4] Second, the measured negative trade impacts of a border are very large, and there is no consensus as to what causes these effects. Their size is likely to be determined partly by how 'soft' the border is. This would be affected by negotiations between Scotland and the rest of the UK and by policy differences on key issues such as immigration and currency. Third, these results come from countries that have been distinct and independent for a long period of time. Whether such an effect would occur as a result of the introduction of a border between two regions initially undertaking high levels of trade is unclear. Also if this is the case, what is the likely time path of any reduction? There are data on the marked reduction in the proportion of trade between the UK and Ireland subsequent to Irish independence, but the comparability between the two cases is again unclear.[5]

All this suggests a number of major problems facing any debate organized around a conventional economic cost-benefit approach to Scottish independence. These include the lack of comparable events, the need to marshal a lot of disparate information, and the many uncertainties surrounding the outcome.

---

[3] For an alternative set of results, see Coughlin and Novy (2011).

[4] There has been work by HM Government (2013d) and Comerford and Rodriguez Mora (2015) using existing trade data to attempt to identify the impact on Scottish–rUK trade if an independent Scotland's trade relationship with the rest of the UK were similar to that of a comparable EU country.

[5] Differences include the introduction by the Irish state of an 'economic war' in the period 1932–8. This involved imposing protectionist measures on imports from the UK, a policy unlikely to be pursued by an independent Scotland.

This last issue was particularly pernicious. This is partly because there were genuine differences of opinion amongst disinterested experts about the likelihood and desirability of alternative outcomes. It is also the case that some of the uncertainty depended on the degree and nature of cooperation that could be expected between an independent Scotland and the remainder of the UK. At its most charitable, one could say that each side was adopting a negotiating position. In the end, the amount of information, and the diversity of perspectives, seem to have overwhelmed any attempt at a public debate carried on along standard cost-benefit lines.

Advocacy

A full cost-benefit approach would therefore be a challenging process in a highly political environment, so it was perhaps to be expected that the public debate was structured in a different way. There was a large amount of information uncovered and much discussion, but the debate took the form of advocacy, rather than an attempt to reach agreed cost and benefit figures.

The White Paper from the Scottish Government reads more like a Yes campaign election manifesto than a document setting out the alternatives for an extremely important constitutional decision. The non-neutral tone can be assessed from the very first page where, after a very brief account of the advantages of having the governance of Scotland solely in the hands of the Scottish Government, the document states: 'This is what being independent can deliver for Scotland and it is why the Scottish Government believes the people of Scotland, individually and collectively, will be better off with independence' (Scottish Government, 2013f: i). This is before the reader has reached any of the subsequent 648 pages of text and annexes. The HM Treasury position was a bit different. Their communications were even more voluminous but also more factual and analytic. However, they were prefaced with the claim that the UK Government was in favour of the Union. In the very first of their Scottish independence research documents, HM Government (2013c: 5) states: 'The UK Government, along with many others, believes that both Scotland and the UK are better served by maintaining their partnership.' In other words, there was no official body holding the ring to set a neutral framework.

Given the political nature of the decision, it was unavoidable that the issues should be framed in an adversarial manner. What was lacking, from an economics perspective, was a basic plan of how the economy would develop with and without the fundamental changes that would accompany independence. On the Yes side, one major lever that an independent country could have—the ability to run an independent monetary policy, with the attendant power to set interest rates and have a flexible exchange rate—was ruled out.

The White Paper (Scottish Government, 2013f: 85) asserted that 'Scotland will continue to use the pound, providing continuity and certainty for individuals and businesses in Scotland and the rest of the UK' and states that the Scottish Government's Fiscal Commission 'commends to the Scottish Government retaining sterling as part of a formal monetary union, and believes that this provides a strong overarching framework for Scotland post independence' (Scottish Government, 2013f: 111). As shown in Chapter 4, monetary union turned out to be a major issue in the debate and one that, as shown in Chapter 10, influenced the result. It is ironic that this revolved around the Scottish Government demanding the right to be denied one of the key macro-economic powers that independence traditionally provides.

A second issue central to an independent Scotland would be the fiscal position. With independence, Scotland would move from being part of a large economy whose public expenditure per head is higher than the national average, and funded primarily by a block grant determined in Westminster, to relying on locally raised taxation and much more strongly dependent on oil revenues. The broader implications of this shift did not form a major element of the debate. In so far as they did, this involved the validity of projected future oil prices and the extent of existing reserves and future oil and gas discoveries. In particular, the implications of the uncertainty and unpredictability of the fluctuating oil price, and the way in which this would have to be dealt with by an independent Scotland, were not central to the debate.

This is even clearer in retrospect. The referendum took place when oil prices were historically high. With oil prices falling by up to 50 per cent just months after the referendum vote, the response of the Scottish Government was not that such fluctuations are to be expected and would be dealt with effectively under an independent Scotland. An oil fund, such as that operated by Norway and the Shetlands Island Council, which would act as a buffer to such price movements, has been suggested; but of course oil revenues invested in this way cannot simultaneously be used to maintain current public expenditure.

One implication of the fiscal autonomy which accompanies independence is that this should incentivize economic growth as any increase in future economic activity will generate increased tax revenue which will now remain in Scotland, rather than flowing to the UK Treasury. For an economist this is a sound argument and appears in the Scottish Government White Paper. However, it did not pay a major role in the debate, perhaps because there is an opportunity cost. The devolved Scottish Government already claims to prioritize growth and has a higher per capita expenditure on industrial development than the UK as a whole. Whether devolved or independent, if Scotland is to spend more on growth it needs to spend less on other priorities.

This is an instance of the recurrent conservatism of the mainstream Yes campaign. There is reassurance given that being a small country does not mean being poor and that an independent Scotland could be viable and successful. There is also much rhetoric about having control over valuable natural resources and also levers of power. Yet there is no clear discussion of the way in which independence not only allows, but also requires, radical changes in strategic economic decisions.

On the No side the problem is in some ways even more serious. It is true that Scottish GDP per head and average household income is very close to the UK average. On these criteria Scotland is in an intermediate position between the South of England and the other regions of the UK. However, the UK Government is unable to tell a coherent story as to how the UK economy operates over space. It therefore had no narrative as to how the UK economy was to develop in the future and the role that Scotland would have in that if it stayed in the union. Successive UK governments have been ambivalent about the degree and nature of economic interaction between regions. In the recent past, the rhetoric underpinning spatial policy has been about rectifying the failure of lagging regions to achieve their potential (HM Government, 2010a). Traditional regional policy, which was about equalizing resources, has been virtually abandoned in favour of regional competitiveness. This characterized both the 'new localism' of the Labour government and the conceptual framework adopted by the subsequent Conservative-led coalition in introducing Local Economic Partnerships (Hildreth and Bailey, 2013).

Before the financial crash, if there was an overall view of the spatial development of the UK economy it might have been that the national economy is essentially driven by London and the South-East and that the other regions benefited from the resulting spread effects (Lees, 2006). The crash seemed, at least temporarily, to have undermined this position with the coalition government expressing the view that the economy needed, amongst other things, spatially rebalancing though what this actually meant is difficult to discern (Clegg, 2010; Hildreth and Bailey, 2013). We know that there are strong interregional migration, trade, and capital flows. This is actually highlighted in work that HM Treasury (HM Government, 2014c) performed as part of the appraisal of the impact of Scottish independence. Theories of regional growth suggest positive or negative feedback effects between regions; Gardiner et al. (2013) gives a survey of this literature. However, the UK Government seems to have no overall theoretical framework that incorporates these interregional effects into a coherent narrative of the UK spatial economy.

Behavioural Approaches

The lack of a clear blueprint for the future on either side of the debate has meant the recourse to a piecemeal and rather fragmented evaluation of the issues. Standard economic approaches proved of limited value, given the difficulties of prediction in conditions of uncertainty and the assumptions that the standard approach makes about actors' motives and behaviour, notably that they appraise the long-term implications of options and compare them systematically. In this context insights from behavioural economics are instructive. This is an approach which has become increasingly prevalent in the past three decades, seeking to incorporate into economics the ideas of psychologists concerning the way in which decisions are made. Daniel Kahneman (2011: 20), a Nobel Prize winner in economics, outlines the difference between two types of thinking, which he labels System 1 and System 2. 'System 1 operates automatically and quickly with little or no effort and no sense of voluntary control. System 2 allocates attention to the effortful mental activities that demand it, including complex computations. The operations of System 2 are often associated with the subjective experience of agency, choice and concentration.' Conventional economics assumes that all decisions are taken using System 2 thinking. That is to say, that we continually rationally optimize, given constraints.[6]

Kahneman claims, on the basis of sophisticated experiments, that we do not and that our default option is the automatic and effortless System 1 thinking. People have several difficulties with System 2 thinking. First, we have difficulty holding a lot of information actively in the brain simultaneously. Second, the brain has difficulty dealing with probability and particularly issues of joint probability (where two or more possible events have to be taken into account) and evidence. Third, in decision-making we are influenced disproportionately, and sometimes wholly irrationally, by the last piece of information we received; we give statements more weight or validity if they are experienced repeatedly. Fourth, we are risk averse and value the cost of a loss much more highly than the benefit of an identically sized gain. Finally we have difficulty taking decisions where one set of attributes needs to be weighed against another.

From our discussion of the nature of the economic issues involved in the Scottish independence debate, they would seem to require System 2 thinking, being long-term and complex. However, the disparate nature of the debate allowed System 1 thought to dominate. This is apparent in the following characteristics. First, there was extensive discussion of many topics, especially where these impacted on particular groups, and much information was generated and disseminated, but decisive public arguments were narrowly focused on a small number of issues. Second, the irreversible decision as to whether to vote for independence clearly should logically be influenced by long-run issues, rather than by existing economic difficulties or policies; but much of

---

[6] A more sophisticated approach is that we act 'as if' we are optimizing all the time (Friedman, 1953).

the debate was dominated by current political and economic issues, such as financial stability and the policy of austerity that had been central concerns of UK politics since the financial crash in 2008. Third, in important respects both the Yes and the No campaigns adopted negative approaches. Typically, those favouring the status quo have an advantage in that there is generally more risk involved with changing the situation (although the Treasury Green Book on appraisal and evaluation emphasizes that doing nothing is an active decision, not a default position). However, more than this, both sides emphasized especially the downside risk of voting for the opposition. That is to say, they attempted to play on the loss aversion of the electorate.

We do not want to give the impression that trained economists always approached the debate with System 2 thinking; they were not immune from making the decision in advance of the evidence. For example, in April 2012, very early in the debate over the independence referendum, the *Economist* magazine, reflecting the projected future demographic position and assuming declining oil revenues, published a front cover with a map of Scotland renamed 'Skintland', with puns instead of place names, such as 'Glasgone', 'Edinborrow', and the 'Highinterestlands'. This suggests a less than sober and rational approach to the independence decision. Second, economists are very late in incorporating behavioural insights in their theories of how choices are made; marketing, public relations, and political special advisors got there first. It would be rather naïve to think that those engaged on both sides of the independence campaign were not primarily interested in winning the vote rather than informing the electorate.

It is useful to look at the way in which topics ultimately get onto the agenda. One was the level of debt that Scotland would inherit. As part of the UK, Scotland at present pays a share of the interest and any repayment of the UK debt. An independent Scotland would be a small open economy whose government would have no existing reputation in the financial markets. Scotland might well have had to pay an interest rate premium over the rest of the UK (Armstrong and Ebell, 2013), but the precise level of initial debt taken on by the Scottish Government would be subject to negotiation. We do not know what criteria would have been adopted as again there is no precedent, except for the Irish Free States, which inherited minimal debt. A further complication is that in order to borrow at advantageous rates, the UK Government has taken legal responsibility to service all of the present UK debt, which might seem to release Scotland from legal responsibility for it. The position favoured by the nationalists (which would minimize the Scottish debt) would be based on Scotland's past contributions to UK tax revenue, starting from the point where North Sea oil revenues began. The position favoured by the remaining part of the UK in a hypothetical negotiation would base Scotland's share of debt on its share of public expenditure. Some intermediate position, based on the population or GDP share seems reasonable. However, there clearly is uncertainty and the then Scottish First Minister, Alex Salmond, threatened to accept no share of the debt if the Government of the rest of the UK refused to agree to a monetary union.

The Yes campaign framed the vote for independence as resistance to austerity, and particularly resistance to welfare cuts and reforms imposed by the UK Government. The first page of the body of the Independence White Paper asserts that independence would 'mean an end to impositions on Scotland of policies like the bedroom tax' (Scottish Government, 2013f: xii). There is a legitimate link to that element of the independence debate that relates to the democratic deficit. Where the tax and expenditure interests and policy preferences of the rest of the UK diverge from those of the Scottish population, then there are clear possible benefits from independence. There are also potential benefits from perceived enhanced local accountability. Again, however, this related to conditions affecting the economy over the relatively short term, and promised to get rid of unpopular present policies imposed by the UK Government when the debate should have been focused on very long-term issues, given the irreversibility of a Yes decision (Goudie, 2013).

While the No campaign stressed the risks of independence, the Yes campaign sought to defend existing policies against what they presented as the risks of union. An increasingly important theme was the claim that within the union the welfare state, and in particular the National Health Service, was under threat. Although this might be seen as a non-economic issue, it concerns the way in which resources are allocated and used. A specific claim was that the policies of the present UK Government were leading to the privatization of the NHS in England and this would ultimately undermine the Scottish NHS by reducing transfers under the Barnett formula. In July 2014 Alex Salmond warned of a 'growing threat' to the Scottish NHS from an agenda of 'privatization and fragmentation' at Westminster. Prominent consultants and health officials supported these claims (Burns, 2014).

Again the short-run policies of the existing UK Government were presented here as relevant to the long-run decision over whether to vote for independence. It is arguable whether moves to private delivery (but with public funding) affect overall spending levels and therefore the transfers to Scotland under the Barnett formula. Moreover, the NHS is fully devolved to the Scottish Government and it is possible for it to use its own tax powers to maintain spending levels.

Net Financial Benefits/Costs to Scottish Households

A key element of the independence campaign was the '£500 test', in which respondents were asked how they would vote if it were revealed that independence would make them £500 a year better or worse off. It was posed in different ways by a number of polling bodies and several times over the years by the Scottish Social Attitudes Survey. The results published in January 2014 for the polling period June to October 2013 showed overall support for independence at around 30 per cent while 54 per cent would vote for remaining in the union (SSAS, 1999–2014). However, if the respondents' income were to rise by £500 per annum after independence, the proportion who would vote Yes increased to 52 per cent whilst if independence were associated with a £500 fall in annual income, it fell to 15 per cent.

Inspired by this finding, the two sides produced their own estimates. HM Treasury calculated the benefit for people in Scotland of remaining part of the UK—the 'UK Dividend'—at £1,400 per person for every year over the twenty years from 2016 to 2037 as a result of lower taxes and sustained public services (HM Government, 2014c). This calculation solely concerns public finances. It includes the additional taxes that the Treasury calculated would be necessary to fund the SNP's firm policy commitments, notably improved childcare—possible changes to welfare payments being too uncertain to cost accurately. They then added the public finance implications of the proposed reductions in corporation and air passenger duty, the higher cost of borrowing, and the costs of setting up independent Scottish institutions. Added into the mix is the effect of lower estimated oil revenues and the higher welfare costs of a more rapidly ageing Scottish population. Whilst there are expected to be costs of independence and much of the analysis that has gone into the Treasury figures is rigorous, the presentation is disingenuous. The main problem is that the benefits of the increased public expenditure or the effect of the reduced taxes on individual's real incomes are not incorporated into the calculations.[7] Also given that these figures depend on projections some distance into the future, there is a precision which is unwarranted.

The Scottish Government (2014a) produced quite a different figure. Again they consider solely the fiscal position but calculated that in fifteen years' time each person in Scotland would be £1,000 better off under independence rather than remaining in the union. The report contains an initial highly technical section concerning the short-term debt position for an independent Scotland. But the key to the headline future public finance benefit is driven by assumed improvements in the economy's performance in three areas: increased productivity growth; increased working-age population; and increased labour market participation rate. However, these improvements

---

[7] Illustrating their presentation with Lego men, the Scotland Office and HM Treasury misguidedly represented this dividend as corresponding to a set of consumption opportunities, one of which was the purchase of 280 hot dogs at the Edinburgh Festival.

reflected Scotland's aspirations rather than being strongly supported by empirical evidence linked to specific policies. They were dependent on Scotland improving not towards the performance of the rest of the UK, against which it has broadly a comparable record, but towards other, better performing, countries. There is no overall policy blueprint to underpin these improvements, rather a piecemeal set of measures whose effectiveness is as yet unproven.

Both sides clearly felt a need to present figures favourable to their own position. In this case, both were misleading to a certain extent and roundly criticized by the opposite camp. The issue here is not that the information is incorrect, but that the two figures are based on completely different assumptions and are carefully curated to produce completely different headline figures.

Conclusion

There were many positive aspects to the economic debate that accompanied the Scottish independence referendum. It engaged the population at large and produced a lot of valuable information and economic analysis. At the very least there is now a clear understanding that Scotland could operate successfully as an independent country, in a similar way to countries such as Iceland or Denmark. However, there were a number of worrying characteristics to the debate.

The fact is that we cannot predict what the economic effects of Scottish independence would have been. There are too many uncertainties and much would depend on how economic actors would behave. As John Maynard Keynes (1936: 161–2) noted in Chapter 12 of the *General Theory*, 'a large proportion of our positive activities depend on spontaneous optimism rather than mathematical expectations, whether moral or hedonistic or economic. Most, probably, of our decisions to do something positive, the full consequences of which will be drawn out over many days to come, can only be taken as the result of animal spirits—a spontaneous urge to action rather than inaction, and not as the outcome of a weighted average of quantitative benefits multiplied by quantitative probabilities.' The question of national independence could be seen as a paradigm case in which animal spirits could be the decisive factor. Yet the debate focused on a small number of issues, often somewhat orthogonal to the central economic issues concerning independence and typically driven by short-term political considerations. Even on these limited terms, the debate frequently obfuscated issues rather than clarifying them, characterized by negative, adversarial arguments aimed squarely at System 1 thinking in a setting in which System 2 thought is required. From an economic policy perspective, the UK Government lost an ideal opportunity to present alternative plans for the future spatial development of the UK economy as a whole and the role of Scotland within this. After the financial crash, the UK Government called for a geographical rebalancing and the information that HM Treasury prepared for the referendum debate could have been used as the basis for a policy to achieve that end. It might even have secured a degree of cross-party support. It certainly would have allowed the UK Government to have made a more positive case for the union.

The full economic legacy of the effects of the referendum campaigns and vote are ambiguous (Curtice, 2015c). As a result of the immediate pre-referendum promises there will be more economic powers to Scotland, but the legislation has been rushed and is challenged by the Scottish Government as not fully delivering on those promises. Further, discussion around the Smith Commission (2014) has tended to focus on the additional fiscal powers rather than what the Scottish Government should actually do with these powers.[8] At the time of writing, William Hill bookmakers are offering odds of 7:2 that there will be a second Scottish independence referendum before 2020 and the Scottish Government clearly see this as a possibility. Could things be done differently a second time round? The real challenge is to present the complex issues involved in independence in a balanced, straight-forward, and simple enough way so that ordinary voters can understand. One clear weakness of the last debate was the perceived politicization of the civil service. When two branches of the UK Government's Economic Service produce contradictory headline assessments of the impact of Scottish independence on the Scottish public finances there is a genuine problem (HM Government, 2014c; Scottish Government, 2014a). This stems from the present policy that whilst the civil service is politically neutral, it is not policy neutral—it supports the Government of the day.

In this case, the Scottish and UK Governments have diametrically opposite policy objectives. In other areas of public policy, where there is a conflict between the informational and policy supporting role of the civil service, the UK Government has set up independent organizations to scrutinize government activity. Examples are the UK Statistics Authority, an independent authority answerable to Parliament, which oversees the Office for National Statistics; the Office for Budget Responsibility which gives independent estimates of the impact of HM Treasury budget proposals; and the National Infrastructure Commission which is to oversee planning for energy and transport schemes. In a future referendum a similar independent, perhaps

---

[8] In fact, the Scottish Government did recommend two policy changes: improvement in child care and a reduction in corporation tax rate. Both of these were assumed to be self-funding. Lecca et al. (2015a, b) analyse various aspects of the impact of greater income tax powers.

necessarily international, body, such as the World Bank or the OECD, could be asked to give factual, informed comment. This would not concern the detailed minutiae of alternative policies, but on broad issues that independence raises and the challenges and opportunities it would necessarily pose. Such a framework might act as a useful focus for a more positive and informative economic debate.

3

Public Finance and Taxation

David Bell and David Eiser

Introduction

Opinion polls regularly highlighted the importance of taxation, pensions, public spending, and currency in influencing voter opinion during the referendum debate. Key issues within the fiscal debates included: whether an independent Scotland's public finances would be sustainable; how to allocate public debt between Scotland and the rest of the UK (rUK); North Sea oil and its importance to the Scottish finances; the role of taxation in stimulating the Scottish economy; and how pensions would be managed in an independent Scotland. Another related debate focused on the interaction between monetary policy and fiscal policy, notably whether an independent Scotland could be part of a sterling monetary union without conceding control over taxation and spending to rUK. Civil service economists in both London and Edinburgh, working respectively for the UK and Scottish governments (but all officially part of the UK Government Economic Service), argued the economic case against and for the break-up of the UK. Other, variously well-informed, commentators produced arguments in support of one or other campaign. Most tried to base their projections on the known features of Scotland's historic economic performance. As noted earlier (Chapter 2) these tended to reflect the immediate context—the fiscal difficulties that the UK currently faces and the consequent short- to medium-term implications for taxation and public spending—even though the economic implications of an independence vote would be long term. Thus, most fiscal projections accepted that an independent Scotland's short- to medium-term fiscal policy would have to follow the UK, with a commitment to reduce or eliminate the budget deficit. Longer-term issues, such as how to maximize sustainable economic growth (which is the Scottish Government's principal policy objective) were largely absent from the debate.

This was a missed opportunity for the No campaign, which failed to highlight the many powers that Scotland already had that could influence growth. Towards the end of the campaign, supporters of independence became more aligned with 'anti-austerity' policies based on the argument that the deficit would be self-correcting if economic growth could be enhanced and therefore spending cuts were unnecessary. This line of argument resembles developments elsewhere in Europe where political opposition to the austerity policies that emerged in the aftermath of the Great Recession have gained strength and some credibility.

What currency Scotland might use and how it would manage its monetary policy were pivotal in influencing voter sentiment. The interaction between monetary and fiscal policy also figured prominently in the arguments for and against independence. Analogies between the difficulties faced by the euro-zone in managing a single monetary policy alongside disparate fiscal policies and that which might be faced by a 'sterling zone' comprising Scotland and rUK were not perfect, but neither were they irrelevant.

This chapter explores these arguments. It recalls some of the key events and arguments that played into the fiscal debate. It describes key players and their contributions, explaining why some topics attracted attention, while others did not. It also discusses the style and evidence base of the arguments that were deployed.

The Protagonists

As noted in the introduction, civil servants played a key role on both sides of the independence debate. The Scottish Government work was coordinated through the Office of the Chief Economic Adviser (OCEA), while the UK Government's case was coordinated through HM Treasury. The Treasury had access to a much wider pool of expertise than was available to the Scottish Government and was therefore able to produce a substantial set of papers covering many of the economic implications of independence. The purpose of the series was to 'provide comprehensive and detailed analysis of Scotland's place in the UK. It set out the facts about a range of constitutional, economic and policy issues that are critical to considering Scotland's future' (HM Government, 2013c). The papers on macroeconomic and fiscal perform-ance (HM Government, 2013d), fiscal sustainability (HM Government, 2014c), and work and pensions (HM Government, 2014d) constituted an extensive analysis of the Scottish economy. Nevertheless, their impact was probably less than the Treasury hoped, partly because the language and presentation of the papers was rather technical and therefore unlikely to influence the average voter. Whether they had an indirect influence through the broadcast and print media is not clear. One suspects it had very little effect on social media where views tended to be highly polarized. The Treasury message was simplified towards the end of the campaign, perhaps best illustrated by Danny Alexander's claim that Scottish families would be £1,400 a year better off with the Union (see Chapter 2).

The main fiscal arguments from the Scottish Government were contained in the White Paper (Scottish Government, 2013f). Several ad hoc publications produced by OCEA covered issues such as the devolution of corporation tax (Scottish Government, 2011), an oil fund (Scottish Government, 2012), economic regulation (Scottish Government, 2013b), pensions (Scottish Government, 2013e), and principles for the tax system (Scottish Government, 2013d). The output of OCEA was supplemented by the work of the Council of Economic Advisers, set up by Alex Salmond in 2007 with the remit to advise the First Minister on increasing Scotland's rate of 'sustainable economic growth'. Some of the advisers believed that independence would provide a growth stimulus. Thus, for example, Professor Andrew Hughes Hallet argued that Scotland would be more affluent if it were financially independent (Hughes Hallet, 2014). Other Council members did not comment on the implications of independence for growth and did not become involved in the referendum debate.

Other commentators tried to take an impartial view of the evidence but this evidence inevitably related to Scotland's experiences within the Union. In contrast, analysis of the economic implications of independence had to be based on projections of the future, which were subject to considerable uncertainty. The Yes campaign was perhaps at a disadvantage in this battle since it is generally easier to make a plausible case that the future will bear many of the characteristics of the past. It is more difficult to argue that the future will involve a substantial improvement in economic performance compared with previous experience. The Yes campaign did try to argue that the past had been riddled with mistakes and missed opportunities: the future would be better even with relatively minor policy changes. This balance of change and continuity perhaps underlay the Yes campaign's tactic to suggest that Scottish independence would only involve a breaking of the political union, but would have no effect on the currency union or on the shared markets for goods, capital, and labour.

The majority of the sixteen questions in the Hunter Foundation e-book (see Chapter 1) covered economic issues with those on pensions, welfare, debt, and finances directly relating to the fiscal debate. It was downloaded about 120,000 times. The Economic and Social Research Council's Future of UK and Scotland programme was intended to make an objective assessment of the political, social, and economic issues associated with changes in Scotland's constitutional status. Several of the ESRC projects (see Chapter 1) dealt with the fiscal consequences of independence; the Institute for Fiscal Studies produced commentaries on Scotland's post-independence fiscal position. The

Centre for Public Policy and Regions (later Fiscal Affairs Scotland) at Glasgow University also tackled this theme. The National Institute of Economic and Social Research produced a number of analyses relating to the post-independence Scottish economy, some with ESRC funding. Though focusing mainly on monetary policy, issues of debt and fiscal sustainability were inevitably discussed. Additional ESRC-funded contributions focusing on debt, spending, pensions, border effects, migration, and tax design were produced by the ESRC-supported Centre on Constitutional Change at Edinburgh. Other ESRC-funded bodies without a specific remit to analyse the referendum dipped into the debate: for example, in 2014, the Centre for Macroeconomics asked its expert members (UK academic and private sector macroeconomists) whether Scotland would be better off in economic terms as an independent country. Weighting responses by self-assessed confidence, 77 per cent of the respondents thought Scotland would not be better off. The Scottish Parliament's information centre (SPICE) also played a useful role in collating the main contributions to the fiscal debate (Scottish Parliament, 2014).

Understandably, politicians found it difficult to accept some of the more objective analysis and bitterly contested the findings. For example, Alex Salmond described the analyses of the Institute for Fiscal Studies thus:

> They look at the balance sheet impact of the policy and nothing more. The focus that is required is not just on Budget deficit but on the deficit of ideas, the deficit of empathy and deficit of imagination which afflicts the Westminster parties and the whole decrepit system that they reflect.
>
> Alex Salmond (2015)

Each of these organizations may have attempted to take a dispassionate view of the fiscal issues that an independent Scotland would confront, but their views were inevitably framed by the current economic context both in the UK and in Europe. The referendum campaign coincided with a period of continuing fiscal adjustment both in the UK and in several other European countries following the financial crisis of 2008. Had the independence debate taken place after the 2003 or 2007 elections, the fiscal context would have been much less intimidating. However, issues such as the financial crisis and the fall in the oil price would have confronted an independent Scotland had an earlier referendum voted in favour of independence, and it would have had to find its own ways of dealing with these problems.

Business organizations largely avoided commitment to either side of the referendum campaign, and though taxation and currency were important issues to the business sector, their voice was largely muted (Bell and McGoldrick, 2014). However, some organizations, such as the Institute of Chartered Accountants in Scotland (ICAS) were more proactive, seeking clarity over some of their concerns. We return to these subsequently.

The Data

The referendum campaign exposed the weakness of much of the economic data available for Scotland. There were three main data sources:

- Scotland's national accounts. The Scottish National Accounts Project (SNAP) has resulted in considerable improvement in estimates of Scotland's macro-economic aggregates. The estimates have been constructed by Scottish Government statisticians and are available on the SNAP website.[1]

- Government Expenditure and Revenue in Scotland (GERS). This is a statistical exercise conducted by the Scottish Government to estimate Scotland's government spending and tax revenues. It shows Scotland's annual fiscal surplus or deficit based on the taxes raised in Scotland (including North Sea oil revenues) on the one hand, and the quantum of public spending both in Scotland (such as on education and health) and for Scots but not necessarily in Scotland (such as defence and debt interest) on the other.

- Public Expenditure Statistical Analysis (PESA). This is a statistical exercise carried out by HM Treasury, which tries to allocate all identifiable public spending to the component parts of the UK. This is the main source of evidence for higher per capita public spending in Scotland compared with the UK as a whole.

The quality of these data has improved in recent years but the estimates may still be prone to error. For example, the amount of corporation tax generated in Scotland is extremely difficult to estimate, given that many enterprises operate on both sides of the border. There are also some conceptual issues with the estimates: for example, it is argued that GERS estimates of Scotland's fiscal deficit/surplus are misleading because they partly reflect the spending priorities of the UK rather than the Scottish Government. However, each of the datasets have the National Statistics kitemark, which guarantees that their collection has been free of political interference and has been conducted to a high professional standard.

There were some areas where the scarcity or absence of data weakened the quality of the economic assessment of the economic implications of independence. These included:

- Information on indirect taxes. VAT is an important source of government revenue, but it is difficult to accurately calibrate exactly where VAT revenues are generated. Related data on consumer spending and on business to business transactions are also rather weak.

---

[1] Scottish National Accounts Programme (SNAP), http://www.gov.scot/Topics/Statistics/Browse/Economy/SNAP (access 5 Aug 2016).

- Information on Gross National Product as opposed to Gross Domestic Product. Gross domestic product measures the value of goods and services produced within an economy: Gross National Product measures the value of goods and services produced by individuals and companies based, but not necessarily located, within that economy. This issue is critical for Ireland, which has a large number of US multinationals located within its territory, but who may reallocate their profits outside Ireland to their headquarter location. These profits do not enhance consumer or government spending or investment within Ireland's boundaries. The same argument was made for Scotland in relation to the profits made by North Sea oil companies and would have affected the Yes campaign's claim that Scotland is the fourteenth richest country in the world.

- Information on high earners. Scotland's top 1 per cent of earners contribute around 20 per cent of income tax revenues. The main Scottish and UK household surveys fail to pick up sufficient numbers of these individuals to infer how they might react to Scottish independence, which could have significant implications for Scotland's tax revenues.

- Trade data—one of the glaring data omissions for a potentially independent state was the absence of robust data on trade. At present there are only experimental data on the trade balance (Scottish Government, 2013a).

Absence of data did not hamper speculation on the effects of independence, some of it implausible. Many individuals and organizations were prepared to base their arguments on data that had no convincing statistical support, notably in the debate around North Sea oil revenues. An economics consultancy based in Scotland, argued that:

> On top of the up to £365 billion estimated to be currently obtainable in tax revenues through conventional means between now and 2040, combined with this up to £300 billion from these new sources of oil and gas production would see North Sea oil and gas revenues of up to a staggering £665 billion, more than double the total taxation from oil and gas received to date (£313 billion).
>
> (N-56, 2014)

The problem with such arguments in relation to oil was that they were based on implausible estimates of economically viable reserves, and based on the oil prices at the time. In retrospect, given the fall in the oil price, they seem wildly unrealistic.

Nevertheless, the referendum debate has revealed important lacunae in Scotland's data infrastructure. Some of the Treasury analysis revealed new data that has been collected but not released at a Scottish level. Given that new powers are coming to the Scottish Parliament following the referendum, further improvements in Scotland-specific economic data will be necessary and may change the nature of any subsequent referendum debates.

What Did They Argue About?

As protagonists on both sides of the debate pored over available data, the question most frequently asked was whether Scotland could continue to support its public services without increasing taxation. A number of other debates were linked to this issue. How important would North Sea oil revenues be in an independent Scotland? How would pensions be affected by independence and would they be affordable? What level of debt would Scotland inherit and what would be the annual cost of servicing that debt? The level of debt could not be separated from the currency issue, the other main economic question raised in the campaign. High levels of debt would have implications for the structure of the monetary union: this also became a highly contested area. In what follows we deal with these issues.

Scotland's Fiscal Balance

The referendum debate coincided with the UK Government imposing the most dramatic fiscal tightening on its citizens for at least a century. In his April 2014 budget, the Chancellor of the Exchequer, George Osborne, plotted a course for the UK budget deficit to fall from 11 per cent of GDP in 2009–10 to 5.5 per cent in 2015–16, and to eradicate it by 2018–19. Cuts to welfare for working-age people such as tougher assessment procedures, benefit caps, and reduced upratings of benefits in line with inflation were particularly salient for the Yes campaign. The infamous 'bedroom tax'—a reduction in benefits for social tenants deemed to have surplus rooms in their accommodation— became a shibboleth to the Yes campaign for the ills meted out to Scotland by Westminster. Much of the fiscal debate during the referendum focused on whether an independent Scotland would have to engage in similar fiscal tightening immediately post-independence.

The Fiscal Commission Working Group (a subset of the Council of Economic Advisers to the First Minister) argued that an independent Scotland, like many advanced countries, should use both a deficit and a debt rule to underpin its medium-term tax and spending plans (Scottish Government, 2013c). However, though its report discussed examples such as the EU Stability and Growth Pact, which mandated governments to hold deficits below 3 per cent of GDP each year and the ratio of public sector debt to GDP below 60 per cent, it was careful not to tie itself to particular numbers in relation to Scotland's budget deficit or to its share of debt in GDP. This meant that the debate in Scotland did not focus on the achievement of specific budget outcomes that had the implicit support of the SNP government.

Given their non-political status, members of the Council of Economic Advisers and the Fiscal Commission Working Group were not heavily involved in the referendum debate. However, in its White Paper, the Scottish Government did produce estimates of Scotland's projected fiscal deficit, albeit only for 2016–17. The essence of these calculations, which are based on projections using the GERS dataset, is shown in Table 3.1 below:

Table 3.1. Estimates of Scotland's Public Finances in 2016–17

	2016–17
Total government spending	£63.7bn
Debt interest (population share)	£4.3bn
Onshore receipts	£56.9bn
Offshore receipts	£7.5bn
Net fiscal balance	−£4.9bn
Deficit as share of GDP 2016–17	
Scotland	−2.8 per cent
UK	−3.4 per cent

Source: Scottish Government (2013f: 75)

Where the White Paper provides a range of possible outcomes, the midpoint of that range has been selected in Table 3.1. Further, some key assumptions underlie these numbers:

- Debt interest is based on Scotland's *population* share of expected UK debt in 2016–17. The Scottish government argued that it would be more appropriate to base debt interest payments on a *historic* share. We discuss this issue in the section on debt.

- Implicit in the spending total is an estimated £3 billion for defence. The Scottish Government's intention was that an independent Scotland would only need a defence budget of £2.5 billion, which would shave £0.5 billion from the deficit. Along with some further changes to taxation, the intention was to reduce the deficit by a further £0.6 billion.

The White Paper includes a commitment to fiscal rules as set out by the Fiscal Commission Working Group, but again there is no commitment to particular deficit or debt levels. So it was not possible to conclude how far spending would have to be cut or taxes raised. It also suggested that post-independence, a Scottish government would:

- Set up an Energy Fund on the lines of the Norwegian wealth fund to manage its oil revenues and act as a buffer against fluctuations in oil revenues.

- Provide universal childcare for 30 hours per week for 38 weeks per year for under-5s.

- Cut Air Passenger Duty by 50 per cent.
- Cut Corporation Tax by up to three percentage points below the UK level.

These commitments were uncosted and seemed to indicate that an independent Scotland could both increase spending and lower taxes sustainably. In retrospect this inference seems implausible.

The White Paper implicitly accepted that after independence currency union with the rest of the UK would require an agreement between Scotland and rUK to ensure fiscal sustainability:

> That is why such a monetary framework will require a fiscal sustainability agreement between Scotland and the rest of the UK, which will apply to both governments and cover overall net borrowing and debt. Given Scotland's healthier financial position we anticipate that Scotland will be in a strong position to deliver this.
>
> Scottish Government (2013f: 117)

This argument was not accepted by the UK Government and indeed, it was partly the fiscal risk associated with monetary union that prompted Sir Nicholas MacPherson to write to the Chancellor recommending against a currency union with an independent Scotland. In particular, he argued that Scottish and rUK fiscal policy would become increasingly misaligned because:

> ... recent spending and tax commitments by the Scottish Government point in the opposite direction, as do their persistently optimistic projections of North Sea revenues, which are at odds not just with the Treasury but with the Office of Budget Responsibility and other credible independent forecasters.
>
> Sir Nicholas MacPherson, Chief Secretary
> to the Treasury, letter to the Chancellor of
> the Exchequer, 11 February 2014.

If an independent Scotland could not credibly commit to a sustainable fiscal policy, then the Treasury view was that the gains from lower transactions costs and increased trade in a monetary union would be more than offset by the risks to sterling posed by the possibility that Scotland would not adhere to its fiscal agreement with the rest of the UK. Mark Carney, Governor of the Bank of England, commented on this issue in a speech in Edinburgh in January 2014. He effectively argued that a 'sterling' currency area covering an independent Scotland as well as rUK would require 'deeper fiscal integration between members', which would imply a centralized fiscal authority with spending power equivalent to a sizeable share of GDP. This suggested that for the Bank of England to be satisfied that a currency union was workable, Scotland would have to give up control over a significant share of its power over taxation and spending. This mirrors the arguments being made by the stronger economies in the eurozone of the need for closer 'fiscal coordination'—code for effectively taking control over the tax and spending policies of the weaker eurozone economies—to stabilize the euro.

Several other independent commentators argued that the White Paper's fiscal projections were overly optimistic. For example, Institute for Fiscal Studies (IFS) economists Amior, Crawford, and Tetlow (2013) argued that:

> A significant further fiscal tightening would be required in Scotland, on top of that already announced by the UK government, in order to put Scotland's long-term public finances onto a sustainable footing.

This would imply implementing all of the austerity measures planned by the UK Government in 2013 and adding some further public spending savings or tax increases. The IFS economists took a much longer view than had the White Paper. Rather than focusing on a single year (2016–17), their analysis extended to 2060.

Their argument was that public spending in Scotland would be more difficult to control because of a more rapidly ageing population than in the rest of the UK, caused in part by lower net migration into Scotland. Disaggregated analysis of public spending patterns suggested that health care costs in Scotland would therefore rise much more rapidly than those in rUK. In the short to medium term, their pessimistic view of the Scottish budget was partly driven by the view that oil revenues would be less buoyant than predicted by the Scottish Government. Their forecast of oil revenues followed Office for Budget Responsibility (OBR) predictions up to 2017–18, which were considerably lower than those of the Scottish Government. Subsequently, they assumed that oil revenues would grow at the same rate as real GDP.

There were other currency options, the most persuasive being that Scotland should establish its own currency. So instead of fiscal discipline being engineered through an agreement with rUK it would be imposed by the markets, which would also pose challenges. MacDonald (2014a) argued that the decision (or forced choice) to establish a new Scottish currency would affect the fiscal balance because the Scottish central bank would need to build a substantial stock of foreign exchange reserves to smooth out currency fluctuations. Without such a buffer, trade would be exposed to exchange rate volatility, which in turn could impede economic growth. How large a stock of foreign exchange reserves Scotland would inherit from the UK could not be determined *ex ante* because its value would likely form part of the wider negotiation around the allocation of debt and assets at the point of independence. Inheriting an insufficient quantity of foreign exchange might require the Scottish Government to cut back on spending programs or increase taxes to build up such reserves. The lack of good trade data added further uncertainty to this debate.

HM Treasury's analysis of Scotland's fiscal outlook, published in May 2014, argued that historically higher levels of public spending per head had been broadly offset by revenues from the Scottish sector of the North Sea. Unlike the Scottish Government, it argued that the fiscal position of the UK as a whole was better than that of Scotland and that the gap would continue to grow, partly as a result of declining North Sea revenues. Like the IFS, the Treasury highlighted Scotland's more rapidly ageing population as a concern and concluded that:

> The projections in this paper for persistent and substantial deficits and elevated debt levels in an independent Scotland are one of several key factors that weigh strongly against agreeing to a currency union.
>
> (HM Government, 2014c: 7)

The Treasury went on to estimate that costs associated with the additional spending proposals outlined in the White Paper, involving changes to child-care, air passenger duty and corporation tax, would add £1.6 billion per year to Scotland's deficit, further widening the gap between the budget deficits in Scotland and the rest of the UK. Needless to say, the Scottish Government contested these estimates vigorously.

Towards the end of the campaign, both sides tried to adopt a more simple interpretation of the implications of the fiscal challenges that would confront Scotland on independence. On 28 May 2014, Danny Alexander, Chief Secretary to the Treasury, launched a Treasury paper which argued that Scots would be £1,400 per annum better off within the UK than they would under independence (HM Government, 2014g). This case was based on Scotland's ageing population, higher debt interest charges, declining oil revenues, etc., but the message was reduced to a simple strapline.

The response from the Yes campaign came on the same day. The Scottish Government stated that everyone in Scotland would be £1,000 better off a year under independence, arguing that 'if Scotland was able to increase its population and close some of the gap in its employment and productivity rates with the top performing countries in the OECD, it would boost tax revenues year on year. After 13 years this could provide an additional boost to tax receipts of over £5 billion a year' (Scottish Government, 2014a: 10). The question left unanswered in the paper was how these step-change improvements in employment and productivity might come about.

Pensions

There are already more than one million Scots of pension age, and many Baby Boomers are soon to retire. Pensions are long-term contracts which, as a result of the referendum, could potentially span different constitutional arrangements. The debate on the interaction between pensions and independence had three main components:

- the state pension;
- public sector pensions;
- occupational (private) pensions.

It is not immediately clear how the treatment of pensions might influence the economic case for or against remaining within a political union. There might be a prima facie argument that potential constitutional change added uncertainty to the nature of the pension contract and therefore was unlikely to be welcomed by pension companies and pensioners. Therefore, it was not surprising that the Scottish Government sought to reassure pensioners that their pensions would be safe and they would not be disadvantaged by Scotland breaking away from the rest of the UK.

'An independent Scotland will have the ability to protect and improve state pensions and ensure that private pensions are secure and saving for retirement is actively encouraged' (Scottish Government, 2013: 139).

ICAS, one of the main professional bodies in the pensions sector, posed a number of questions to the Scottish Government in April 2013 (ICAS, 2013). These were:

- Who would make state pension payments in an independent Scotland and take responsibility for any entitlements built up prior to independence?
- Who would be responsible for unfunded public sector pension liabilities built up prior to independence?
- What pension regulation and protection arrangements would an independent Scotland need for private sector pensions?
- How would EU solvency requirements for defined benefit and hybrid pension schemes be met across the UK if Scotland became an independent country?

The Scottish Government (2013e) responded in September 2013. It proposed a mechanism for allocating accrued rights to the state pension based on residence. It suggested that the increase in the state retirement age to sixty-six proposed for 2026 would be reviewed post-independence reflecting Scotland's lower life expectancy. John Swinney, the Finance Secretary, promised to adopt the UK 'triple lock' for the state pension in an independent Scotland even though there is widespread scepticism about its sustainability in the long run. It ensures that the state pension will increase by either the rate of growth of wages, or the rate of growth of prices, or 2.5 per cent, whichever is the greatest. The ICAS (2014) response also emphasized the uncertainty around the affordability of these proposals, given Scotland's ageing population.

The Scottish Government paper promised to take on the liabilities for the pensions of members of UK-wide unfunded pension schemes living in Scotland. This would undoubtedly be a major issue for intergovernmental negotiation and ICAS again raised the issue of affordability. In respect of private pensions, the key issue was that EU regulations suggest that cross-border pension schemes have to be solvent; many existing UK pension schemes are insolvent. ICAS was not satisfied that the Scottish Government properly addressed the question of how any deficits in these schemes would be eliminated on independence. It is true that the schemes will have to be made solvent at some time in the future; the effect of independence would only be to remove the element of choice as to when that time would be. Nevertheless, this would cause significant problems for pension companies, some of whom are located in Scotland while their main markets are in rUK. The ICAS view was that the Scottish Government had failed to adequately address all of the issues regarding post-independence private pension provision in Scotland. However, given their abstruse nature, it is unlikely that the implications of independence for private pension schemes had much of an effect on the overall dynamics of the referendum campaign. Again, the focus was on the short and medium term rather than on the long view.

North Sea Oil and Gas Revenues

The future path of North Sea oil revenues became a hugely contested issue. It was evident that (a) Scotland's dependence on oil and gas revenues to support its public services was much greater than that of the UK as a whole; and (b) these revenues were extremely volatile. Figure 3.1 shows the evolution of UK oil and gas revenues from 1980 to 2013–14 and forecasts for UK revenues made by the Office of Budget Responsibility up to 2020–1. It also shows the White Paper estimate for Scottish oil and gas revenues in 2016–17 of £7.5 billion and the estimated oil and gas revenues accruing to Scotland for the period 2009–10 to 2013–14 assuming that Scotland receives a geographical share of these revenues.

It was largely accepted by both sides that after independence, Scotland's share of these revenues would be determined by the median line principle for allocation of the UK continental shelf—the geographical principle. This would mean that the vast majority of the North Sea oil revenues would accrue to Scotland. This is evident from Figure 3.1 in the proximity of the estimated Scottish revenues from the North Sea to those for the UK as a whole over the period 2009–10 to 2013–14.

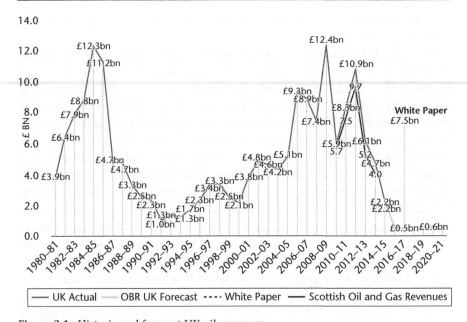

Figure 3.1. Historic and forecast UK oil revenues

Source: Her Majesty's Revenue and Customs, Office for Budget Responsibility and Scottish Government

The estimate of Scotland's oil revenues in 2016–17 used by the White Paper is also shown in Figure 3.1. Given that the average Scottish revenues between 2009–10 and 2013–14 were £6.4 billion, the White Paper estimate appears optimistic, but not absurdly so. The forecast itself was based on assumptions about both the oil price per barrel and North Sea production, both of which became the subject of intense debate. The Scottish government assumed that production would rise by two million barrels of oil equivalent per day and that the oil price would be around $113 per barrel, arguing that the high levels of investment that were observed in 2013 were an indication of the industry's confidence in the future of the North Sea.

Events have not proved very kind to these forecasts. The oil price had fallen to below $50 per barrel by September 2015 and parts of the North Sea were being shut down because the costs exceed the value of the oil being recovered. Figure 3.1 also shows the latest OBR forecasts of oil revenues out to 2020–1, which average around £0.6 billion for the next five years. This substantial decline in oil revenues is not the fault of the Scottish Government nor the UK Government, but it does illustrate that oil and gas revenues are highly volatile. The Yes campaign response was that Scotland could set up an oil fund to buffer the effects of market fluctuations. The No response was that Scotland would not have enough fiscal headroom to establish the fund in the first place without substantial cuts in spending or tax increases. In the event, the size of Scotland's initial fiscal deficit would make the establishment of such a fund extremely problematic in the short run.

Debt

North Sea oil revenues played into the issue of how debt would be allocated between Scotland and rUK at the point of independence. This allocation of debt and the rate of interest that Scotland would pay on its share of debt—and on any new debt that it issued—would have had substantial effects on Scotland's fiscal position. To put this in context, total public expenditure on and for Scots was estimated to be £66 billion in 2013–14: of this, £3.08 billion (4.6 per cent) was debt interest, based on a population share of UK debt. If Scotland did not have any debt and therefore did not need to make any debt interest payments, it would be able to increase health spending by 27 per cent.

The main measure of debt used by the UK Government is public sector net debt (PSND). This rose rapidly during the referendum campaign due to the size of the UK's annual budget deficits. However, although PSND is the most commonly quoted measure of debt, there are variants. Another commonly used measure is so-called Maastricht debt, which more closely approximates gross debt rather than net debt. Choice of measure would have had a substantial impact on Scotland's initial debt. On a population basis, Armstrong and Ebell (2013) estimated that Scotland's net debt in 2015–16 would be £143 billion under the Maastricht definition and £121 billion under the PSND measure.

The rest of the UK has a much wider revenue base than Scotland: thus between 2009–10 and 2013–14, although UK oil revenues were slightly larger than those in Scotland, they only accounted for 1.2 per cent of UK total revenues but more than 12 per cent of Scottish revenues. Hence Scotland's increased dependence on natural resource taxation compared with the UK as a whole—an argument that was also deployed by opponents of a currency union. Figure 3.1 shows that oil revenues comprised a much larger share of UK revenues during the 1980s. Due to the positive effect of historic oil and gas revenues on the UK budget, the Scottish Government argued that Scotland should not have to contribute its population share of the outstanding debt, but rather a *historic* share based on Scotland's aggregate spending and tax receipts (including oil revenues) from 1980–1 onwards. Over that period, the Scottish Government estimated that Scotland ran an annual net fiscal surplus equivalent to 0.2 per cent of GDP, while the UK ran an annual net deficit of 3.2 per cent of GDP. Since 90 per cent of UK public sector net debt had been accrued since 1980, extending the historical calculations before 1980 would not make a significant difference to this allocation of debt. How to allocate the debt between Scotland and rUK became an important point of debate between the Yes and No campaigns, but of course could not be resolved prior to the independence negotiations. Thus, in the White Paper, the Scottish Government (2013f: 348) argued that it should only take on debt of around £100 billion, 55 per cent of Scottish GDP. Nevertheless, it acknowledged that the outcome would be determined by negotiation:

> Will an independent Scotland pay its fair share of shared liabilities? Yes. Scotland and the rest of the UK will agree a share of the national debt. This could be on the basis of our historical contribution to UK revenues or on the basis of our population share. Either way, our projected share of the UK debt will be smaller as a proportion of our economic output (GDP) than for the UK as a whole, which means Scotland is well placed for the future.
>
> (Scottish Government, 2013f: 380)

The Treasury also acknowledged the outcome would be determined by negotiation, but based their analysis of Scotland's fiscal prospects on the assumption that it would inherit a population share of the debt.

> In the event of independence, the allocation of the national debt would be subject to negotiation. The UK Government has stated its clear position that an independent Scottish state would become responsible for a fair and proportionate share of the UK's current liabilities. A population split of national debt at the end of 2015–16, would mean an independent Scotland took on debt of around 74 per cent of its GDP. HM Treasury projections use this as the debt 'starting point' for an independent Scotland. They show that due to the persistently large annual budget deficits, debt quickly reaches unsustainable levels without policy action.
>
> (HM Government, 2014c: 9)

Other commentators (Armstrong and Ebell, 2014b and CPPR, 2014) suggested that the choice of 1980 as the historic debt allocation mechanism was arbitrary and that historical precedent indicated either an allocation based on population or on income.

Neither side acknowledged the role that the creditors might play in debt allocation. Creditors have an interest in ensuring that the debt is placed where it is most affordable. Would private creditors dictate the allocation of debt, as was the case with all of the Eastern European economies when they became independent in the 1990s? This is unlikely, but it would be unwise to assume that they would not have any influence, particularly if they acted together. They might, for example, argue in favour of either the income-based or the historic-based allocation of debt because these would better reflect what Scotland could afford.

It was also argued that, as a new, small state with no credit history and a small bond market, an independent Scotland would have to pay a premium on its debt interest. Armstrong and Ebell (2013) argued that Scotland would pay an interest rate premium of between 0.72 and 1.65 percentage points above UK rates. HM Treasury (2014: 40) took the mid-point of this range (1.2 per cent) as the indicative premium that the Scottish Government would face.

Oxford Economics also argued that the premium would exceed 100 basis points (Oxford Economics, 2014: 20). The Oxford Economics report was commissioned by the Weir Group, one of Scotland's few FTSE 100 companies and one of the few large concerns that took a clear stance against independence.

The assumption around what risk premium Scotland might pay on its debt may seem esoteric, but it would have made a significant difference to Scotland's fiscal position on independence. If it were to inherit a historic share of debt at the end of 2015/16 and pay no premium on its borrowing, Scotland's debt interest payments in 2016/17 would have been around £4.1 billion. If it inherited a population share, its debt interest would have been £5.2 billion. If it inherited a population share and faced a 1.2 percentage point premium on its borrowing, Scotland would face debt interest payments of £6.6 billion in the first year of independence. The difference between the lower and upper estimates of interest costs more than exceeds Scotland's university budget. Again, though clearly important, this was a technical issue that received relatively little attention in the popular debate.

Health Spending

Scotland's record on health spending was questioned by the Institute for Fiscal Studies towards the end of the referendum campaign. This was an unexpected development because spending on the NHS has been completely devolved to Scotland for decades. The Yes campaign argued that independence would protect its status and funding. Nevertheless, Johnson and Phillips (2014) argued that the Scottish Government had increased spending on health less rapidly than rUK even though Scotland's block grant from Westminster had been cut by less than that in the UK as a whole since 2009–10. This was a damaging claim to the Yes campaign. However, Cuthbert and Cuthbert (2014) argued that it was not the spending commitment that mattered to the independence campaign, but rather that an independent Scotland would maintain a fully public NHS. If the UK government chose to privatize health service funding (rather than health service delivery) then Scotland's ability to continue funding a fully public NHS might be jeopardized if Scotland remained within the UK because cuts in NHS spending in rUK would work through the Barnett formula, reducing Scotland's block grant, and thus making it more difficult to fund the Scottish NHS. Independence was desirable because the UK might adopt policies that would reduce the size of the state. Rather than offering a new vision, independence was a means to maintain the status quo. Compared with other jurisdictions, this may seem an unusual reason for seeking independence.

Fiscal Issues That Had Little Traction in the Referendum Debate

We complete this chapter by considering some of the fiscal issues that might have been expected to play an important role in the debate but failed to make a significant impact. Why this was the case is not entirely clear. Some issues were complex; some affected both sides of the argument and it was difficult to determine what difference independence might make; some just seem to lose momentum.

Universalism Versus Means Testing

Prior to the referendum, Scotland's greater reliance on universal benefits rather than means-tested benefits compared with the rest of the UK provoked considerable debate. Universal benefits included prescriptions, bus passes for the elderly, university tuition fees, and personal care for the elderly. While some argued that universal benefits seemed to be subsidies to the better off, others argued that a sustainable welfare system should offer everyone some benefits in order to maintain its democratic legitimacy.

A Scottish Debt Market

One of the new institutions that an independent Scotland would have had to create would be a debt market. How this was structured and managed would have significant implications for public spending and also for pensions. Yet this issue was hardly mentioned in the debates. If Scotland had, by choice, or by the lack of an alternative, set up its own currency, then Scottish pension funds would have to invest heavily in the Scottish debt market to reduce scheme members' exposure to exchange rate risk. If Scotland had stayed within sterling, Scottish bonds would have had to compete with UK bonds and Scottish pension funds could hold a more diversified bond portfolio. If Scottish bonds carried a liquidity premium, Scottish pensioners would gain from the higher yields, since they would have to invest less to get the same return as an rUK pensioner. However, Scottish taxpayers would have to fund these higher debt charges. This implies that a risk premium on Scottish bonds would result in a transfer from Scottish taxpayers to Scottish pensioners relative to the rest of the UK.

Tax Powers and Economic Growth

One argument made by the Yes campaign in favour of Scotland gaining complete control over the fiscal levers was that these could be utilized to increase levels of productivity and therefore its economic growth rate. This also played into the argument that Scotland could avoid the need for austerity policies because enhanced growth would enhance government revenues, improving the deficit and reducing the debt as a share of GDP. The main mechanism for manipulating the fiscal system to increase Scotland's growth rate was included in the White Paper—to reduce the rate of corporation tax by up to 3 per cent. Arguably the No campaign failed to contest this assertion, which seems at odds with much of the evidence. For example, Aghion and Howitt (2009) in their review of growth theory illustrate how complex this issue is and list a number of possible drivers of growth, among which innovation plays a vital role, while competition policy, tax, education, macroeconomic policy, democracy, and levels of trust within the economy may also make a contribution. The recent report of the LSE Growth Commission (2013) focused on investment in human capital, infrastructure, and innovation as being the key elements that needed to be addressed to support and enhance the UK's growth rate. None of these issues played a significant role in the referendum campaign. Rather the assertion was that the addition of tax powers to those that the Scottish Government already possessed would make the difference to moving to a new and more rapid growth path.

Conclusion

The debate on Scotland's fiscal policies took many twists and turns during the referendum campaign. Much of it was highly technical and eventually both sides looked for handy soundbites that conveyed their key messages. This strategy may have produced electoral advantage, but it failed to convey the necessary nuances and qualifications. Making such caveats was ruled out in the heat of the campaign and therefore much of the detailed economic analysis did not reach the electorate. It is not entirely clear whether voters had assimilated this knowledge during the early part of the campaign, perhaps mediated through the press. This may have reflected a lack of economic literacy in the Scottish population. Or perhaps more likely it was a result of the inherent complexity and novelty of the arguments involved in the creation of a new state.

Many of the arguments reflected short- to medium-term issues. Longer-run issues such as whether the Scottish economy might grow faster or slower than the rest of the UK after independence got little attention. Given that constitutional change is for the long haul, the absence of such argument from the debate perhaps suggests a myopic approach from the protagonists, or perhaps their assumption that voters were similarly myopic. Not only was the debate present-focused, on occasion it appeared that the reason for seeking separation was to maintain the status quo. This was clear in relation to the NHS debate, where the Yes campaign argued that the Conservative administration would undermine public funding of the health service.

The quality of the debate was constrained by the adequacy of the available data and it was largely viewed through the lens of UK's current economic structures and fiscal difficulties. Inevitably, debates on Scotland's potential future reflected evidence drawn from its past and inferences drawn about the future. Inferences about the nature of the post-independence Scottish economy were subject to substantial uncertainty; even demographic projections, which played a vital role in IFS arguments regarding fiscal sustainability, have to be treated with caution when looking forward more than a decade. The 2001-based projections for Scotland's population made by the Registrar General suggested that a fall in Scotland's population to 4.94 million by 2016 from its 2001 level of 5.06 million was likely. In fact, it grew to 5.35 million by 2014 and is expected to increase further by 2016. Instead of falling by 2 per cent, it has grown by 6 per cent. Demographic forecasts are subject to considerable error. The uncertainty attached to economic forecasts is significantly greater, given the greater inherent volatility of macroeconomic aggregates. It was clearly understood by both sides that independence was such a unique event that risk-averse individuals might well be deterred by uncertainty relating to their major economic concerns. However, uncertainty was not thought to play well in political debates. Both sides portrayed their point estimates as if there was no room for doubt. This certainly played into the hands of newspaper sub-editors whose life was made easier when parties issued simple claims such as Scots being £1,400 a year better off in the union or being £1,000 per year better off with independence. The room for measured analysis, with plausibly qualified claims, diminished as the referendum date approached, making for a highly polarized debate. These may have stretched the voters' credulity on both sides. The Yes campaign had the difficult task of reassuring voters' concerns about their economic future in the presence of considerable uncertainty, while the No campaign combined point forecasts of better outcomes within the union with arguments that focused on the uncertainty associated with issues such as pensions, taxes, debt, and the currency. Ultimately (see Chapter 10), it was the risks that perhaps played the strongest role in determining the outcome in favour of the No campaign.

4

The Currency Issue

Contested Narratives on Currency Union and Independence

Coree Brown Swan and Bettina Petersohn

Introduction

One of the most contested issues throughout the referendum campaign was the question of which currency an independent Scotland would use. The Yes Scotland campaign asserted its right to continue to use the pound within a formal currency union while the UK Government and the Better Together campaign rejected this claim. These competing narratives culminated in one of the televised debates between the two campaign leaders when Alistair Darling posed a challenge to Alex Salmond on the subject of the insignia of an independent Scotland. He said: 'I presume the flag is the saltire, I assume our capital will still be Edinburgh, but you can't tell us what currency we will have' (cited in Carrell and Brooks, 2014). The First Minister replied, 'We will keep the Pound, it is our Pound as well as England's Pound. This is Scotland's Pound. It doesn't belong to George Osborne, it doesn't belong to you. It has been built up by Scotland for a long time.'

The No side responded that this was not possible and would not happen; one of the rare instances in which they stated clearly what their response to a Yes vote would be. These starkly contrasting claims constituted one of the central arguments of the campaign and the resulting uncertainty was one of the critical elements in the outcome (see Chapter 10). Matters were complicated by the fact that not all Yes supporters were in favour of a currency union and, for many years, the SNP had envisaged an independent Scottish currency.

The debate about currency was marked by significant differences in framing the issue; by contrasting knowledge claims based on different interpretations of the economic analyses; and by tactical moves aimed at winning the argument with the voter and gaining advantage in the polls. For the currency debate, the timing of the independence referendum also mattered with the recent experiences of the European common currency providing ample examples for campaigners and academics alike on potential mistakes when negotiating currency arrangements. Academic contributions were often critical of a monetary union, emphasizing banking risks and the need for fiscal coordination. Although the SNP had contemplated a common European currency fifteen years earlier, joining the euro was also no longer a favourable option for the Scottish Government in light of the recent crisis.

In this chapter, we identify the protagonists and the main issues of the currency debate. We discuss how the idea of an independent currency has historically been central to national sovereignty but may now be in question and how the SNP's policy has evolved. We show how the main protagonists of the currency debate framed the issue, with the No side taking the traditional view that currency is central to national sovereignty while the Yes side emphasized shared authority and partnership. Each side selected particular aspects of the question to support the credibility of their interpretation of what independence means and to thread these into a coherent narrative. We discuss the different knowledge claims made by the two campaigns, in what was a highly technical matter, notably in relation to the wider implications of monetary union. We then examine the tactical games played by the two sides as each sought to prove that the other side was bluffing, in a context of considerable uncertainty. Finally, we show how the currency debate reflects some of the key characteristics of the campaign as a whole.

The Options and the Protagonists

In principle, there were several currency options for an independent Scotland. These options were identified by the Scottish Government's Fiscal Commission Working Group as well as academic studies of the issue, notably Armstrong and Ebell's 2013 report. Post-independence, Scotland could adopt its own independent currency, floating in international markets as Sweden has done, despite its theoretical commitment to join the euro. Alternatively, it could join the euro, perhaps after a transition period. It could also retain pound sterling. This could be done in several ways. It could negotiate a full currency union with the remaining United Kingdom. In this scenario, the Bank of England would remain as the central bank and lender of last resort, while Scotland would 'share' the currency, with some say in its management. Alternatively, it could use the pound unilaterally (sterlingization) in the way that some countries use the US dollar and others the euro. This might involve a currency board arrangement in which Scottish pounds would be backed by Bank of England pounds kept in the Scottish Central Bank. In this scenario, Scotland would have no control over monetary policy. Finally, a Scottish pound could be pegged to the pound sterling much in the way that the Danish krone is pegged to the euro. Again, Scotland would have to accept monetary policy from the rest of the United Kingdom. With the exception of the separate currency, all of these involve forgoing full independence in the traditional sense and accepting shared power and interdependence in macroeconomic and fiscal policies.

The main protagonists were the two governments and the leaders of the Yes Scotland and Better Together campaigns. The SNP-led Scottish Government's position was informed by the recommendations of the Fiscal Commission Working Group (2013), a subcommittee of the Council of Economic Advisors, whose first report pointed out the benefits of an independent currency, including maximum policy sovereignty and an increase in economic sovereignty, but ultimately recommended that the Scottish Government retain sterling in a monetary union with the rest of the UK. The Commission also argued that this was in the UK's interest. The Scottish Government adopted this position in its April 2013 publication, *Currency Choices for an Independent Scotland: Response to the Fiscal Commission Working Group* and the First Minister explained the economic and political rationale in a speech entitled *The Currency Union*: part of a series of speeches on the six unions and presented in the Isle of Man in July 2013. The position was further elaborated in the Scottish Government white paper, *Scotland's Future* (2013f).

The unionist camp, including the United Kingdom Government, the Better Together campaign, and the unionist parties, rejected this claim. The UK Government (HM Government, 2013a) published its analysis of the prospect of a currency union in April 2013: *Scotland analysis: Currency and monetary policy*. The House of Commons Scottish Affairs Committee (2014) also took evidence, publishing its findings in *The Referendum on Separation for Scotland: no doubt-no currency union* in July 2014. In February 2014 Chancellor George Osborne made a speech in Edinburgh on the prospect of a currency union with an independent Scotland. In conjunction with this, his Liberal Democrat and Labour counterparts Danny Alexander and Ed Balls made statements the same week, ruling out the prospect of a currency union by whichever party formed a government following the 2015 General Election. Alistair Darling, head of Better Together, emphasized the issue of currency and the absence of a 'plan B' in the televised debates of August 2014.

The issue was also marked by unusually overt interventions by civil servants as well as business groups. Mark Carney, Governor of the Bank of England, set out the Bank's position in January 2014 at a speech at the Scottish Council for Development and Industry. In *The Economics of Currency Union* he set out the costs and benefits of currency areas while ostensibly maintaining a position of neutrality. 'Any arrangement to retain sterling in an independent Scotland would need to be negotiated between the Westminster and Scottish Parliaments. The Bank of England would implement whatever monetary arrangements were put in place.' The Treasury was less guarded in comparison. In an unusual move, subsequently criticized by a House of Commons Committee (see Chapter 1), Sir Nicholas Macpherson (2014), the Permanent Secretary, published his advice to the Chancellor, describing the prospect of a currency union as 'fraught with difficulty'. The CBI, which endorsed a no vote, issued a statement calling into question the Scottish Government's economic plans and prospects for a currency union.

As the issue was a highly technical one, there were interventions from academic analysts looking at the economics of currency unions (see Chapter 3 for more details). Generally, these analyses avoided taking sides in the independence question and focused on the strengths and weakness of the various options, with many of them stressing the strict conditions that would have to be put on a monetary union and the difficulties it would entail (Armstrong and Ebell, 2013).

Currency, Statehood, and Nationalism

While those arguing against a currency union questioned the viability of a state's independence without its own currency, historical as well as contemporary cases suggest that currency and state do not always coincide. Prior to the nineteenth century, international currencies circulated alongside local ones and little effort was made to consolidate the diversity of currencies in use. With the emergence of the modern state in the late eighteenth century, statehood and territorial currencies became more closely interlinked. Sovereignty over the military and defence as well as over the issuing of currencies and taxation were vital for the state to fulfil its function of providing security and economic growth. Max Weber (1919) emphasized the creation of a centralized bureaucracy with professional and permanent staff as a key characteristic of the modern state enhancing its administrative capacities. Standardization of the territorial currency was part of that process of bureaucratic consolidation and the assertion of sovereignty by the state (Helleiner, 2003).

During the period of state formation in which the activities of the state were directed at regulating trade relations and ensuring that standard rules apply across the territory, a common currency facilitated trade and economic exchange. A shared currency also provided a vehicle for nationalist imagery; it contributed to the construction of an imagined community and strengthened a sense of faith in the nation. As a common medium of communication, currencies also created collective monetary experiences, thus contributing to a sense of popular sovereignty (Helleiner, 1998). Furthermore, paper money issued by the state played an important role in financing wars. The American Civil War, for example, triggered the development of a single national paper money issued by the federal government replacing paper notes from local banks over time. Southern states continued to issue their own notes as one way of revenue raising during the war. In this case, an independent paper note served several functions, a practical and fiscal one and a political one in support of forming an independent community (Schwab, 1892).

Nevertheless, a national currency does not form a defining characteristic of an independent state as the existence of a number of currency unions between states demonstrates. There were currency unions even in the nineteenth century, and states that emerged as a result of more recent processes of decolonization or after the collapse of the Communist bloc have not always moved to establish their own currency. Alesina and Barro (2001: 381) identified sixty small countries or territories which are either members of a formal currency union or have used a larger country's money based on negotiated agreements. Examples of formal currency unions are the eurozone, Central and West African monetary unions, or the East Caribbean Currency Union. The Common Monetary Area encompassing South Africa, Namibia, Lesotho, and Swaziland allows for the simultaneous use of the South African rand forming a legal tender in all four states and separate currencies issued by the three other member states that are nevertheless pegged to the rand.

Currency agreements may be more or less formal and have in the past included the opportunity for some kind of shared rule over monetary issues between the states involved. The currency treaty signed between Switzerland and Liechtenstein in 1980 regulated the use of the Swiss franc in the principality, with the Swiss National Bank determining the monetary policy and the authorities in Liechtenstein being responsible for its implementation. The treaty also provided for the creation of a joint commission responsible for the interpretation of the treaty and for a court of arbitration in case of conflict, each composed of equal members from both states and governments. Other examples which do not allow for influence at the centre include the currency unions between the UK and the British territories with the Falklands, Gibraltar, and the Isle of Man using the pound, or the use of the American dollar in Ecuador and El Salvador for domestic market transactions, also called dollarization (Alesina and Barro, 2001).

Former British colonies, which used sterling formally alongside local currencies, pledged to remain in the sterling zone after independence, but they established their own central banks as part of the transition and eventually adopted their own currencies (Stockwell, 1998: 101). In contrast, former

French colonies maintained the French franc and fourteen countries in Africa now participate in the Communauté Financière Africaine (CFA), which uses the CFA franc and is guaranteed by the French Treasury with a fixed exchange rate against the euro (Gulde and Tsangarides, 2008). The dissolution of the political unions in Soviet Union and Yugoslavia also entailed the dissolution of currency unions.

Within the European Union, adoption of the euro is, at least in theory, obligatory for all members except the United Kingdom and Denmark. Some Eastern and Central Eastern European States which had originally introduced their own currencies soon abandoned them, although others have been tardy in adopting the euro. Non-member states have also moved into the euro area, more or less officially. Montenegro uses the euro without being a member, while Bosnia and Herzegovina's currency, the convertible mark (KM) is pegged to it. Kosovo also uses the euro (Korovilas, 2002). This is another instance of the more general phenomenon in which European integration reduces the cost of statehood, detaches some of its traditional components, and allows for new configurations of sovereignty.

Indeed, many parties favouring independence are generally also supportive of supranational integration and currency unions. Parties seeking self-government in Flanders, Catalonia, and the Basque Country foresee continued integration within the eurozone. We find similar positions beyond Europe and the comparatively highly integrated economic market of the eurozone. The Parti Québécois (PQ) argued, in the context of both the 1980 and 1990 referendums, that it would keep the Canadian dollar, in an effort to bolster support for independence and reduce monetary uncertainty. The 1980 referendum question defined the sovereignty association as an 'economic association including common currency'. The then leader of the Parti Québécois, Jacques Parizeau, said in 1991 that 'We are the co-defenders of the Canadian dollar' (cited in Helleiner, 2007). In the context of the second referendum of 1995, the Parti Québécois maintained the position of a common market, common currency, and common banking system. If a currency union could not be negotiated, it argued, the Canadian dollar would be used unilaterally. Federalists contested this assertion, pointing to both the economic risks and querying the purpose of independence if the economic tools were shared or ceded to another. Following the failed referendum campaign, the Bloc Québécois tabled a discussion of Canada's participation in a North American monetary union or the adoption of the US dollar (Helleiner, 2003).

The Scottish National Party's own position on currency has shifted over time. While always including some degree of coordination with the rest of the UK, the preferred option of own currency, currency union, or later using the euro seemed to be contingent on the level of self-government enjoyed by Scotland and the economic performance of the respective moment. From its origins, the party advocated an independent central bank, allowing for financial and political self-government. In the *Aims and Policy of the SNP*, the party advocated the establishment of a Scottish central bank for the management of the Scots pound, which, in the context of the 1970s oil boom, was expected to gain strength against an English pound (SNP, 1977). However, strong ties were envisaged, with a forum for the negotiation of exchange controls with England and facilities to allow Scottish financial institutions to operate through the London exchange (SNP, 1977).

By 1997 the party had adapted its position on independence to the changed European context including the prospect of a common European currency. While not committing to participation, the party said in its draft document on a constitution for an independent Scotland that 'An SNP led Scotland will be mindful of the benefits of European monetary union and the common goal of economic convergence and would ensure that a referendum was held on any proposal to adopt a common European Currency' (SNP, 1997). This position was solidified in the manifesto for the 1999 Scottish Parliamentary elections as well as in the party's 2001 manifesto, which set out conditions by which Scotland could enter, including acceptable economic conditions, an agreement on exchange rates, and a popular referendum (SNP, 2001).

There were both practical and strategic aspects to the policy as the SNP could avoid the 'situation of an independent Scotland either remaining part of Sterling or creating a separate currency' (MacAskill, 2004). This position was maintained by the party until the euro crisis, which called the sustainability of this arrangement into question. The 2009 National Conversation document, *Your Scotland, Your Voice*, hinted at this shift. 'Scotland would continue to operate within the sterling system until a decision to join the euro by the people of Scotland in a referendum when the economic conditions were right' (Scottish Government, 2009: 31). After the experiences of the eurozone crisis, joining the euro was not promoted as a desirable alternative in subsequent manifestos or over the course of the campaign (SNP, 2010). This left a currency union with the UK as the dominant position for the referendum debate, but several actors on both sides saw this as a restriction to the discussion.

The debate was situated within the context of a eurozone in crisis—a condition which influenced the SNP's position on currency as well as the content of arguments made both for and against currency union. Academic contributions also played a role here, with growing interests in the implications of the monetary union in Europe. As a result, academic contributions were often critical of forming a monetary union, drawing on the recent experience of crisis management by eurozone member states and EU institutions. They emphasized issues of banking risks and the need for fiscal coordination to ensure adequate response to changing economic conditions (Armstrong and Ebell,

2014a), issues that may not have been as salient without the example of the eurozone crisis.

Competing Frames

The debate was shaped both by the position of the two campaigns on the issue—in favour of a yes or no vote—but also understandings of union, independence, and sovereignty in a modern era. Two competing frames came to the fore. The UK Government adopted a positive view of the economic and political union of the United Kingdom, viewing it as a source of strength, stability, and sovereignty. At the same time, the currency union was framed as a negative, that is, something that would increase risk, threaten stability, and undermine sovereignty—not just for the rest of the UK but for Scotland as well. In contrast, the Scottish Government framed the political union of the United Kingdom as a negative one, imposing policies on the Scottish Government that do not match with policy preferences in Scotland, while emphasizing the potential of multiple interconnected and overlapping unions which could be maintained in the event of independence—the social, monarchical, and monetary unions as well as membership to the European Union. This suggested a greater degree of comfort with the idea of sovereignty as being shared between governments of different levels. While these issues of sovereignty, as exclusive or as shared, emerged in other aspects of the debate, it was particularly salient in the way the debate over a currency union was framed.

For the No side, the United Kingdom was seen as the 'most successful monetary, fiscal and political unions in history' (HM Government, 2013a: 18). A currency union, in the view of the UK Government, goes hand in hand, and indeed requires a political union for the coordination of economic policy. In the absence of this political union, 'It would not be possible to recreate today's arrangements' (HM Government, 2013d: 6). For the No side, the pound and the Bank of England were not assets to be shared or divided, but institutions forming part of the Union. Alistair Darling insisted that if Scotland walked away from the political union, it walked away from the pound (*Daily Telegraph*, 24 November 2013) and had no right to pick and choose which bits of the Union it would keep.

A currency union, without the political union as a coordinating mechanism, would serve to undermine sovereignty, not just of the rest of the United Kingdom, which may be called upon to bail out Scottish banks, but for an independent Scotland. The campaign often asked: What was the point of independence, if recently won sovereignty would only be immediately ceded to decision makers elsewhere? George Osborne emphasized this prospective dependency in his February 2014 speech, saying that 'the logic of a currency union would mean that Scotland would have to give up sovereignty over spending and tax decisions'. According to *United Kingdom, United Future*, the UK Government's (HM Government 2014f: 18) final contribution to the *Scotland Analysis* programme, such an arrangement 'would make Scotland's economic policy dependent on another country, in which it has no longer any say or representation'. This would also place limits on the ability of an independent Scotland to pursue economic measures in the event of a shock which affected only Scotland (HM Government, 2014f: 18). As Alistair Darling put it in the first leaders' debate, having a currency union would be 'a bit like getting a divorce and keeping the same joint bank account'. George Osborne also employed this figure of speech, describing the Yes campaign's plan as 'a bit like a couple getting divorced but saying we're going to keep the current account and we're going to keep the joint mortgage. You know that's not what happens in divorce and it's not what happens in separation' (Andrew Marr Show, 2014a). An independent Scotland would not be part of the Union and for the UK Government and Treasury, there could be no question of the United Kingdom sharing control of its monetary policy with a foreign state. Taxpayers in the rest of the United Kingdom would be subject to the risk 'of providing taxpayer support to the Scottish financial sector if the Bank of England was acting as a joint lender of last resort' (HM Government, 2013a: 8).

In contrast, the SNP and Scottish Government saw monetary union as detachable from political union—part of their argument for keeping five of the existing six unions (see Chapter 1). In an interdependent world, independence was not coterminous with an independent currency. The Scottish Government White Paper noted that '[i]ndependent countries around the world share currencies. Countries like France, Germany, and the Netherlands do not have their own currency but are clearly independent and control their own resources' (Scottish Government, 2013f: 27). The rationale behind this choice was based in the desirability and practicality of such an arrangement for both Scotland and the rest of the UK. In contrast to arguments made by unionist opponents, who questioned the value of independence without an independent currency, a currency union would give Scotland more of a say in economic policy than it possesses under the current arrangement. 'For the first time since it was founded by a Scot, Scotland as a country would have a formal stake in the governance of the Bank of England—protecting its independence, but taking our share of responsibility with the rest of the UK' (Salmond, 16 July 2013). A currency union, with provisions for Scottish representation within decision-making bodies, would enhance representation, currently nonexistent. They bolstered this with a moral argument that the pound belonged to Scotland as much as the rest of the UK and that it and the Bank of England should be regarded as assets, to which both sides had a right after separation. For Alex Salmond (2013), 'The Bank of England, despite its name, is actually a shared asset—it was founded by a Scot, and its assets and liabilities belong to Scottish taxpayers just as much as people in the rest of these islands.' The White Paper (Scottish Government, 2013f: 7) stated that 'The Pound is Scotland's currency just as much as it is the rest of the UK's.' Contradicting claims by opponents were rejected as bluff and bluster; in the event of a yes vote, actors on both sides would behave rationally.

Knowledge Claims

On the currency issue, and in particular, the formation of a currency union, both campaigns employed a range of knowledge claims about the feasibility, desirability, and the consequences of such a union. Both drew on evidence from experts in order to enhance the credibility of their claims. The competing knowledge claims of the two sides focused on two aspects: whether a currency union was feasible or desirable and the economic and political consequences of that choice. Neither side sought to present this as an issue pitching Scotland's interests against those of the United Kingdom. Rather they argued that, if independence were to come about, their preferred solution would be in the interest of both sides. As a result, these claims were grounded in a belief in rational self-interest.

For the Fiscal Commission Working Group (2013), which advised the Scottish Government, a monetary union with the rest of the UK would provide 'a strong overarching framework for Scotland post-independence'. The Yes side also argued that the UK would have an interest in monetary union in order to stabilize trading conditions between the two countries and to include Scottish oil in the balance of payments of the sterling zone. In *Scotland's Future*, the Scottish Government (2013b: 7) stated that 'Using Sterling will provide continuity and certainty for business and individuals, and an independent Scotland will make a substantial contribution to a Sterling area.' This argument was based on an analysis of trade between the two territories, with the UK as Scotland's largest trading partner and Scotland as the UK's second largest partner; the cross-border nature of business; labour mobility within the borders of the United Kingdom; and the sterling zone's status as an optimal currency area. The rest of the UK would benefit from Scotland's industries, including oil and whisky, according to Finance Minister John Swinney (cited in Blackhurst, 2014).

In contrast, the unionist campaign's main claims made against the feasibility of a currency union focused on the benefits of scale, especially higher economic benefits due to being part of a larger entity; greater capacities of the UK Government to manage a recession; and the negative implications of separating powers over taxation from powers over monetary policies for dealing with a crisis effectively. In the Scotland Analysis series, the UK Government presented the UK as a success story, having 'brought economic benefits to all parts of the UK because taxation, spending, monetary policy and financial stability are coordinated across the whole of the UK' (HM Government, 2014a: 18). However, this successful monetary union could not be maintained in the event of the dissolution of the other unions which were vital for coordination and cooperation.

Further differences between the knowledge claims employed by each campaign hinged upon what exactly was meant by Scotland continuing to use the pound. The Scottish Government's (2013f) proposals were centred on a full monetary union, in which Scotland and the UK would share the management of the currency. This included using the Bank of England as the lender of last resort should Scottish banks fail. Whatever the merits of this policy, it could only work if both sides agreed. Other options, including sterlingization and pegging a Scottish currency to the pound, could be applied unilaterally. Alistair Darling acknowledged this in the second televised debate, saying 'Of course we can use the Pound . . . we could use the rouble, we could use the dollar, we could use the yen. We could use anything we want' (cited in Swanson, 2014). He then made clear that these options were second best to the status quo of remaining part of the United Kingdom and having a shared currency. A currency union between Scotland as an independent state and rUK was not a viable alternative.

During the course of the long campaign, the deeper implications of monetary union were drawn out: the union would include shared financial regulation as well as monetary policy. Monetary union would also have implications for broader issues of macroeconomic policy, further questioning the reality of independence. The experience of the eurozone was crucial here and was employed by unionists to illustrate the risks of diverse fiscal policies and a common monetary policy (HM Government, 2013a). The euro had been launched as a monetary union but without a deeper political or fiscal union. National governments would be responsible for maintaining fiscal discipline within limits stipulated at European level and there would be no bail-outs for failing governments or banks. The idea was that monetary union would be accompanied by economic convergence so that a single interest rate would be appropriate across the whole of the union. However, this scenario depended on a number of untested assumptions, which were exposed with the eurozone, global economic, and sovereign debt crises from 2008. In response to the crisis, governments of EU member states agreed to tighten European controls over national debts and deficits and introduce stronger mechanisms for enforcing them, including a series of stability pacts culminating in the Treaty on Stability, Coordination and Governance signed by all EU countries except for the United Kingdom and the Czech Republic. The widely drawn implication in the context of the Scottish referendum was that a monetary union between an independent Scotland and the UK would require similar mechanisms, thus curtailing the leeway of action of the Scottish state.

Interestingly, much of this analysis was in fact shared by the Scottish Government and its idea of how a monetary union with rUK would function. The Bank of England would continue to be a lender of last resort in Scotland, thereby ensuring that the entire sterling area would be responsible in case of another bank failure such as occurred in 2008. The Scottish Government stated that the 'Bank of England Financial Policy Committee will continue to set macroprudential policy and identify systemic risks across the whole of the Sterling Area. There could be a shared Sterling Area prudential regulatory authority for deposit takers, insurance companies and investment firms' (Scottish Government, 2013f: 133). Moreover, the Scottish Government recognized that in a currency union, a sustainable fiscal framework was important and significant divergences in fiscal balances were to be avoided. 'That is why such a monetary framework will require a fiscal sustainability agreement between Scotland and the rest of the UK, which will apply to both governments and cover overall net borrowing and debt' (Scottish Government, 2013f: 137). Within these constraints, however, Scotland would be free to set its own economic policy, including overall levels of public spending.

Based on the interconnectedness of fiscal and monetary policies, the debate about a currency union also stimulated a discussion on the degree of independence and freedom that Scotland, as a smaller partner in this union, would actually have. The No campaign seized on the constraints acknowledged by the Scottish Governments with Alistair Darling telling the BBC's *Newsnight Scotland* programme that a post-independence currency union with the rest of the UK would be 'desirable', but he added: 'But you have got to understand there would be consequences. A currency union means you have both got to agree your budgets, you've both got to agree how much you can tax, spend and borrow. The point I am making is that's not freedom' (cited in Buchanan, 2013). This perspective was shared by the independent economic think tank, Fiscal Affairs Scotland, arguing that negotiating a currency union with the rest of the UK would put restrictions on an independent Scotland to decide over monetary and fiscal policies, including setting its own corporation tax rates (McLaren and Armstrong, 2014).

Much of the economic case for independence had long rested on Scotland being able to pursue a macroeconomic strategy suited to its conditions and not those of the south of England, where deflationary and restrictive policies had been periodically applied to dampen demand. The SNP also argued during the 2015 General Election campaign that the UK Government had applied excessive austerity and that there was room for further borrowing. So accepting a fiscal pact as part of currency union did represent a significant move. Even some analysts far from the pro-independence movement seemed to believe that the SNP may have conceded too much. Armstrong and Ebell (2014a) argued that a full currency union including banking union and a fiscal pact would be worthless in any case, so that in practice it would amount to sterlingization (which they, following economic convention, call 'dollarization'). On the other hand, they were also very critical of sterlingization as a solution, given the high levels of Scottish debt. Another academic, Ronald MacDonald (2014b) similarly argued against all the sterling options.

From within the Yes camp, the Scottish Greens (2014a) and the pro-independence left were also less convinced that a currency union formed the best option. In advance of the campaign, Green MSP and party co-convenor Patrick Harvie questioned the exclusion of an independent Scottish currency from the debate, saying 'We seem to be told that our only choice is between the Euro and the Pound. I think we should open up the debate and look at whether an independent Scotland could have an independent currency, even if it might take years to reach that point.' Writing in the *Edinburgh Evening News*, former SNP MP Jim Sillars (2014) presented an alternative: a currency aligned, at least in the early stages of independence, to the pound. This would allow for 'a genuinely independent country, not controlled economically by another'. Responding to the intervention by the Governor of the Bank of England, Harvie urged the Scottish Government to make preparations for a Scottish currency considering the likelihood of diverging economies north and south of the border. In the account of the Scottish Greens, economic independence was only possible with an independent currency (Scottish Greens, 2014a).

These divisions were exploited by the Better Together campaign, with Alistair Darling asking on *Newsnight Scotland*: 'How on earth can they ask people to vote for independence when they can't even agree amongst themselves the most basic and fundamental things like what currency we would use?' (cited in Buchanan, 2013). Despite these objections, the campaign maintained its focus on its Plan A, maintenance of sterling within a formal currency union in the knowledge that this was the most reassuring option and the one most favoured by public opinion (Panelbase, 2014). In the final weeks of the campaign, Crawford Beveridge, senior economic advisor to Alex Salmond and chairman of the First Minister's Fiscal Commission Working Group, made a statement that a currency union might not be negotiated and that Scotland might not be sharing the pound after all. In his view, 'sterlingization' would be only a transitional step towards an independent currency for Scotland (cited in Riley-Smith, 2014).

Due to the contrasting knowledge claims made by the two campaigns and governments, as well as internal inconsistencies within the camps, implications, and consequences of a currency union remained uncertain. Campaign tactics aimed at reducing the credibility of the claims made by the respective other side and at stirring doubts with regard to what currency arrangement would be negotiable after a Yes vote.

Tactics

For the Yes campaign, the goal was to present a certain and safe position on currency—a currency union negotiated between the United Kingdom and Scotland. This position would provide the stability of remaining part of a larger monetary unit whilst allowing an independent Scottish government to pursue its own policy goals. The unionist campaign, in contrast, emphasized the inherent uncertainty of their rivals' proposals, a tactic strengthened by their willingness to categorically rule out a currency union. On many of the issues during the campaign, the No side refrained from suggesting that independence would be impossible, fearing that it would be seen as running Scotland down, or lacking in credibility. So, for example, they never claimed that Scotland would be excluded from the European Union, but merely listed reasons why it might be and focused on the risk and potential uncertainty (see Chapter 5). On the issue of currency, however, they were trenchant. A currency union would not work and would not be negotiated by the United Kingdom. The three unionist parties issued statements to that effect in concert, with the Permanent Secretary of the Treasury backing them up. Speaking on *The Andrew Marr Show* (2014a) on 7 September, as polls indicated a narrow lead for Yes, George Osborne stated unequivocally: 'No ifs, no buts; we will not share the Pound if Scotland separates from the rest of the UK.' In response to these arguments, the Yes side accused them of bluffing and insisted that, as it would be in the interests of both sides, it would happen. The First Minister described the UK Government's initial objections to the currency union as 'contrived scepticism' (Salmond, 16 July 2014). Speaking on *The Andrew Marr Show* (2014b) just days before the referendum, the First Minister said that he expected to see 'a more constructive approach' on Friday 19 September, when the 'referendum incentive to provide obstacles in the path of Scotland will be dissipated'.

During the referendum debate, the unionist campaign focused on the risks of currency union, while the Scottish Government and Yes campaign emphasized the negative effects that a refusal on the part of unionist parties would have on the economies of both Scotland and the rest of the United Kingdom. Contesting the position of the UK Government and the Better Together campaign, the Scottish Government argued that not having a currency union would entail costs for the taxpayer and businesses thereby damaging the economies of both Scotland and the UK significantly. Its analysis suggested costs of £500 million per year for industry and business in the rest of the United Kingdom (Scottish Government, 2013a). In a speech on the Isle of Man, which incidentally uses the pound without a formal currency union, the First Minister described the economic folly of rejecting a currency union. He asked 'Can you seriously imagine any Chancellor telling businesses in England, Wales or Northern Ireland that they planned to put up such a ridiculous and unnecessary barrier?' (Salmond, 16 July 2013). In a speech following George Osborne's intervention, the First Minister noted that by forcing Scotland to adopt an independent currency, a tax would be imposed on English businesses, a tax he described as 'the George tax' (Salmond, 17 February 2014).

Coordinated statements were made in February 2014 by Chancellor George Osborne, Shadow Chancellor Ed Balls, and Chief Secretary to the Treasury, Danny Alexander, which promised that all three unionist parties would move to block a formal currency union. As these challenges to the Yes campaign's position on currency mounted, the campaign adopted a dismissive position—rejecting unionist statements as bluff and bluster and linking them with the unpopular Conservative government. Interviewed on *Good Morning Scotland*, the Deputy First Minister described the position as 'absurd' (cited in Watt, 2014a). A refusal to enter into negotiations would 'cost their own businesses hundreds of millions in transaction costs, it would blow a massive hole in their balance of payments, it would leave them having to pick up the entirety of UK debt' (cited in Watt, 2014a). Speaking on 17 February 2014, the First Minister described George Osborne's speech as 'not an economic assessment but a campaign tactic' (Salmond, 2014). Interviewed on the *Today* programme (2014), the First Minister described the Chancellor's speech as 'bluff, bluster and bullying'. He said: 'Well that's my assessment of the position. It's bluster because George Osborne described it as keeping the Pound. Of course the Pound is an international tradeable currency. It's not a question of keeping the Pound. It's a question of whether there would be an agreed currency union. That's the bluster aspect. And the bullying aspect is obvious: it's a dictate from on high.' This message was echoed by Deputy First Minister Nicola Sturgeon, who described the Prime Minister as having gone from 'love bombing' to 'bullying and intimidation' (cited in Watt, 2014a). Campaigners appealed to both the pride and the common sense of voters, with Nicola Sturgeon assessing the tactic as: 'It will backfire spectacularly on the No campaign because they are treating people like fools. People are not fools. People can see the sense of the position we are putting forward for Scotland and the rest of the UK' (cited in Watt, 2014a). Scottish Green leader Patrick Harvie also noted that 'discussions over currency are for post-Yes negotiations, and nobody even knows who'll be in Government at Westminster from 2015' (Scottish Greens, 2014b).

The criticism focused on Chancellor George Osborne specifically, both for his role in delivering the key speech and for his position within an unpopular government. Alex Salmond described his intervention as the 'sermon on the pound';[1] both 'insulting' and 'demeaning to Scotland' (Salmond, 2014). Transaction costs incurred by rUK businesses should the UK refuse to enter into a formal currency union were attributed to a 'George Tax'. Nicola Sturgeon reminded voters that 'Neither George Osborne nor anyone else can stop Scotland using the Pound.' This persisted throughout the campaign, and in the televised debate Alex Salmond appealed to the audience, stating 'This is Scotland's Pound. It doesn't belong to George Osborne.'

The goal of the unionist campaign was to undermine the credibility of the Yes Scotland campaign's position—that following the referendum, a currency union would be negotiated in the best interests of all involved. The issue came to a head in the first televised debate between Alex Salmond and Alistair Darling, when Darling scored against Salmond on the grounds that he had staked everything on an option that had been ruled out by his necessary partners and that there was no Plan B. This was taken as a serious defeat for the Yes side. Although there was no post-debate surge in support for No, there was an added element of uncertainty as voters had to put the assertions of one side against those of the other, with no hard basis of evidence. By the second debate, Salmond was better prepared and more flexible, insisting that there was a Plan B and a Plan C in the various ideas put forward by economists. Although it was never made explicit, observers from this point assumed that there was a *de facto* Plan B and that it was sterlingization. This provided something of a fall-back position as the UK Government could not prevent it from happening, but it also weakened the position of the Yes side. If, as they had argued, the UK had a strong interest in a common currency, it could gain these advantages through sterlingization, without having to enter into a full monetary union and giving Scotland a say over monetary policies. In that case, Scotland would simply have to accept monetary policies made in England. So Plan B unstated an assertion that the UK could not actually stop Scotland from using the pound. The Yes side made no effort to elaborate on sterlingization, attracting sharp criticism from the strongly unionist House of Commons Select Committee on Scottish Affairs (2014), which called on the Scottish Government to publish research on all the alternatives.

In response, the SNP and Scottish Government sought to indicate that a currency union would not be entirely at the discretion of the UK. Not only did the UK have a shared interest in currency union, but Scotland would have an additional bargaining chip. Both sides agreed that, in the event of independence, Scotland had to take on a share of the accumulated debt, although the

---

[1] This is a play on the phrase Sermon on the Mound, used by critics of Margaret Thatcher's 1988 address to the General Assembly of the Church of Scotland, in which she asserted the primacy of individual responsibility.

percentage was disputed. This might involve Scotland issuing new debt to buy out its share, or for the UK to continue to own the debt, with Scotland paying its share of the loan charges. In an effort to assure market stability and assure rating agencies during the campaign, the UK Treasury issued a technical note in January 2014 in which it set out the UK Government's guarantee for the entirety of the UK debt (HM Government, 2014e). This gave the Yes side the opportunity to suggest that, if a full currency union were not on offer, then Scotland would refuse to pay its share. A moral justification was the argument that, if the asset of the pound and the Bank of England were to go only to one side, the division of other assets should also be called into question. In response to the Chancellor's Edinburgh speech, Salmond said 'if there is no legal basis for Scotland having a share of the public asset of the Bank of England then there is equally no legal basis for Scotland accepting a share of the public liability of the national debt' (Salmond, 2014). This was raising the stakes since, while the Treasury had now seemingly given Scotland a legal basis to repudiate its debt share, it would risk exclusion from borrowing markets or at least having to pay a premium on its interest rates were it to be seen as effectively reneging on its obligations.

Because independence did not happen, it is impossible to test the credibility of the assertions by either side. Their formal positions were very hard, but even during the campaign there were some signs of weakening. An item in *The Guardian* reported an unnamed UK Government minister as saying that 'you simply cannot imagine Westminster abandoning the people of Scotland. Saying no to a currency union is obviously a vital part of the no campaign. But everything would change in the negotiations if there was a yes vote' (Watt, 2014b). On the other side, the Yes campaign, while insisting on currency union, did by the end of the campaign have a fall-back position or Plan B in the form of sterlingization.

Conclusion

The currency question illustrates the role of uncertainty and the way in which the two sides played upon it. It is of the nature of arguments about monetary policy, debt limits, and bail-out provisions that any pledges should be credible since they will influence the behaviour of actors. In this debate, neither side wanted to do anything that might have upset markets, either during the campaign or in the aftermath, hence their categorical assurances of stability. The credit rating of the UK and a potentially independent Scotland were both at stake. On the other hand, in a situation like this, certainty is never possible and it is easy to criticize assurances as mere bluff. Modelling scenarios with a view to predicting outcomes in situations like this usually start from the position that all sides are rational utility-maximizers in possession of the relevant knowledge, pursuing their own interests (see Chapter 2).

Both sides in this debate used this rational actor assumption as the basis for their predictions on the implications of independence. The Yes side insisted that shared interests would bring both sides to the table to agree on the terms of currency union; the No side argued that what was proposed was in the interest of neither side and would not happen, adding a rare categorical pledge, underpinned by all three potential UK governing parties. Yet the rationality assumption is not always to be trusted, especially in cases of political conflict. The multiplicity of actors, including the two governments, international institutions and the bond markets created further uncertainty. When the Yes side raised the stakes by threatening not to accept a share of the UK debt, they gained a bargaining chip but at the cost of highlighting additional risk and uncertainty.

There was little common ground in the debates about the currency but contrasting frames and different knowledge claims. The Yes side believed that the various components of the union were separable and that independence entailed gaining political sovereignty but sharing the functional responsibilities and institutions. Rather than undermining its independence, the currency union would allow for an independent Scottish position within the Bank of England and influence over fiscal policy. This cooperation was linked rhetorically with a larger partnership of equals, a renewed relationship between Scotland and the rest of the United Kingdom. Critics, however, asked why the UK, as by far the larger partner, would agree to sharing authority in this way (Armstrong and Ebell, 2014a). The No side insisted that independence means the dissolution of the union as a whole, without any common policies or institutions to be negotiated afterwards between independent units.

More widely, the proposal for currency union tests our understanding of the meaning of independence in the modern world. For the Better Together campaign, independence and sovereignty were overlapping concepts; genuine independence required sovereignty—over currency, over foreign policy, and borders. The campaign often asked what was the point of independence, if recently won sovereignty would only be immediately ceded to the Bank of England or the European Union? For the Yes Scotland campaign, sovereignty could be shared, as long as partners chose to do so willingly. This was a fact of life in an interdependent world. The idea of interdependence was expressed in matters beyond the issue of currency, with the Yes Scotland campaign continuing to propose coordination of certain public services—the DVLA, the Civil Aviation Authority, the system of research council funding—as well as the maintenance of a social union and open borders, leading to McEwen (2013) to describe the SNP's vision of an independent Scotland as 'embedded'.

It was noted in Chapter 1 that there was a certain convergence between the two sides in their practical proposals, with the SNP offering 'independence-lite' and the unionist parties conceding more devolution. Important differences between the two sides remained, notably on foreign affairs and participation in Europe, and the post-referendum Smith Commission proposals fell short of most definitions of devolution-max. The most radical 'devolution-max' proposals, however, envisage the Scottish Parliament in control of all taxation, and paying a contribution to UK services, while monetary policy remained in the hands of the UK level. Within the realm of economic policy, this does begin to resemble the version of 'independence-lite' offered by the SNP, providing for fiscal autonomy but within a monetary union.

It is difficult to pronounce who were the winners in this debate. The failure to specify a Plan B in the first referendum debate was a key factor in Alex Salmond's acknowledged loss of it (Salmond, 2015). Yet neither this nor the strong all-party unionist pledge not to allow currency union seemed to sway public opinion. As shown in Chapter 10, the percentage of voters believing that the UK would allow Scotland to keep the pound went up from 33 per cent to 40 per cent, to outnumber those who believed the opposite; but this was still not a majority. This may be attributable to there being more trust in the Yes campaigners than in the No side as represented by the UK Government and London politicians and the pledge against currency union may have been politically counter-productive. This failure of public opinion to respond either to negative assessments or to warnings from the unionist side in turn encouraged the Yes side not to elaborate on Plan B, apart from assurances that nobody could stop Scotland from using the pound. On the other hand, Yes Scotland did not win the argument overall; there remained a considerable doubt on the matter and our data (see Chapter 10) show that this was one of the key uncertainties influencing the result at the margin. In any future referendum campaign, the Yes side will need to have a stronger story about the currency if it is to assemble a winning majority.

5

Welfare

Contesting Communities of Solidarity

Nicola McEwen

The defence of a social democratic vision of welfare was a key issue in the independence referendum campaign, just as it had been in the devolution referendum seventeen years earlier. For the Yes camp, independence promised the power to create a more equal society and a fairer, more progressive welfare state, built upon Scottish social solidarity and the 'common weal'. Promises included protecting and expanding pensions and benefits and abolishing the 'bedroom tax', halting welfare retrenchment and some other aspects of UK welfare reform, defending the NHS, and building a more Nordic-style welfare state reflecting the solidarity and social values (assumed to be) shared by Scots. For its part, the No campaign questioned the financial ability of an independent Scotland to afford current levels of spending on pensions, benefits, health care, and social care, let alone build a more generous system. No campaigners stressed that the UK's 'broad shoulders' meant that resources could be pooled and burdens shared. The Labour Party appealed to a conception of social solidarity that crossed the internal territorial boundaries of the UK. It championed the UK 'social union' as the essence of its political union, reflecting and reinforcing UK-wide solidarity and mutual belonging. These competing claims and aspirations were set against the backdrop of controversial UK welfare reforms and a state-driven narrative that presented welfare as an unsustainable burden rather than a source of collective solidarity and pride. This weakened Labour's arguments about social union and gave the Yes side the opportunity to present independence as the best way to preserve the social and economic entitlements associated with the post-war welfare state.

At the heart of these debates lies the interplay between policy choices, identity politics and contested communities of solidarity. The territorial politics of welfare is a common feature of nation-building and nationalist mobilization across advanced democratic nations and states. This chapter contextualizes and evaluates the competing welfare claims made by both sides in the independence referendum campaign. It first explores the relationship between territorial politics and the welfare state, arguing that the nation-building role once played by UK welfare has been undermined by both the transfer of competences over key welfare institutions and services to the devolved institutions, and the retreat from state welfare at the centre. Second, it identifies the key protagonists in the welfare debate. Drawing on a range of documentary sources from the long referendum campaign, including campaign documents, archived website material, government documents, speeches, news articles, and online footage, it then analyses the core dimensions of the referendum welfare debate. The key analytical device is that of 'frames', defined by Gitlin (1980: 6) as 'principles of selection, emphasis and presentation composed of little tacit theories about what exists, what happens, and what matters'. In political communication and campaigning, frames help to interpret and lend meaning to policy and political challenges, and to guide and motivate political behaviour (Entman, 1993; Hallahan, 2011). In the context of the referendum, framing helps us to identify how political actors perceived and represented the key issues on welfare, raising its salience in campaign discourse. The chapter draws upon Benford and Snow's threefold categorization of framing to elucidate the ways in which different constitutional options were invoked to present the *diagnosis* and *prognosis* for the future of the welfare state, and to *motivate* supporters and shape vote choice (Benford and Snow, 2000).

The terms 'welfare' and 'welfare state' require clarification. For some, welfare may be a general set of social programmes delivered by the state, and the term is sometimes used in a derogatory way to refer to a narrow set of social security benefits, largely for people outside of the labour market. The broader definition used in this chapter conceptualizes the welfare state as a kind of *statehood*—'a state in which organized power is deliberately used (through politics and administration) in an effort to modify the play of market forces' (Briggs, 2000; Wincott, 2003). In this sense, 'welfare' captures the broad range of social services, institutions, transfers, and entitlements provided to individual citizens to protect them against social and economic contingencies, for example, related to age, ill health, unemployment, or low pay, and to promote their social, educational, and economic development and well-being. It includes institutions like the National Health Service, specific policy programmes, and provisions for social housing, schooling, education, social care, and health care, as well as benefits and tax credits provided through the social security and tax system. The welfare debate in the referendum campaign also invoked a societal vision—of the kind of country the UK is and had become, and the kind of country an independent Scotland could be.

The Welfare State and the Nation-State

Historically, the development of the *welfare* state and the *nation*-state went hand in hand. The expanded role of the state in providing for the day-to-day needs of its citizens helped to reinforce its legitimacy among those it governed and justified the levying of taxes on the population. The national symbolism that accompanied such interventions strengthened the perception that the state represented a community of mutual belonging (Mishra, 1999). Depending on the nature of the welfare regime, welfare states could generate social solidarity and mutual belonging across class groups, conferring an equality of status and set of entitlements on citizens irrespective of their market value and reinforcing that the better off had obligations towards their poorer compatriots (Marshall, 1950; Titmuss, 1958).

Intentionally or otherwise, welfare state institutions and services also served the politics of nation-building in plurinational states where the boundaries of national communities are contested. The nation-building function of the welfare state may be both symbolic and instrumental. Symbolically, welfare institutions can provide an institutional focus for national solidarity, representing a symbol of mutual belonging, risk-sharing, and common security. It was not by accident that UK welfare developed a *National* Health Service and a system of *national* insurance, contributing to what Billig (1995) referred to as the 'unmindful reminders' of the boundaries of nationhood that are subtly presented and represented in every day discourse and experience. More instrumentally, the welfare state may serve a nation-building purpose by protecting citizens against risk and providing for their social and economic security, as well as focusing political organization and mobilization towards the institutions of state. A state that provides social protection for its citizens may also secure their loyalty, strengthening the ties that bind and heightening the risks associated with changing the constitutional order (McEwen, 2006: 62–79; Banting, 1995; Béland and Lecours, 2008).

In the UK and elsewhere, the relationship between the welfare state and the nation-state has faced two key challenges in recent years: the development and expansion of multilevel government; and a retreat from state welfare in the face of ideological pressures and growing financial and demographic burdens. First, in multilevel states where political authority is dispersed across levels of government, often there isn't a *national* welfare system at all, but variations on social welfare provision across the internal units of the state (McEwen and Moreno, 2005). The development of distinctive policies, social programmes, and entitlements for citizens of the same state depending on the region in which they live poses a challenge to the principle of social citizenship and the equality of status for all citizens, potentially undermining interregional solidarity ties.

The regionalization of welfare can, of course, boost welfare state development at the regional scale, and lead to the development of systems of welfare that are more responsive to regional needs and preferences. The state need not be the only appropriate level of social citizenship (Keating, 2009: 504–6). In multinational states, substate nationalist and regionalist party governments have exploited the opportunity to use their command of social welfare to try to shift loyalties away from central institutions and to reinforce the boundaries of the national communities in whose name their territorial claims are made (McEwen, 2006; Béland and Lecours, 2008; Vampa, 2014). Where the welfare state becomes a tool deployed in the competitive nation-building strategies of state and regional governments, it can 'ratchet up' social welfare provision as each level of government competes for recognition in similar policy spheres (James and Lusztig, 2002; Banting, 2005; Allen, 2012).

The second challenge to the nation-building potential of welfare comes in the form of welfare retrenchment. In some countries this may be ideologically driven; rooted in a neoliberal desire to escape a perceived dependency culture, an over-burdened and overly interfering state, and to promote enterprise and individual responsibility. For many, it is a response to increased levels of social expenditure across advanced democratic states, faced with ageing populations, low fertility, and, consequently, less favourable dependency ratios between non-workers in need of care and tax-paying workers with the ability to fund it. This is often compounded by a belief that citizens are less willing to pay higher taxes for redistributive welfare (Bonoli, 2000). Welfare retrenchment, where it occurs, undermines the extent to which state-wide welfare institutions can represent symbols of interregional and class solidarity. It may also undermine perceptions that the state can act as the guarantor of citizens' social rights and entitlements. As a consequence, attachment to the nation-state may weaken, as may the risks and potential losses associated with major constitutional change. Substate nationalist or regionalist parties who demand greater self-government or independence for their territorial communities have exploited state welfare retrenchment, developing a narrative which questions the willingness and ability of the existing state to meet social and economic need, and promises a better future in the wake of territorial self-government. In the 1995 Quebec sovereignty referendum, for example, the Yes campaign exploited federal government cuts to unemployment insurance, pensions, old age security, and transfer payments to the provinces, which they contrasted to the social democratic *projet de société* associated with a sovereign Quebec (McEwen, 2006; Béland and Lecours, 2008). Similarly, in the 1980s and 1990s, the welfare retrenchment of the Thatcher/Major governments was used by advocates of Scottish self-government to reinforce the need for a Scottish Parliament—to protect public services, develop 'Scottish solutions to Scottish problems', and to guard against the regressive policies of a right-wing government (McEwen, 2006). Ideological, demographic, and political pressures on the welfare state may of course be evident equally at the regional scale of government as at the centre. Where welfare competences are shared, these pressures can generate both burden-shifting and blame-shifting between levels of government.

The Scottish independence referendum was set against a backdrop of these twin challenges. The once broadly integrated UK welfare state has given way to divergent systems of welfare as a result of devolution, while the one remaining area of welfare—social security—that remained the responsibility of the UK Government was being reshaped and partially eroded by controversial welfare reforms.

The Scotland Act 1998 transferred significant areas of the welfare state to the Scottish Parliament, and has allowed divergence in the substance and delivery of social services, with a greater preference toward universality and public provision in Scotland as compared to England. The most visible areas of distinctive social policy—'free personal care', the abolition of tuition fees, free prescriptions, free bus travel for pensioners—assumed a symbolic significance in underpinning devolved Scotland's distinctiveness within the union. Although the UK welfare state always entailed variation between and within the UK's four nations, alongside many other inequalities in access to service provision (Wincott, 2006), devolution has rendered territorial variations more visible, and created the structures to facilitate the growth of distinctive welfare regimes. Social entitlements across many areas of provision now vary according to the territorial community in which UK citizens live, generating concerns among some academics on the liberal left that the absence of national, UK-wide frameworks may weaken interregional solidarity and social citizenship (Hazell and O'Leary, 1999; Jeffery, 2002: 193–4).

However, the reservation of social security and most tax policies meant that the capacity to shape redistributive welfare remained principally with the UK Government and parliament, while a good deal of interdependence between devolved and reserved competencies created jagged edges in social provision, for example, between housing and housing benefit, or social care and disability benefits. Thus, UK welfare reforms intended to simplify the social security system, to reduce the financial burden social welfare imposed on the state and to promote (through cuts and curtailing entitlements) an ideologically driven transition from welfare to work for working-age adults, had direct and indirect consequences for devolved welfare competence. UK welfare reform also led to Scottish policy developments and commitments in response to what both the SNP government and the Labour opposition perceived as injustices in the system. For example, a system of discretionary housing payments was established by the Scottish Government to mitigate the effects of the UK Government's 'spare room subsidy' (bedroom tax) imposed on those living in social housing in receipt of housing benefit. Following the termination and subsequent devolution (with a 10 per cent cut) of the UK Social Fund, the Scottish Government set up its own, more generous Scottish Welfare Fund to give grants to those in crisis or in need of community care. UK welfare reform may have further weakened the relationship between the welfare state and the nation-state, further undermining a conception of Britishness founded upon social welfare that had resonated in Scotland since the Second World War (Finlay, 1997), and had already been weakened during the Thatcher years. The bedroom tax and a punitive sanctions and benefits regime implemented by the UK Government helped to make welfare and 'fairness' central themes of the independence referendum campaign, enabling nationalists in particular to contrast the cuts and retrenchment in the new British welfare state with the promise of progressive welfare under independence.

The Protagonists

The social democratic case for independence has long been evident on the left of the SNP. While there was no significant ideological divergence between Deputy First Minister Nicola Sturgeon and First Minister and party leader Alex Salmond, he tended to place more emphasis on the claim that independence was necessary to achieving Scotland's economic prosperity, whereas Sturgeon's comfort zone lies in social policy and welfare. The welfare state—couched within the broad objective of creating a 'fairer' society—was one of the three themes which made the Scottish Government's case for independence (alongside the democratic and economic case), set out in the White Paper, *Scotland's Future* (Scottish Government, 2013f). The White Paper gave some pointers to what that fairer society might look like, but the details of the independent Scottish welfare state were left to an independent expert group appointed by the government. Chaired first by Darra Singh, formerly Chief Executive of Jobcentre Plus and the second Permanent Secretary of the Department of Work and Pensions (DWP), then by Martyn Evans, Chief Executive of the Carnegie UK Trust, the expert group involved academics, senior public servants, and business and third-sector representatives. Its first report set out the transition to an independent welfare system, focusing on the bureaucratic challenges of transferring powers over social security from the UK to the Scottish governments (Expert Working Group on Welfare, 2013). Its final report presented a vision of an independent Scottish social security system which could be 'fair, personal and simple' (Expert Working Group on Welfare and Constitutional Reform, 2014).

The vision of a more progressive, socially just Scotland also lay at the heart of the case for independence across the broader Yes movement. Though much the smaller party within the Yes Scotland campaign, Scottish Green Party shared with the SNP a vision that independence could have a transformative effect on Scotland, including by creating a system of progressive taxation that would help to promote social justice, albeit one that promoted sustainability over economic prosperity, and decentralization and local empowerment over state control. Within the wider, more grassroots, movement, groups such as the Radical Independence Campaign, Common Weal, National Collective, Women for Independence, and outlets like Bella Caledonia also campaigned for independence as a means to a more progressive future. They championed 'hope over fear', 'the politics of sharing', and 'a Scotland of social justice', articulating aspirations of preserving public services, eradicating poverty, income and gender inequality, and securing a redistributive welfare state (Radical Independence Campaign, 2013; McGarry, 2013).

The No campaign was more fragmented when it came to the welfare theme. In spite of the post-war welfare consensus, the relationship between the nation-state and the welfare state has never been central to Conservative notions of Britishness, which instead rely on more traditional institutions and conventions of state. The potential of state welfare to promote solidarity across class and territorial groups has always been recognized and used more by the Labour Party. Long before devolution, Scottish Labour politicians traded Scottish political autonomy for access to the levers of power at the centre, with the promise that they could defend Scottish territorial interests and deliver the goods. After devolution, Labour maintained a commitment to a UK welfare vision, even promoting the NHS as a *national* symbol in spite of its growing divergence under a system of multilevel government. It was the Labour Party, then, who championed a positive welfare case for union in the referendum campaign, one of the few areas where Labour could carve out a distinctive voice for itself in the Better Together campaign. However, it did so from a position of political weakness given the party's opposition status in the Westminster and Holyrood parliaments and the dependence of the vision on a future Labour-led government promoting UK welfare solidarity.

The No campaign was more united in talking up the risks that independence posed to pensions, benefits, and social service provision. The UK Government's *Scotland Analysis* paper on work and pensions (HM Government, 2014d) set out the scope and costs of existing social security provision for Scotland and the benefits of being part of UK-wide systems. It provided estimates of the costs of setting up new independent welfare bureaucracies and emphasized the increased financial burden that would face an independent Scottish Government in light of demographic projections and other cost pressures. As in other policy spheres, this risk analysis provided the basis for the more negative case for a No vote, enabling Better Together to focus on the costs and potential losses independence could generate for citizens in need.

Framing the Debate

Benford and Snow's (2000: 615) categorization of the way political actors utilize frames to lend meaning to policy and political issues provides a useful lens through which to understand the way welfare issues were framed in the referendum debate. They drew a distinction between diagnostic framing, used to identify a problem and assign blame; prognostic framing, where campaigners offer an alternative to the perceived problem; and motivational framing intended to shape and motivate action in pursuit of campaign goals. Such framing was evident in the referendum among both the Yes and No campaigns, though in rather different ways. Only the Yes campaign perceived and represented the Union as the source of the problems facing the welfare state. Moreover, the welfare issue gave the Yes campaign an opportunity that was less evident in other parts of the campaign. UK Government policies on welfare reform and retrenchment were used as symbols of all that was wrong with the Union, in contrast to an alternative, aspirational prognosis for welfare offered by an independent Scotland where social democracy could flourish. For No campaigners, independence presented a rather bleaker prognosis in light of demographic trends and economic and social risks. The motivational appeal came in both negative exposure of risks and a positive appeal to the sense of community and solidarity that allowed those risks to be pooled and shared across the UK.

Four thematic areas highlight the ways in which both sides of the debate framed the issues of welfare. Each is discussed in turn below. For the most part, both campaigns talked past each other on welfare, appealing directly to the hearts and minds, aspirations and fears of the electorate.

Independence and the Defence of the Welfare State

From the outset, the coalition government's welfare reforms were used both as a symbol of how the UK had moved ideologically from its own past and Scotland's present, and a rationale for the powers of independence to restore and advance social justice. These themes were signalled in the early stages of the campaign in the First Minister's Hugo Young lecture, delivered in London in January 2012, when he suggested that:

> ... anyone who accepted the Union partly because of the compassionate values and inclusive vision of the post-war welfare state may now be less keen on being part of a union whose government is in many respects eroding those values and destroying that vision ... And looking at the problems of health reform now, I thank the heavens that Westminster's writ no longer runs in Scotland on health

issues. But the looming issues of welfare reform exemplify why Scotland needs the powers to make our own policies to meet our own needs and values.

(Salmond, 2012)

Such interventions highlight the twin challenges of welfare retrenchment and devolution confronting the traditional nation-building role of the welfare state. The critique is levelled both at British welfare institutions, deemed unable to embody social solidarity and represent shared British values, and at service provision. The British state was presented as no longer offering social protection, and the First Minister stressed a growing divergence between British and Scottish systems of social welfare.

Social justice was also a recurring theme of Nicola Sturgeon's referendum campaign. In a speech in December 2012, she acknowledged that the creation of the post-war welfare state had been a defining feature of Britishness, but argued that the institutions that underpinned British distinctiveness 'are under attack from the Westminster system of government' which is 'eroding the social fabric' (Sturgeon, 2012). In March 2013, she spoke of the efforts that the Scottish Government was undertaking to mitigate the detrimental effects of UK welfare reform, but argued: 'in order to deliver meaningful and long lasting change, and to deal effectively with an issue as complex as child poverty, with its many layers and its various causes and effects, we do need the levers currently reserved to Westminster to be returned to Scottish hands' (Sturgeon, 2013). Speaking to business leaders in March 2014, she highlighted 'the need to protect the post-war welfare state' as a core ambition of Scottish independence, arguing that 'far from pooling risk and sharing resources, the current Westminster government is intent on nothing less than the dismantling of the social security system' (Sturgeon, 2014a).

Framing the debate in this way diagnosed the constitutional status quo and the constraints of political union as the underlying problem. Devolved Scotland could take some steps to develop distinctive policies in those areas of welfare under its jurisdiction, but so long as Scotland remained within the United Kingdom, it could not fully escape the welfare retrenchment of the UK Government. From the perspective of the Yes campaign, independence offered a better, more progressive prognosis. Independence would give Scottish political institutions the tools to address Scotland's social and economic problems, to preserve those elements of the *British* welfare state that Scots still hold dear, and to create a policy landscape reflective of Scottish values, which it is presumed are founded upon social democracy. These campaign themes also built upon an egalitarian myth that has deep roots in Scottish institutions and political discourse. The enduring belief that 'we're a' Jock Tamson's bairns' (in spite of evidence of deep inequalities in the social structure) was central to the reframing of Scottish nationalism during the Thatcher years

(McCrone, 1992; Hearn, 2000; Morton, 2011), and coloured the discourse of Yes campaigners in the independence referendum.

The presentation of independence as a route to social justice was even more evident in the aspirations of the broader Yes movement. The Radical Independence Campaign (2013) underlined the impact of welfare reform on the poorest communities in Scotland, and claimed that independence was an opportunity for radical social change. In the wake of George Osborne's rejection of a currency union, they issued a 'message to the victims of austerity' and embarked upon a grassroots engagement strategy taking their message—and voter registration forms—to those poorer communities in urban Scotland where alienation is high and political participation low (Radical Independence Campaign, 2014). The left-wing think tank, Common Weal, linked its support for independence to a comprehensive, universal, and interventionist welfare state designed to support wealth redistribution, class and gender equality, constitutionally enshrined socio-economic rights, and the pursuit of social justice. The creative arts group, National Collective, presented an aspirational vision of an independent Scotland with the powers to create a 'fairer, more compassionate welfare system' and used concerts, posters, and Twitter to mobilize the sympathetic and inspire optimism for a future under independence.[1]

Within the official campaign, the possibilities of self-government, as well as the threats from union, were illustrated with reference to the NHS, which became an increasingly prominent theme in the final weeks of the campaign. Health care is fully devolved in Scotland, although funding has been dependent upon spending decisions in England and the Barnett consequentials this generates. In her final speech in parliament before the launch of the short campaign, Sturgeon claimed that protecting the NHS was 'a fundamental reason for independence. So that cuts from Westminster don't damage our NHS and instead we have the opportunity to decide for ourselves the resources we give to the NHS and other public services' (Sturgeon, 2014b). The focus on the threats to the NHS was a departure from what had hitherto been a deliberately positive campaign, and a drift towards the negativity and language of risk more familiar to their opponents. From the summer of 2014, the Yes Scotland campaign website ran a page with a headline asserting that 'A Yes means real gains for Scotland's people—but it's our NHS that will see the biggest cost if it's a No' (Yes Scotland, 2014). It went on to argue that:

All of the Westminster parties are signed up to yet more swingeing austerity, sucking money out of Scotland's budget and people's pockets. Particularly at risk

---

[1] For example, a #YesBecause hashtag, led by National Collective in the final days of the campaign, attracted 101,238 tweets in 24 hours, and according to its coordinator, reached over 3 million people and was trending in Scotland, the UK, and worldwide (Colquhoun, 2014). Many of the contributions expressed hopes of a better, more equal society.

from a No is our NHS, where the privatization of the health service south of the Border could trigger cuts to Scotland's budget.

The prominence of the threat to the NHS in the Yes campaign may seem surprising given that the UK parliament has no constitutional competence over health care in Scotland, and health spending in England had not declined so there were few adverse effects on fiscal transfers (see also Chapter 2). But the NHS has always had symbolic significance in the debate, and had itself been a symbol of Britishness. Presenting it as threatened by continued political union helped to reclaim the *national* in the National Health Service. The NHS was not the only devolved area at the heart of the Yes campaign. At the launch of the White Paper on *Scotland's Future*, Nicola Sturgeon's flagship policy commitment was to initiate a 'transformational' expansion in child care provision in the event of the SNP being elected to lead the first post-independence Scottish Government. Although this is wholly within the devolved sphere, the Scottish Government argued that only independence would enable this commitment to be financed through the increased tax take from an expanded female workforce. The policy was clearly also a naked attempt to make independence more appealing to women, given the gender gap in support for independence.

An Appeal to the Social Union

Whereas the campaign for a Scottish Parliament in the 1980s and 1990s had the social democratic terrain largely to itself, in the independence referendum, the Yes campaign had to compete for this space with the leading players within Better Together. The Labour Party included a vision of social solidarity embodied in the welfare state as central to a social democratic case for union. They appealed to social solidarity at the British scale, implicitly framing the UK nation-state as a UK welfare state, and defending the Union as, in Gordon Brown's phrase, 'a Union of social justice'.

The nation-building impact of the welfare state can be traced back to the early post-war years, and the impact the post-war welfare state had in creating new cherished *national* institutions, protecting citizens against social and economic risk, and at least for two decades marginalizing the home rule issue in political mobilization and debate (Finlay, 1997; McEwen, 2006). Its use in framing political discourse and explicitly presenting the UK as a social union is a more recent phenomenon, however, and largely an invention of Gordon Brown. He has been articulating the idea of the UK as a social union reflecting interregional solidarity since the onset of devolution (Brown and Alexander, 1999). These sentiments influenced the Commission on Scottish

Devolution (Calman Commission; 2009)—set up in the wake of the SNP's first election victory in 2007 by the opposition parties with the support of the UK Government to review the existing devolution settlement—and justified its recommendation to retain social security as a responsibility of the UK parliament. In a speech in 2012, Brown set the tone for Labour's referendum campaign in his defence of the 'union of social justice', supported by the spread of Scottish values across the UK:

> We have guaranteed that no matter whether you are Scottish, English, Welsh or Irish you will have not just the same political rights but the same economic and social rights – to health care, to the same level of child benefit, to minimum wage, and to pensions. We have guaranteed that when one part of the UK is in difficulty the rest of the UK will come to their aid...In the last hundred years the union *thanks to Scottish ideas of fairness and opportunity* has become a union for social justice.
>
> (Brown, 2012, italics added)

The assumption of uniformity in health care was an exaggeration—even before devolution, there were some variations in the delivery of health care across the nations and regions of the UK. But the bigger problem was that such a discourse was being articulated against a backdrop of cuts to social security and fears of privatization in the NHS in England. It risked appearing nostalgic, potentially reinforcing the message of the Yes campaign that it spoke to a vision of the UK welfare state that no longer existed. For Labour, however, the diagnosis of the problem facing the UK welfare system was not political union but the Conservative-led coalition government. The solution was not to tear up 300 years of union, but to vote for a Labour government at the next General Election.

These themes of cross-border social solidarity became a key feature of the Better Together campaign. One of its campaign documents, entitled *A Sharing Union*, appealed to a vision of social solidarity implicitly founded upon a shared sense of *Britishness*, and reflected a belief in the principle of social citizenship irrespective of where in the UK one lived (Better Together, 2014a):

> The principled case for social union across the UK reflects *our history*. The welfare state was drawn together on the grounds that people across *our country* should have a minimum standard of living regardless of where they live. This is shown by the young person in work in London supporting the child benefit of someone growing up in poverty in Glasgow, and the revenues from oil receipts off the coast of Aberdeen supporting the person looking for work in Aberystwyth. We share with those across the UK a single system of unemployment assistance, a single old age pension, a uniform NHS, and more recently a common national minimum wage. These principles underpin our argument for the benefits of pooling resources across a wider community [italics added].

Speaking to a third sector audience, Alistair Darling, Labour MP, former Chancellor of the Exchequer and chair of the Better Together campaign, underlined that pooling and sharing resources was a 'fundamental part' of the UK, and the best way to respond to social inequality: 'The United Kingdom is far more than an economic and political union; the social union is a fundamental part too and these three elements are what makes the UK what it is' (cited in Third Force News, 20 February 2014). Gordon Brown, who assumed a more prominent role in the latter stages of the campaign, returned to these themes of shared social citizenship and the pooling of resources and sharing of risks it implied (see Brown, 2014a). In a powerful speech on the eve of the referendum, he invoked the shared sacrifices and a shared peace, embodying a shared solidarity across the nations of the UK: 'The vote tomorrow is whether you want to break and sever every link and I say let's keep our UK pension, let's keep our UK pound, let's keep our UK passport, let's keep our UK welfare state' (Brown, 2014b).

Thus the Yes and No campaigns made similar appeals to social justice, but targeted them to distinctive communities of solidarity, one Scottish, and one in which Scottishness co-existed alongside and strengthened Britishness. They drew upon a similar set of social values, and a similar set of assumptions about the egalitarian nature of Scottish values, but envisaged these as best reflected within different bounded communities. These were primarily sentiment-based, rather than fact-based; appeals to feelings of identity and belonging. These appeals were aimed directly at voters, and largely talked past each other. Only latterly did Brown explicitly try to counteract the framing of the Yes campaign, evidently concerned at its apparent impact on the referendum vote. In an article in *Prospect Magazine*, Brown criticized the tax and social policy commitments in the independence White Paper:

> One of the propaganda devices of the Scottish National Party has been to persuade left-of centre opinion that breaking free from London rule would create a 'northern light' for social justice...However, a Scotland which followed the policies outlined in the SNP's white paper for independence and ended the system of pooling and sharing resources across the United Kingdom would quickly find that income and wealth would be more unequally distributed than in the country they abandoned.

The Costs of the Welfare State Under Independence

The social democratic case for union was mainly the preserve of the Labour Party and Better Together. While the UK Government also reiterated the advantages for citizens and employers of a shared UK social security system, it was on more comfortable ground in framing the debate around the risks independence posed, including to the welfare state. From the perspective of the UK Government, there was no welfare problem to diagnose, but the prognosis for welfare in an independent Scotland looked bleak. The Scotland Analysis paper on Work and Pensions, which like other outputs of the Scotland Analysis series sought to present a fact-based analysis and defence of the Union, claimed that 'An independent Scottish state would face a more acute challenge than the UK as a whole, both in terms of demographic change, and its ability to absorb the impacts from a narrower tax base' (HM Government, 2014d: 10). The paper highlighted the increased relative costs of pensions and benefits resulting from demographic pressures, suggesting that Scotland was especially vulnerable because it had proportionately fewer children (and therefore fewer workers in the future), fewer immigrants, and a population that was consequently ageing faster. This was only partly corroborated by independent analysis. Parry (2014) pointed out that social protection spending per head in Scotland was now barely above the UK average (2 per cent with the gap narrowing), while demographic and economic projections resulting from migration, life expectancy, rates of disability, and housing rents are too contestable and in any case have hitherto broadly balanced out revenue and spending disparities. Bell et al. noted that the disparity related more to relatively high spending on ill-health related benefits such as Disability Living Allowance and Pension Credit rather than the state pension. Whilst Scotland's population is expected to age more rapidly than that of the UK as a whole, the gap is projected to narrow again after 2032, and could in theory be offset partially or wholly by immigration were Scotland and the rest of the UK to pursue high and low immigration policies respectively (Bell et al., 2014).

Framing independence as the problem, and exposing the risks to social and economic security posed by a Yes vote, was also central to the broader Better Together campaign. Using—and arguably abusing—figures from the Institute of Fiscal Studies, Better Together highlighted the risks associated with lower tax revenues and the set-up costs of a new welfare state. A pamphlet presenting a unionist case for the NHS noted: 'The impartial experts at the Institute for Fiscal Studies (IFS) have shown that a separate Scotland would face between £3 billion and £10 billion of cuts or tax increases... Some of these cuts would inevitably come out of our NHS budget. We don't have to take such a big risk with our health service if we stay in the UK' (Better Together, 2014b).[2] The Better Together pamphlet on social security similarly raised

---

[2] In fact, the IFS estimated Scotland's net fiscal deficit in 2012–13 to have been 8.3 per cent of GDP, compared with 7.3 per cent for the UK, but in the year previously, Scotland had a relatively smaller net fiscal deficit. Using the OBR's forecasts for the UK as a whole and assuming an independent Scotland would accept a population share of debt, they estimated that Scotland's net fiscal deficit would decline to 2.9 per cent by 2018–19, assuming that the independent Scottish

doubts about the affordability of pensions and benefits in an independent Scotland, given the level of deficit and demographic trends: 'With so much doubt over what would happen to these payments, how they would be paid and who would pay for them, the only responsible choice in September is to vote to remain in the United Kingdom' (Better Together, 2014a).

Welfare Bureaucracies and Cross-Border Cooperation

As noted above, many of the pillars of the welfare state are already devolved to the Scottish Parliament, with institutional foundations that long predate devolution. Independence may have posed challenges and opportunities in maintaining, financing and expanding these, but there would be no new set-up costs. In social security, by contrast, the challenge of disentangling Scottish and UK entitlements and liabilities, and setting up a separate Scottish welfare bureaucracy, was acknowledged by both sides, although they differed on the scale and cost of the task.

For No campaigners, the costs of setting up new bureaucracies to deliver social security benefits (and to collect the tax revenues to fund them) added to the grim prognosis for welfare in an independent Scotland. The Scotland Analysis paper asserted that establishing a social security bureaucracy for an independent Scotland would require investment in a new IT system in the region of £300–400 million. In addition, it estimated operating costs of at least £720 million per year, and extra costs associated with developing, or procuring, relevant expertise to enhance policy-making and bureaucratic capacity, and to deliver and manage a large-scale welfare system. The paper also stressed the complexity and costs of disentangling Scottish and UK pension liabilities, disentangling and replacing other hitherto integrated tax and benefit systems, contracts and services, and negotiating ownership of, and access to, historical records of social security and tax claims (HM Government, 2014d: 79–83). The emphasis was on the costs, risks, and difficulties inherent in such a change, especially within the eighteen-month time scale that the Scottish Government had envisaged for the transition to independence. It assumed bureaucracies would have to be established from scratch, without factoring in the possibility of transferring ownership of existing Scotland-based DWP bureaucracies to the Scottish Government as part of independence negotiations.

The Scottish Government delegated the task of setting out a path towards transition to its Expert Group on Welfare. In its interim report, the expert

Government pursued austerity policies similar to those planned for the UK, putting it in a relatively worse position than the UK as a whole, which was projected to produce a net fiscal surplus of 0.2 per cent of GDP by 2018–19 (Amior et al., 2013).

group recommended that the Scottish and UK governments work together, in the spirit of the Edinburgh agreement, to deliver pensions and benefits on a shared arrangement basis for an unspecified transitional period, to minimize the disruptive impact for those dependent on benefits. The group also recognized the geographic interdependence in the current welfare bureaucracy. The bodies delivering public pensions and benefits are all under the control of the UK Government, but they are scattered across the UK. Most—though not all—benefits applied for by Scots are processed in Scotland. These Scotland-based offices also provide this service to claimants in England. For example, the Child Maintenance Service, based in Falkirk, processes applications for the North East of England. DWP centres in Scotland deliver working age benefits for applicants in Yorkshire, the North West of England, and London. The emphasis on continuity was intended to reassure citizens of a smooth transition to independence and there are clear advantages—in terms of continuity of service to those dependent on welfare benefits and job security for those who deliver them—to shared service agreements even after independence.

Yet, the greater the interdependencies and continuities, the less scope there would be for doing things differently. At present the social security system is deeply integrated, with corporate functions and IT systems managed centrally. Service delivery is dependent upon an integrated payment and accounting system run by the UK Department for Work and Pensions. This core engine at the heart of the system calculates benefit entitlements based upon a UK policy framework. Such a system can accommodate relatively minor modifications, as in Northern Ireland, but in practical terms, it would be extremely difficult to share the administration and delivery of services in the context of markedly different entitlements north and south of the border. Sharing welfare bureaucracy may not have comfortably coincided with the social welfare aspirations of many independence advocates.

The UK Government's Scotland Analysis paper also questioned the viability of shared systems after independence. It suggested that the UK Government would be unlikely to see such arrangements as beneficial to 'the continuing UK' and that they would be difficult to envisage in light of the rejection of a formal currency union by all UK parties, since the payment systems were based on Sterling. Where a negotiated agreement to share social security service delivery could be reached, the analysis paper insisted it would mean that an independent Scottish state 'would not be able to make changes to existing social security policy or processes or to opt out of Great Britain-wide reforms' (HM Government, 2014d: 79). Intriguingly, this pressure to conformity and uniformity was not emphasized by the UK Government in deliberations over the Scotland Bill 2015/2016 on devolving more limited social security powers, although many of the arguments still held. In the referendum context, the purpose was clear: expose the risks, emphasize the costs, and draw attention to the complexity of the task of disintegrating one system and creating another. The problem for the UK Government in the area of welfare, however, was that its own programme of cuts to benefits and tax credits meant that, for those favouring comprehensive social security and redistributive welfare, a vote to remain in the Union was not risk-free.

Conclusion

In the independence referendum, voters were given conflicting messages of the implications of both independence and union for a social democratic welfare state, with one side talking up the promise and opportunities of independence and the other warning of its dire consequences. The Yes campaign capitalized on divergence in the welfare regimes north and south of the border since devolution, and the trajectory of UK welfare reform and retrenchment, to advance a social democratic case for a Yes vote. Threaded throughout the Yes campaign were three themes explicitly linking the past and future of the welfare state with the goal of independence. First, the UK welfare state could no longer reflect Scottish values or be trusted to provide social security to Scottish citizens, as evidenced in ongoing welfare reform. Second, the apparent direction of travel in the health service south of the border posed a threat to the devolved NHS in Scotland. And third, independence offered the prospect of a comprehensive welfare state that would reflect better the assumed needs and priorities of the Scottish people. For its part, the No campaign linked the welfare state and the defence of the union with both a defence and celebration of the 'union of social justice' and its embodiment of social solidarity on a UK scale, and a threat to the ability of an independent Scotland to maintain, let alone, expand social welfare provision.

The *Risk and Constitutional Change* survey, conducted by Delaney, Henderson, and Liñeira as part of the Centre on Constitutional Change research programme, suggests that the mixed messages were met at best with a mixed response, with limited evidence that they helped convert voters to either side (see Chapter 10). In particular, if the social democratic appeal and emphasis on welfare issues on the part of Yes campaigners was intended to appeal to women, in light of the gender gap in support for independence, there is little evidence to suggest that it succeeded. More men than women expected independence to lead to better care services for children, the elderly, and people with disabilities just as more men than women supported Scottish independence. Nonetheless, even if this campaign discourse had only a limited direct impact in converting opinion toward the Yes vote, its motivational effects mattered. A vision of a progressive social democratic country, made possible by the powers and opportunities offered by constitutional independence, helped to motivate and mobilize the grassroots Yes movement, perhaps reinforcing the social bases of support for independence.

There is little evidence, too, to suggest that the Gordon Brown and Better Together vision of a UK social union and UK social solidarity still has deep resonance in Scotland. Although a prominent theme among some key players, the social democratic case for union was not as central to the No campaign as was the social democratic case for independence. UK welfare reform and the UK Government's austerity programme gave these claims a nostalgic air, potentially reinforcing the claims of Yes campaigners that progressive welfare at the UK scale was a thing of the past. There is strong evidence from the aforementioned survey and many others suggesting that Scots believe the Scottish Parliament should control all areas of the welfare state, even if they don't necessarily believe this should lead to a markedly distinctive set of entitlements. In the referendum campaign, however, the core message of the UK Government and Better Together campaigners revolved around the risks to social security and the welfare state, alongside the broader set of risks and uncertainties associated with independence, and these may have contributed to the general unease among No voters at the consequences of a Yes vote.

6

The European Question

Michael Keating

Europe in the Independence Debate

The proposals for Scottish independence placed it firmly in the context of the European Union (EU). This took some of the sting out of charges of separatism and provided an external support system for an independent Scotland. Yet it also opened up a new line of attack by unionists, who questioned whether, how and on what terms Scotland could become an EU member state. The argument at times was reduced to obscure legalisms, made all the more difficult by the lack of European law and precedent. The No side used doubts over EU membership to increase risk and uncertainty, while the Yes side argued, with less effect (at the time), that the greater risk was of Scotland being taken out of Europe against its own will in a future EU referendum.

Europe and Nationalism

Supranational integration in Europe and the secession of 'stateless nations' might appear to be in contradiction to each other; the one aspires to larger units, the other to fragmentation. Yet, in another sense, they are complementary, seen as two aspects of spatial rescaling and state transformation, as functional systems and policy community migrate to new territorial levels. While some stateless nationalists have opposed European integration as a violation of sovereignty, others have embraced it as a new framework for independence, providing the external support system that small states require (Lynch, 1996; Keating and McGarry, 2001; McGarry and Keating, 2006; Hepburn, 2010). Europe gives small states a large internal market, restrains the predatory behaviour of large countries, and provides a common regulatory framework (Baldersheim and Keating, 2015). The Basque Nationalist Party came out for a united Europe as long ago as the 1930s, while Catalan nationalism has always had a European dimension. From the 1980s an increasing number of nationalist and regionalist parties adopted the slogans of 'Europe of the Peoples', or 'Europe of the Nations'. How far EU membership does entail a loss of sovereignty depends on what vision of Europe one adopts. In an intergovernmental Europe of nation-states (de Gaulle's *Europe des patries*), sovereignty is retained while states cooperate on matters of mutual interest. In the supranational vision, they pool and share sovereignty. Some nationalist parties have aspired to take their place as players in an intergovernmental Europe of the nation-states. Others have taken their Europeanism to the point of accepting shared sovereignty and the supranational principle, seeking a post-sovereign political order in which authority is shared across multiple levels (MacCormick, 1999; Keating, 2001).

Scottish nationalism has always had a European wing, but by the time of UK entry into the European Communities in 1973, the SNP was opposed. Its success in North East Scotland in the elections of 1974 owed something to fears of the impact of the common agricultural and fisheries policies. In the referendum on membership in 1975, the SNP supported a No vote, although the pro-European minority was allowed quietly to dissent. Jim Sillars' breakaway Scottish Labour Party was the only one to link the issues, arguing that, if the UK were to remain in Europe, then Scotland would need sufficient self-government to represent itself; in practice, this meant independence.

By the late 1980s the party had changed tack, adopting Sillars' policy as Sillars himself joined the party. Since direct elections to the European Parliament in 1979, the SNP had been present (in the person of Winnie Ewing) and the party began to discover Europe. This was also the time that the Labour Party turned back to Europe, impressed by the 'social dimension' introduced by Commission president Jacques Delors and the increased hostility to Europe of Margaret Thatcher. By the 1992 General Election, the SNP advocated 'independence-in-Europe', which has been its policy ever since. It has tended to take an intergovernmental view of Europe, although it has long had a post-sovereigntist wing, inspired by the work of Neil MacCormick (1999). By time of the referendum, the broader movements for Europe of the Peoples (or Regions) had waned in the face of the lack of opportunities for non-state actors in the emerging European space but remained attractive for people seeking a third way between independence and union.

Scottish public opinion on Europe also shifted from the 1980s onwards. At the 1975 referendum, Scotland, like the rest of the United Kingdom, voted to remain in the EC, but by a smaller majority than England or Wales.[1] Since the

---

[1] England voted Yes by 68.7 per cent; Wales by 66.5 per cent; Scotland by 58.4 per cent; and Northern Ireland by 52.1 per cent.

1990s the British Social Attitudes Survey and opinion polls have consistently shown that Scotland is not passionately pro-European but is a little less Eurosceptic than the other UK nations. A great deal was made during the 1980s and 1990s of the benefits of European regional funding for Scotland, although this has now largely been phased out as the new member states have priority.[2] It is likely also that Scottish voters have followed the lead of their parties. Surveys have shown that voters for all parties in Scotland are less Eurosceptic than in England, notably Labour voters. This still leaves a lot of Eurosceptics in Scotland, including a sizeable minority of SNP voters.

There is, however, a Scottish elite consensus on Europe, including the main political parties, the business community, the trade unions, and most of civil society. The United Kingdom Independence Party (UKIP) remains a minor presence, and Europe is not used as a weapon in inter-party competition. Scottish organizations have been active in Europe, using opportunities provided for a 'regional' presence while successive Scottish governments have emphasized the need to promote Scotland's interests in Brussels. All of this has allowed the old 'permissive consensus', or passive support for European integration, to persist longer in Scotland than in England.

Dramatis Personae

The debate on Europe involved more players than other aspects of the campaign, since it brought in non-UK individuals and institutions. It was another valence issue, with all the parties agreeing that Scotland should be within the European Union but disagreeing on whether, and how, this would be possible after independence. The Yes side shared a pro-European vision and presented Europe as an answer to many of the thorny questions about how an independent Scotland could survive in a dangerous world. The Labour Party also took a pro-European line and during the debates the leader of the No side, Alistair Darling, said to SNP leader Alex Salmond that they could be campaigning on the same platform in a future European referendum. The Scottish Conservative Party is not particularly Eurosceptic and its leader Ruth Davidson was committed to remaining in Europe. Wider Conservative divisions over Europe were kept under wraps during the campaign to allow the No side to present possible Scottish exclusion from the EU as a danger. To the left of Labour, the Radical Independence Campaign said very little about Europe, despite the historic Euroscepticism of this sector of opinion. Foley and Ramand (2014), the most

---

[2] It is debatable whether Scotland really did benefit from EU regional funds as the Treasury has always refused to recognize that these are additional to existing funding, but they were given great prominence.

complete statement of the radical case, say nothing at all about it while Gall (2013: 33) criticizes the SNP for 'not exploiting the greater freedom that being outside the EU would give' but does not elaborate.

The UK Government's position was presented in one of the Scotland Analysis papers, prepared by the Foreign and Commonwealth Office (HM Government, 2014b). This did not assert that Scotland would be rejected by the EU but rehearsed every argument to the effect that accession would be difficult, uncertain, and costly. The Scottish Government's position was set out in the independence White Paper and elaborated in a separate document (Scottish Government, 2014b).

There were several interventions from EU figures, notably José Manuel Barroso, president of the Commission and Herman van Rompuy, president of the European Council, all supporting the proposition that Scottish membership would be a difficult proposition. These were seized on by the No side as definitive pronouncements, although neither of these individuals has official standing on the matter, so they were in practice no more than expressions of opinion. Joaquín Almunia, a Spanish member of the European Commission, went even further, urging Scots to vote No. It is highly unusual for a member of the Commission, which is supposed to be politically impartial, to intervene in a matter of domestic politics in a member state, but Almunia was also thinking of the independence debate in Catalonia. In 2014 Barroso was succeeded as president of the Commission by Jean-Claude Juncker, who owed little to the UK Government (which had tried to block his nomination) and took a less aggressive line, reverting to the position that this was a matter for Scotland and the UK. In July 2014 Juncker stated, in an explicit reference to the Balkans, that the EU would not enlarge during the next five years. This was seized upon by the No side as a declaration that Scotland could not be admitted. Shadow Foreign Secretary Douglas Alexander described it as a 'hammer blow for the nationalists', while Scottish Conservative leader Ruth Davidson said that it confirmed that Scotland would have to join the queue (Daily Express, 15 July 2015). Juncker's office immediately corrected this. It was in any case apparent that the context for Juncker's remarks was the south-east of Europe and that admitting Scotland would not in fact enlarge the EU's territory.

Other member states exercised the usual diplomatic discretion, stating that this was an internal matter to be resolved by the people of Scotland and the UK, but there is no doubt that they preferred a No vote. In some cases, this was because they have their own internal nationalist movements, while in others their instinct was to support fellow member-state governments. In practice, it seems that most had resolved to follow whatever the UK decided, mindful of the Edinburgh Agreement.

There was a series of academic interventions, by constitutional lawyers and political scientists, coming to rather different conclusions. Some insisted on a literal reading of the treaties, taking silence as evidence that seceding territories cannot join the EU, others sought a deeper interpretation of the spirit of the treaties, while a third group argued that the issue was primarily political and that, if the political will is present, the EU institutions and member states can usually find a legal way to realize it.

For some, this was a legal argument, to be resolved by resort to the relevant treaties. The treaties, however, are silent on the matter and there is no precedent. The European Free Alliance, a coalition of 'stateless nations, regions, and traditional minorities' (http://www.e-f-a.org/about-us/whats-efa-and-history/) in Europe, with which the SNP is affiliated, has proposed the idea of 'internal enlargement' through which nations seceding from their host states could accede directly to the EU, but this has made no progress given the obvious reluctance of member states. Under the Lisbon Treaty, countries can leave the EU but only on their own volition. Greenland was allowed to leave the EU but remain within Denmark, while eastern Germany became part of the EU by joining Germany. Neither of these cases is really relevant, but they do at least suggest that European law can be creative in dealing with unanticipated events when it needs to be. Both sides in the debate showed a reluctance to get a definitive legal ruling, which indicates a certain lack of confidence in their case. The UK government declined to get a ruling from the European authorities, on the grounds that it did not plan for a Yes vote but instead commissioned a report from two academic lawyers (Crawford and Boyle, 2013). The Scottish Government maintained a bluff by implying that it did have legal advice but only actually got it when it was challenged under Freedom of Information law, and the advice came from its own legal advisors, not the European authorities (to which it did not have direct access in any case). A move in the European Parliament to get a legal opinion was blocked by Parliament president Martin Shultz, who did not want to get involved in what was a matter of domestic politics.

Some guidance was provided by the Vienna Convention on the law of succession for new states, which allows them to accede to existing international treaties by declaring their intention to abide by them. Most observers, however, considered this insufficient and, in any case, that the relevant law was not international but European. The consequence of all this was that there was no definitive legal guidance and a great deal of legal interpretation and invention.

The Independence Proposals

The SNP's proposals for Scottish independence placed it clearly in the context of continued membership of the European Union. Although there had been some earlier suggestions that Scotland would automatically remain within the

EU, the Scottish Government's (2013f) independence White Paper accepted that the remaining UK would retain continuous membership and that Scotland would have to accede. This was accompanied by assurances that Scotland would play a positive role in Europe, with an implicit criticism of successive UK governments for their uncooperative attitude. The timetable for accession to the EU would run in parallel to that for independence, that is eighteen months, so that the two would coincide.

Two ways in which an independent Scotland might gain entry into the EU have been proposed. One is by the normal process of accession under Article 49 of the Treaty of European Union, although this in the past has been used only by countries coming in from outside the Union. The other is by a change in the treaty itself, under Article 48, which would recognize Scotland as a member state with continuity of effect. Some legal experts insisted that only Article 49 would be appropriate. Others supported the use of Article 48, notably Sir David Edward (2012), a former judge at the European Court of Justice. Edward's position, that an independent Scotland could and would secure EU membership, was subsequently cited frequently by Alex Salmond, drawing strength from the fact that Edward was himself a staunch unionist.[3]

The SNP and Scottish Government preferred Article 48. They further stated that Scotland would seek, and obtain, the same terms of membership as the UK currently enjoyed, including the various opt-outs from common policies. One of these concerns the single currency (the euro); instead, Scotland would retain the pound (as discussed in Chapter 4). Scotland would remain outside the Schengen passport-free travel zone, so keeping the borders with England and Ireland open. The SNP also opted to retain opt-outs in Justice and Home Affairs although it had earlier been critical of some of these.

There followed three levels of argument, over whether an independent Scotland would be in the EU at all; on the process for becoming a member; and on the terms of membership and costs.

Arguments of Principle

The hardest argument against Scottish membership came from people who insisted that Scotland would not get in and, on principle, should not. Legal scholar Joseph Weiler (2014) argued that, by leaving the UK, Scotland would forfeit its moral right to be part of the European family. He had earlier made the same argument about Catalonia, although the legal arguments there are

[3] Edward (2014) at one point complained about becoming the poster child of the independence movement but did not waver from his position that, *if* Scotland becomes independent, it would be in the EU.

quite different (Weiler, 2014). Interestingly, Weiler brushed aside many of the practical objections to independence in Europe, agreeing that it could be done. The argument rather was, as Europe represented a higher moral order, separating from a large nation-state must represent a lower one; he added some gratuitously disparaging remarks about Scottish and Catalan nationalism.[4]

Another extreme position was taken by José Manuel Barroso, president of the European Commission. In an interview on British television (Andrew Marr Show, 16 Feb 2014), he declared that it would be 'extremely difficult, if not impossible', for an independent Scotland to join the EU. The 'difficult' part of this was widely accepted by observers, but the suggestion that membership might be impossible put Barroso in the company of Weiler in suggesting that there are certain nations that could not get in no matter what, while other European nations had the right, subject to meeting the criteria, to join the family (even if they were secessionist creations themselves). He caused further provocation by comparing Scotland to the case of Kosovo, which had experienced civil war and ethnic cleansing and which was unrecognized by several EU member states because it was unrecognized by Serbia. This is a different matter from an independent Scotland, which would be recognized by the United Kingdom under the terms of the Edinburgh Agreement. While the No camp seized on Barroso's remarks as definitive, it is not clear what standing he had. He did not have an elective mandate in Europe, and the Commission's role in the decision on admitting new countries is purely technical so that, were Scotland to meet the criteria, Barroso or his successor would be obliged so to report. As Neil Walker (2014) put it, Barroso may have had a political motive to argue against Scottish accession but failed to give reasons. Some former EU officials, including Graham Avery, Hugh McLean, and Jim Currie gave different views on the matter and questioned Barroso's standing (Scottish Parliament European and External Affairs Committee, 2014). It was recalled that former Commission Secretary General Emil Noël had stated back in 1979 that, if Scotland and England were ever to separate, both would remain in the EU (Douglas-Scott, 2014). Indeed, given the nature of the EU and its various institutions, there is arguably nobody and no institution that could definitively speak for it on this matter (Walker, 2015).

Against Weiler and Barroso, some legal scholars argued that Scotland would have a moral and legal right to EU membership. Matas, Gonzalez, Jaria, and

---

[4] Weiler's argument ran: 'These arrangements were well intentioned but lacking in political imagination and eventually, let us not hide the ugly facts, feeding and leading to that poisonous logic of national purity and ethnic cleansing. Again, make no mistake: I am not suggesting for one minute that anyone in Scotland or Catalonia is an ethnic cleanser. But I am suggesting, that the "go it alone" mentality is associated with that kind of mindset.' If Weiler is not accusing Scottish nationalists of ethnic cleansing, one wonders why he introduced the phrase, other than to poison the debate.

Roman (2011) had earlier argued that the EU is based in principles of democracy, equal citizenship, and rights and so would be obliged to respect an act of self-determination. They cited the judgement of the Supreme Court of Canada (1998) which had noted, in the Quebec secession case, that Quebec did not have a unilateral right to secede, but then argued that the democratic principles that underpinned the constitution would oblige Canada to respond were Quebec to give a clear majority for a clear question on independence. Douglas-Scott (2014) similarly argued that Scottish self-determination was an expression of precisely the values of democracy to which the EU is committed and which it has exported to eastern Europe and beyond.

Some legal scholars drew on the concept of citizenship, arguing that Scots had acquired rights under the EU (and EU citizens have acquired rights in Scotland), and have EU citizenship, which cannot unilaterally be withdrawn (Douglas-Scott, 2014). Against this, was the argument that EU citizenship is derivative of state citizenship so that it is a state's membership of the EU that confers European citizenship on its people not the other way around. Crawford and Boyle (2013) merely called the issue speculative; something that would have to be resolved in the European Court of Justice.[5] On more political and moral grounds, it was argued that not allowing Scotland into the EU would be equivalent to expelling Scots from the Union since they and their territory have been part of the EU and its predecessors for over forty years (albeit not as a member state), and a Yes vote in the referendum, far from expressing a desire to leave the Union, was linked to a strong commitment to membership. Another argument was that common citizenship could be used as a means to bridge an interim between independence and EU accession (Tierney and Boyle, 2014).

The Process

Most opponents of independence focused less on the principle of EU membership than on the practicalities, including the process. They tended to discount the use of Article 48 as inappropriate for accession of a new member and insist that it would have to be done under Article 49. The Scottish Affairs Committee of the House of Commons (composed entirely of unionists) insisted that Scotland would be outside the EU for an indeterminate period of time while accession was negotiated, and could not dictate terms.[6] The

---

[5] While they were regularly cited by the No side, Crawford and Boyle's argument was really quite nuanced and guarded.

[6] This report was weakened by the fact that the Committee had taken no evidence of its own but used only evidence submitted to other inquiries, including that of the Scottish Parliament, putting its own interpretation on it.

European and External Affairs Committee of the Scottish Parliament (with a nationalist majority) came to a different conclusion, but the unionist minority dissociated itself from all the crucial paragraphs. David Cameron insisted that Scotland would have to join a 'queue' of would-be members.[7] He and others also suggested that Scotland would have to work through all the necessary chapters to meet the *acquis communautaire*, the body of existing EU law and policy, citing the recent case of Croatia and implying that this would take years.

In practice, there is no queue and applicant countries are accepted when they are ready, which makes it much easier for northern European countries that already meet the criteria. As the UK Government (HM Government, 2014b) analysis itself concedes, Swedish and Finnish accession was indeed accomplished in about two years while the Norwegian negotiations took only a year (although a subsequent referendum meant that Norway did not actually join). The UK Government argued that Scotland could take longer as it was asking for opt-outs but, as it was merely asking for a continuation of present arrangements and was already compliant with the *acquis*, this might suggest that negotiations could actually be shorter.

One reason for the No side to insist on Article 49 was that they could then say that Scotland would be obliged to leave the Union and negotiate from outside. This implied a period in the wilderness, with no guarantee of getting back in at any particular time or on any particular terms. All were agreed that this would indeed be very costly. However, in a number of interventions, Graham Avery (2014a, b), a former senior EU official without a stated position on the merits of Scottish independence itself, argued that the practical problems could be overcome and that the issue was essentially political. Avery had himself negotiated several accessions and insisted on the European tradition of finding solutions and ways around apparent obstacles, in contrast to the purely legalistic approach.

Veto Points and National Interests

Whichever route and independent Scotland would have taken to join the EU, whether by Article 48 or 49, would have required the agreement of all

---

[7] 'The strictly factual answer is that if Scotland vote for independence, they are no longer members of the European Union and it has become clearer and clearer since this campaign started that they would have to reapply to join the European Union. And as such, as an independent country, they would have to queue up as it were behind other countries, for instance those in the Western Balkans, that are already on the path towards membership.' http://www.theguardian.com/politics/blog/2014/jun/02/newark-byelection-politics-live-blog#block-538c6489e4b01a015a59fbc3 (accessed 5 Aug 2016).

twenty-seven other member states. Agreement to accession has not normally been a problem and member states have generally respected the idea that European states satisfying the criteria have a right to join. Exceptions were the French veto on UK membership in the 1960s, which was down to the personal objections of President de Gaulle, and objections from several countries to Turkey, although that could officially be put down to the fact that Turkey was not ready. Even Cyprus had been admitted, in spite of the internal and international dispute about its territorial integrity. Scotland posed problems mainly because it could set a precedent encouraging secessionist movements elsewhere, including Spain, Cyprus, Belgium, and Romania. The No side repeatedly suggested that other member states might well veto Scottish membership although at no point did they (as opposed to commentators) say which these might be. Nor did the No side or the UK parties ever say that they would veto Scottish entry, while also refusing to say if they would support it. Their strategy was rather to use the EU question to raise the level of risk and uncertainty, always their strongest card.

It is clear that other member states instinctively backed the UK side in the referendum, if only out of solidarity. They tended, however, to do this discretely and insist that it was a matter for the people of Scotland under the Edinburgh Agreement. Asked by the BBC, half the member states declined to comment on the issue, while five indicated that Scotland would have to apply (http://www.bbc.co.uk/news/uk-scotland-scotland-politics-21602456). None of them threatened to veto Scotland's accession to the EU and their representatives usually said that they would follow the UK's lead; the inference is that they would recognize an independent Scotland. In that case, it is difficult to see on what grounds they could veto Scotland's EU membership.

Particular attention was given to the case of Spain, because the government of Catalonia was planning its own referendum on independence in November, drawing heavily on the Scottish precedent. It is no secret that the Spanish Government worried a lot about the outcome in Scotland because, politically, it would serve as a precedent for Catalan and other nationalists. Prime Minister Rajoy and Foreign Minister García Margallo said repeatedly that Scotland, if it became independent, would thereby put itself outside the EU, face catastrophic consequences and find re-admission difficult (Garea, 2015). On the other hand, Spanish ministers at no point indicated that they would veto Scottish membership. This made strategic sense, since if they insisted too strongly that no seceding state could join and lost that argument in the case of Scotland, they would indeed have set a precedent for Catalonia. Instead, they argued that, while Scottish membership would be difficult, it was in any case not a precedent for Catalonia, since the Edinburgh Agreement permitted Scottish independence, while the Spanish constitution expressly prohibits any secession from Spain. This subtlety was lost on José Manuel Barroso, who put Scotland and

Catalonia in the same camp, insisting that they would be outside the EU if they became independent, thus conceding that Catalonia could become independent. The more consistent position would be to say that Catalonia will remain in the EU for ever, since it can never leave Spain, an argument put by Spanish Prime Minister Manual Rajoy (*El Economista*, 19 August 2015). When pressed, Foreign Minister José Manuel García-Margallo followed other EU states in stating that Spain would, like other member states, take its lead from the UK.[8]

Of course, there are wider issues at stake. Spain's position within the EU was a weak one, as it sought to fend off a financial bail-out, and it would have found it difficult to stand up if the other large states wanted to accommodate Scotland. It also had its own problems with the UK Government, notably over Gibraltar, which the Spanish Popular (conservative) party regularly uses to distract attention from domestic difficulties. On one occasion, the outspoken Foreign Minister, after insisting that an independent Scotland would be outside the EU, pointed to a 'paradox', that should the UK leave the EU, Scotland would hold an independence referendum to remain in—the occasion was the launch of a book about Gibraltar (Política, 06 March 2013). So the Spanish strategy was to dissociate Scotland from Catalonia by stressing the legal and constitutional differences, while linking them through the proposition that both faced painful and costly isolation if they persisted with the demands for independence.

Those arguing that Scotland would indeed remain in the EU tended to point away from legalistic reasoning and towards politics and the self-interest of the key actors. So it was to the mutual interest of all member states and the Commission to maintain the integrity of the Union and the single market (Avery, 2014a). If Scotland were forced out, it would create a hole in the geography of the EU and cause endless problems for traders, investors, mobile workers, students, and governments. A whole range of treaties, institutions, and laws would have to be negotiated with the new state. The experience of Switzerland's relationship with the EU had convinced policy-makers that such ad hoc arrangements should be avoided, an argument repeated in relation to the proposed EU referendum in the United Kingdom. Particular criticism was reserved for the idea that Scotland should exit the EU and then come back in again. This threatened years of disruption for no good purpose and was against the spirit of maintaining the integrity of the EU territory (Tierney and Boyle, 2014). Given the economic crisis, the troubles with the euro, the need to deal with Greece, the refugee crisis, and the instability in Ukraine, it did seem unlikely that Europe would want to inflict another problem on itself by

---

[8] 'España no trabaja sobre hipótesis. Lo que sí le digo es que sería determinante a la hora de decidir nuestro voto cuál fuese la actitud del Reino Unido', *La Vanguardia*, 16 December 2013.

negotiating the extraction of Scotland from the single market and European citizenship and then negotiating to get it back in again.

Terms and Opt-outs

Beyond the debate about whether and how Scotland could become a member state of the EU was the third level of debate, on the terms. Matters here were even less clear. The UK has, over the years, negotiated a number of opt-outs from European laws and policies. Such opt-outs are not open to new member states, which must accept the *acquis communautaire* as it is. The issue then arises as to whether Scotland is to be treated as a new member state or a continuing one. The No side insisted that Scotland, if it got in at all, would be treated as a new member state. Once again, there is no legal provision and no precedent.

The UK, along with Denmark, has an explicit opt-out from the single currency, the euro; all other member states are expected to join, although only when they are ready. At one time, the SNP contemplated entry into the euro, although that might have required it to have its own currency for a time in order to satisfy the criteria. With the crisis in the eurozone, this became politically unsustainable and the decision was taken to retain a currency union with the UK (although not all the Yes forces agreed, see Chapter 4). The No side argued that Scotland would be obliged to join the euro, while at the same time insisting that it could not (for other reasons) keep the pound. The main riposte to this was that based on the argument that joining the euro was not an automatic consequence of EU membership and was actually rather difficult. The Scottish Government's (2014b: 3.14) line was that 'an independent Scotland will not be in a position to seek, or . . . to qualify for, membership of the eurozone in the foreseeable future. Accordingly, the transition to full EU membership will include specific provisions that ensure Scotland's participation in the sterling currency area does not conflict with wider obligations.' Scott (2012) concurred that accession to the euro is a difficult process and that, while new member states are expected to start the process, there is no legal requirement and no state has ever been obliged to join the single currency. Sweden does not have an opt-out but has been under no pressure to join. The crisis in the eurozone has made existing members rather wary of admitting new members, so it is difficult to see why they would make a priority of pulling Scotland in, but the issue of principle remains. Avery (2014a) agreed that in practice Scotland could avoid joining the euro.

The Schengen zone is the common passport-free travel area, to which EU members are expected to adhere, along with some non-EU states. As with the euro, states need to meet certain criteria for entry. The UK has an opt-out while

Ireland also took one in order to maintain the existing free travel area with the UK (and the Channel Islands and Isle of Man). As the UK has no intention of joining Schengen, Scotland's adhesion would require it to set up a border with the rest of the UK, with passport controls. Given the choice, the Yes side opted for the existing common travel area and opting out of Schengen. As with the euro, the requirement to join Schengen is subject to eligibility criteria and it is clear that, if Scotland were to keep open the border with England and Northern Ireland, it would not qualify. It is difficult to see why other member states should object to this if the United Kingdom itself wanted to keep things that way. The Scottish Government had made it clear that it would not erect border posts with England, so any initiative to do so would have to come from the UK side and it is difficult to see why they would want to do something so damaging to the interests of UK citizens and business. Once again, neither side could give promises as to the outcome of this, but the uncertainty played to the advantage of No.

The other principal opt-out concerns the area of Justice and Home Affairs (JHA). The UK has a complex relationship with this field but had an obligation to decide by 2014 whether to opt in fully or opt out. This is a divisive matter within the Conservative Party, and the UK Government decided to opt out but then negotiate to get back in to individual items. The SNP-controlled Scottish Government had been rather critical of this approach, preferring a more positive one but it also had its concerns about JHA, which it considered did not pay enough attention to the particular features of the Scottish legal system. In the event, it stated that an independent Scotland would also pursue the approach of opting in. Again, there was an argument as to whether it could inherit the UK exception but also a question as to whether Scotland would want a different set of opt-ins to the UK, a matter that was never really resolved.

Costs

There was some argument about the costs of EU membership and non-membership. The Yes side accepted that Scotland, like the UK, would be a net contributor but suggested that it could get a better deal in agriculture than it did as part of the UK. The No side warned that Scotland, being outside the EU, would lose out on agricultural and regional funds although, being presently a net contributor, this would surely be balanced by not having to pay in. There was some debate about the rebate that the UK gets from its automatic contributions to the EU (negotiated by Margaret Thatcher in the early 1980s). The UK Government insisted that Scotland would get none of this, while the Scottish Government said it would get a proportional share. According to

Avery (2014a), both were wrong and the issue would have to be resolved at EU level. Once again, this might be seen primarily as a political matter. The UK is under constant pressure over the rebate and could have an interest in ensuring that Scotland gained a share of it in the present and future budgetary cycles, if only to secure an ally and to demonstrate that the rebate was a response to objective conditions faced by both states.

There was a series of arguments about the impact of EU membership and exclusion on particular sectors. So the No side claimed that, because cross-border pension schemes had to be solvent, some occupational pensions in Scotland would have to be cut to bring them into balance (this would presumably also apply in the rest of the UK). The Yes side argued that a way around this could be found, although citizens may have been less concerned about the cross-border issue than the fact that their pensions were under-funded at all.[9]

Both sides tended to agree that Scottish exclusion from the EU would be extremely costly, given the economic gains of membership. This was the main burden of the No side's message given its suggestion that Scotland would find it impossible or at least difficult to remain in the Union. The Yes side sought to turn this argument on its head by pointing to the Conservative promise to hold a referendum on UK membership of the EU and suggesting that a pro-European Scotland could be dragged out of Europe by a Eurosceptic English majority. That it could use this threat shows how far being pro-EU had become the common property of the parties in Scotland and did not attract the political penalty it did in some parts of England. The threat was indeed a real one. Although Scots are only slightly more pro-Europe (or less Eurosceptic) than the English, polls showed that they could end up on opposite sides, something that did actually happen in 2016.

What Vision for Europe?

The Scottish Government consistently argued that Scotland would be an active player in Europe, suggesting that it would engage more positively than the UK does. Yet by accepting the same membership terms as the UK, including the opt-outs, it could put itself into the club of semi-detached members. A large member state can perhaps remain somewhat aloof from Europe and threaten to veto measures it does not like. Small states best secure their interests by being actively engaged and contributing to the common pool of ideas, rather than just pursuing their national interests (Panke, 2010).

---

[9] Shortly after the referendum, one of these UK-wide systems, the Universities Superannuation Scheme, was drastically curtailed.

They need to find allies and form coalitions. This issue was explored in some of the academic contributions to the debate (RSE and BA, 2014) but scarcely featured in the campaign.

Nor was there much of a debate about what sort of Europe the various parties favoured and how Scotland might contribute to it. There are different visions of Europe, which are vigorously debated within other member states. Some aspire to federalism with 'ever closer union', a position explicitly rejected by the UK Government; others prefer a more intergovernmental union, with power in the hands of member states. British Conservatives saw the EU as primarily a single market and have opposed the idea of 'social Europe', which includes labour market regulation and protection from those who might lose out from the process of change. The Scottish Government reaffirmed its support for the more social vision, but only in very general terms.

The Balance of Opinion

In the absence of clear law or precedent, much of the debate about an independent Scotland's place in Europe was speculative. At one end were those who sought a clear legal provision for secession within Europe and, in its absence, assumed that it was impossible. At the other were those who considered it all a matter of politics and sought to predict how the various parties would respond, based on their own self-interest. These tended to the view that mutual self-interest would lie in keeping the single market and the integrity of EU territory. At the political level, views about admission to the EU largely followed people's opinions about independence itself. Academic analysis was more complex; for example, there were people who opposed independence but nevertheless believed that an independent Scotland would, under whatever conditions, be within the EU (Edward, 2014; Tomkins, 2014).

Given that few people definitively claimed that Scotland would leave, and remain outside, the European Union, the debate focused on the procedures, the transition, the terms of membership, and the costs involved. In this, it echoed the referendum campaign as a whole. The case of Scotland is in many ways simpler than that of other nationalist movements, such as Catalonia, since the UK Government had accepted that Scotland could be independent. In another way, it is more complicated since the Catalan nationalists aspire to join the EU as a normal member state, with the whole *acquis communautaire* and the euro while the SNP wanted to replicate the UK's special position in Europe. This allowed opponents of independence huge scope to argue about what Scotland could get; interestingly, nobody on the Yes side disputed the claim to the same terms as the UK or proposed to abandon the opt-outs.

The history of European integration would suggest that, when the EU is under a political imperative to do something, it can usually find a way, but the way is often untidy and creates further problems later on. This is the experience, for example, of the eurozone, where rules have been abandoned when necessary but without putting in place a satisfactory alternative. Whatever the EU did about Scotland would have had repercussions across the Union. Had there been a blanket refusal of Scottish membership, it would have demonstrated that democratic, peaceful, and constitutional nationalism was fruitless, giving sustenance to other forms of nationalism (a point that seems to have escaped Joseph Weiler). In parts of Europe where peaceful and violent nationalism compete, this would have been highly dangerous. More likely, given the democratic nature of the Scottish process and the desire to minimize disruption, a way would have been found to accommodate Scotland, but this too would have had major political repercussions. It is true that the case differs from those in Spain and elsewhere in being agreed between the two governments, and both member states and European institutions would no doubt have used this to differentiate the cases, but this is a legal distinction, not a political or moral one. Nationalists in Catalonia and elsewhere followed the Scottish example closely, and it would set a destabilizing political precedent.

There is a hiatus in European law, which regulates huge areas of economic, social, and environmental policy but has no capacity to deal with matters of national self-determination. The EU tends to favour the integrity of states but, when they break up, has usually accepted the fact (Avery, 2014b). Practice has been inconsistent since the end of the Cold War. The response to the break-up of Yugoslavia was improvised and badly coordinated. Member states have still not agreed on whether to recognize Kosovo. There was an EU-regulated referendum on independence for Montenegro, but it was ad hoc rather than part of a consistent strategy. Cyprus was allowed to enter the EU as a divided country, with only the Greek side enjoying membership rights, although it was the Greek Cypriots who had rejected the proposed settlement, which the Turkish Cypriots accepted. It was easy to refuse recognition of Russia's annexation of Crimea, which was brought about through force and subversion; it is not clear what the attitude of the Europeans would have been had Crimea followed the 'Scottish path' to secession. The Scottish experience again suggests the need for some principles and rules.[10]

The EU issue was not particularly salient during the campaign but did contribute to the uncertainty. While this may have favoured the No side, the Yes side also sought to take advantage over the uncertainty about the UK's membership. Our pre- and post-referendum surveys show a small fall in

---

[10] At a minimum, these could distinguish between unilateral secessions and those agreed by the state as a whole.

the numbers of people who thought that nobody knew whether Scotland could have become part of the EU although they still amounted to 51 per cent of respondents. The numbers believing that Scotland would have been able to retain EU membership on the same terms as the UK went up slightly, from 27 per cent to 29 per cent, while the numbers doubting it went down from 45 per cent to 41 per cent. This suggests that considerable uncertainty remained at the end of the campaign. The EU issue may have been marginal and was certainly less significant than the issue of the currency, but the research does show that, if the EU had made it clear that Scotland would be a member, Yes and No could have been level. The argument of the Yes side that the risk lay in staying in the UK, and thereby being dragged out of Europe, seemed to gain little traction. The hypothesis that the UK might withdraw from the EU depressed both the Yes and No vote by similar amounts and increased the Don't Knows, suggesting that the argument was too complex and speculative. A month before the vote, an ICM poll tempered the picture of Scots as Europhiles, showing that while 59 per cent of Yes voters wanted Scotland to apply to join the EU, 27 per cent disagreed. There was a more longstanding scepticism about claims that Scotland would have to join the euro, with three-quarters of voters rejecting this claim already in 2013 (What Scotland Thinks/Panelbase). Overall, the evidence is that the EU issue did contribute to risk and uncertainty, to playing to the advantage of the No side and vindicating their strategy of emphasizing doubt, but that its role was less than that of other factors, notably the currency (see Chapter 10).

The campaign, in which both sides argued about the best way to stay in Europe, reinforced the pro-European consensus in Scottish politics, with implications for the promised UK referendum on EU membership. When this was announced in 2015, First Minister Nicola Sturgeon demanded that withdrawal should be allowed only if all four UK nations had agreed, a position shared by Northern Ireland's Deputy First Minister Martin McGuinness. This was never going to be accepted by Westminster, but the idea that Scottish self-determination aspirations affected not just the UK but the broader relationships within Europe was reinforced. The result of the 2016 European referendum in which the UK voted to leave by 55 to 45 per cent, while Scotland voted to remain by 62 to 38 per cent, ensured that the two issues remained closely linked, complicating any constitutional accommodation.

7

Defence and Security

Colin Fleming

The Defence Issue

Defence and security are central to the very idea of a sovereign, independent state, but these issues had played a relatively marginal role in the debates and literature on Scottish independence before the referendum campaign. During the campaign itself, they were considerably less prominent than economic issues, but a number of questions were posed about the choices facing an independent Scotland. A range of parliamentary committee inquiries examined defence and security issues relating to possible Scottish independence. These were followed in October 2013 by the UK Government's (HM Government, 2013b) Command paper *Scotland Analysis: Defence*, and in November 2013 with the publication of the Scottish Government's White Paper on Independence, *Scotland's Future*, which set out its vision for Independent Scottish defence and security models.

The two sides applied quite different frames to the issue. While the No side assumed the needs of a large state, the Yes side approached the question from the perspective of a small state, while stressing collective security. Consequently, they often talked past each other. Key issues included the viability and cost of an independent Scottish defence force; nuclear weapons, notably the UK's nuclear deterrent; membership of NATO; security needs in the face of new threats; and the economics of defence spending. As in other fields, uncertainty and risk played an important role. Where there were clear differences of opinion on the same issues, such as the timescale for independence or the economic impact, the arguments tended to be speculative or technical, so that it was difficult for the general public to get a purchase on them. Much would also depend on the outcome of negotiations. Both sides might focus on common interests. On the other hand, if Scotland were to take a hard line (for example on Trident), it could render the hope of a smooth, phased, transition of Scottish forces from the rest of the UK (rUK) highly problematic (Fleming, 2014).

The Protagonists and Framing the Issue

The issue divided the Yes from the No side but there were differences within each camp, which the official campaigns sought to de-emphasize. For example, the Scottish National Party (SNP) and Scottish Government proposed that Scotland should be a member of the North Atlantic Treaty Organization (NATO) while sections of the SNP and the non-SNP left and the Greens dissented. The UK Government supported the continuation of the independent nuclear deterrent in the form of the Trident missile system, although sections of the Labour Party disagreed. The issue also drew in outside actors with an interest in the UK's security strategy, including the United States and the NATO alliance itself. While these actors sought discretion and insisted that it was a matter for the people of Scotland, there was no doubt that they saw Scottish independence as potentially destabilizing (W. Walker, 2014).

Underlying the debate about defence and security was a fundamental difference in conceptions of Scotland's position in the world. The No side adopted a large-state perspective, making broad assumptions about what was desirable and achievable. This essentially saw the UK as a global power, capable of defending itself, maintaining an autonomous military capacity, able to project itself across the world, and meeting the expectations of a permanent member of the United Nations Security Council. An independent Scotland would lose the safety of being an 'integrated' part of a 'major power', with a consequent diminution of its security being the likely result of independence. In the UK Government (HM Government, 2013a, b) reports on the defence and security implications of independence, this position was reinforced with warnings about the ability of an independent Scotland to finance its defence requirements and recruit sufficient personnel to make a fledgling Scottish Defence Force operational. From this perspective, Scottish independence would have resulted in a loss of capability for Scotland and, presumably, as a consequence, for the remainder of the UK. Scotland would lose its influence as part of a UN permanent security member, lose the strength in depth of UK power in the European Union (EU), and lose out on UK defence spending. This would strip Scotland of the tools to pursue its international advantages as part of the UK. As argued at the time by the then Secretary for State for Scotland, Michael Moore, 'being part of the UK provides an incredible platform from which Scotland can do more, go further and aim higher in the wider world'. He continued:

The real effects of walking away from this unique global advantage need to be fully explained to people in Scotland... part of that would be swapping our collective strength in the UK for an uncertain alternative as a separate country.

(Moore, 2013)

This was a position explicated by other Government Ministries and was underlined in official Government Reports and House of Commons inquiries into the consequences of Scottish independence (House of Commons Scottish Affairs Committee 2012; House of Commons Scottish Affairs Committee 2013; House of Commons Defence Committee, 2013). The UK Government's response to the Scottish Affairs Select Committee contends that:

The UK stands out as having one of the most extensive and effective diplomatic networks in the world, with around 270 diplomatic posts in nearly 170 countries, employing over 14,000 staff. This network provides a platform for promoting the international, political, economic and commercial interests of the UK as a whole, in every major city of the world. From Scotland's perspective, the network draws considerable strength from combining global influence with local connections and knowledge to promote and protect Scotland's interests.

(Foreign Affairs Committee of Session, 2013)

The basic argument was clear: Scotland would be unable to shape world events or safeguard Scottish interest in the way the UK could.

The Yes side, by contrast, envisaged Scotland as an independent European state embedded in collective security systems. In place of global ambitions, an independent Scotland's focus would be on the defence of its territorial integrity and territorial interests as well as taking on a regional role contributing to the security of the strategically significant High North. This would be in conjunction with limited contributions to UN-sanctioned international commitments. There was a strong emphasis on ridding Scotland of nuclear weapons; indeed, a ban on nuclear weapons was to be part of the constitution. As these visions were so far apart, the two sides often talked past each other rather than engage directly.

Defence and security were also issues in which risk and uncertainty were prominent. The No side argued that independence would create a security gap and emphasized Scotland's vulnerability to international attack, terrorism, espionage, and cyber warfare (HM Government, 2013e). Independence was presented as a threat to Scotland's security; it was better protected as part of a large state with extensive military and security capabilities. George Robertson, former Scottish Labour MP and NATO General Secretary, was particularly outspoken, claiming in a speech in the USA that 'The loudest cheers for the break-up of Britain would be from our adversaries and from our enemies. For the second military power in the west to shatter this year would be cataclysmic in geo-political terms' (*The Herald*, 8 April 2014). For its part, the Yes side reminded voters of the Iraq war and the detrimental impact its fall-out has had for national and international security, warning that Scotland could be dragged into similar risky ventures if it remained part of the UK. As the Scottish Government's (2013f: 232) White Paper put it:

> ...improving the way defence is delivered in and for Scotland is one of the most pressing reasons for independence. For decades we have been part of a Westminster system that has sought to project global power, giving Britain the capacity to engage in overseas military interventions and to deploy nuclear weapons.

Speaking to Scotland's vocal anti-war movement the message that Scotland would not be dragged into what it saw as illegal wars, the White Paper continued: 'It will be the people of Scotland, through our Parliament, who decide whether or not our young men and women are sent to war' (Scottish Government, 2013f: 234).

In principle, a range of defence options could be open to an independent Scotland as a small state. It might have chosen neutrality, which itself could take different forms. Ireland provides one model. It is formally neutral but during the Cold War was firmly in the Western camp and has been a member of the European Union (formerly Community) since 1973. In practice, Ireland was able to shelter under the NATO security umbrella since the alliance would never tolerate a hostile power establishing a foothold there. Scotland could have effectively had a free ride on security, knowing that it would be looked after. Sweden and Switzerland opted for armed neutrality during the Cold War, while Finland had to observe a balance between East and West, due to its history and geostrategic position. At the other extreme from neutrality, the independence side might have proposed a security union with the United Kingdom analogous to its proposals for monetary union, effectively trading off autonomy against security and stability.

In fact, they choose neither, but rather to embrace collective security in Europe and the north Atlantic zone. The Scottish Government emphasized its intention to develop close defence cooperation with the rest of the UK (which would be its primary ally) and with its near neighbours in the North Europe, particularly the Nordic states, as well as within NATO. At the same time, the White Paper provided a commitment that Scottish forces would not be allowed to become involved in foreign wars unless such action was sanctioned by the United Nations, was supported by the Scottish Government, and had the backing of the majority of the Scottish Parliament (the so-called Triple Lock).

The Proposals

The Scottish Government's defence and security blueprint thus presented a very different model from that currently pursued by the UK. Despite significant cuts to the UK defence budget following the Coalition government's Strategic Defence and Security Review (HM Government, 2010b) the UK continues to provide a full spectrum of military capabilities (land, air, and sea) with the capacity to be involved in military interventions such as those in Iraq and Afghanistan. The UK armed forces underwent a series of personnel cuts following the 2010 Strategic Defence and Security Review (SDSR), with numbers dropping from 178,000. They are expected to settle at around 145,000 following the 2015 SDSR, continuing to represent a formidable integrated military system. By contrast, according to the Scottish Government's White Paper, an independent Scottish Defence Force would consist of 15,000 regulars and 5,000 reserves, and would adopt niche capabilities necessary to ensure Scotland's security. It would thus have more limited strategic goals determined by its own regional interests.

The Scottish Government and the SNP underlined their commitment to northern European defence. Scotland's main strategic interests would have lain in maintaining security in the North Sea, Eastern Atlantic, and across the High North. While there was a range of small states that might inform the design and capabilities of any future Scottish defence force, both parties also highlighted their interest in Nordic defence models (Robertson, 2013). Norway and Denmark were of particular interest and were presented as the most likely models that Scotland could emulate. Both have close similarities with Scotland in population size and national GDP, and both have regional interests in oil and gas, fishing, and the emergence of the High North as an area of geostrategic interest. Denmark, in particular, was seen as a comparable example of how Scottish defence forces could be adapted, although Scotland would likely have less interest in the type of overseas stabilization operations in which Denmark has recently been involved.

Reflecting the change in emphasis from being part of a large state to that of a small state, the Scottish Government's proposed defence budget was set at £2.5 billion at the point of independence excluding set up and/or transitional costs. This was in line with other small European states, such as Denmark, but would be unable to match the economies of scale that a larger state could manage.[1] However, despite claims that this figure would not provide the type

---

[1] Individual commentators placed caution over the ability of the Scottish Government to pay for high-tech assets such as Typhoon aircraft. In fact, Stuart Crawford argued that the Scottish defence forces would only require training aircraft such as the Hawk aircraft, suggesting Tornado or other high-end aircraft would be too advanced and too expensive (Crawford and Marsh, 2012: 11).

of capabilities envisaged in the Scottish Government's White Paper, there was tentative acceptance that this was credible and sufficient to enable Scotland to build modern, flexible defence forces over and beyond the transition phase, capable of responding to regional and global challenges in cooperation with allies (Chalmers, 2013). There would inevitably have been a transitional period as Scotland's defence capabilities would not be fully operational by 2016, or possibly longer, by when the Scottish Government assumed independence negotiations would be completed and Scotland could formally become an independent state.

The White Paper (Scottish Government, 2013f) identified five 'defence priorities' for an independent Scotland: (i) commitment to the annual budget of £2.5 billion; (ii) ensuring the speediest safe withdrawal of nuclear weapons from Scotland; (iii) a focus on maritime capabilities, such as air and sea-based patrol, and specialist forces; (iv) progressively building a total of 15,000 regular and 5,000 reserve personnel over the ten years following independence; and (v) reconfiguring the defence estate inherited at the point of independence to meet Scotland's needs. This would have included the transition of Faslane in the west of Scotland (currently used for the UK's Trident nuclear weapons) to a conventional naval base and joint headquarters of the Scottish Defence Forces (SDF). There was a further commitment to undertake a feasibility assessment of whether the dockyards at Rosyth on the east coast of Scotland could be brought back into use as a naval base, giving the Scottish Defence Force the flexibility to deal with potential incidents in the North Sea.

The Scottish Government prioritized naval and air forces able to protect Scotland's vast coastline, as well as a mobile army brigade capable of being deployed as part of larger operations if required. At the point of independence the proposals for a Scottish Defence Force estimated a total of 7,500 regular and 2,000 reserve personnel, to be increased further to approximately 10,000 regulars and 3,500 reserves by the end of the initial phase of transition—five years following independence. The Scottish Government estimated that it would meet its maximum strength of 15,000 regulars and 5,000 reserves within ten years. With respect to naval and air forces, the proposals in the White Paper expected naval capabilities would comprise 'one naval squadron to secure Scotland's maritime interests and Exclusive Economic Zone (EEZ) and contribute to joint capability with partners in Scotland's geographical neighbourhood'. The squadron would consist of two frigates from the Royal Navy's current fleet; a command platform for naval operations; up to four mine countermeasure vessels from the Royal Navy Fleet; offshore patrol vessels; and up to six patrol boats and auxiliary support ships. A second naval squadron would be developed during the transition period, providing the Scottish Government with the naval capabilities to contribute to NATO or EU operations out with Scotland's immediate strategic ambit of the North and Eastern Atlantic.

Core elements of a Scottish air force would be equipped with a share of UK assets, and would be tasked with policing Scottish airspace. In addition, it would be equipped with a Quick Alert (QRA) Squadron of twelve Typhoon jets to be based at Lossiemouth, although this was a contentious issue and several commentators felt that the Typhoon was too sophisticated and thereby too expensive for Scotland to use in the long term (Crawford and Marsh, 2012).

Scottish land forces in 2016 would have had an army HQ function and an all-arms brigade, with three infantry/marine units, equipped in the first instance from a share of UK assets. It is estimated that this would comprise 3,500 regular and 1,200 reserve forces, rising to an estimated 4,700 regular personnel throughout the transition period. The first task of a Scots army was to be territorial defence; however, Scottish soldiers would have participated in overseas operations if sanctioned by the Scottish Government and parliament (as highlighted above in relation to the Triple Lock). The decision to provide the possibility of Scottish personnel serving overseas fed into and was based on its requirement to bring capabilities to the table should it seek membership of NATO and close cooperation with its near neighbours. However, in the main, the Scottish Government proposed that it could bring added value over the long-term by concentrating on filling capability gaps in the Nordic region and Atlantic, such as maritime air surveillance and naval surface fleet dedicated to a regional role.

Although the White Paper provided details of a Scottish Order of Battle, as a new state Scotland would be in the position that it could work from a blank canvas and indicated that it would undertake a Strategic Defence and Security Review in 2016. This was important for several reasons. Scotland would be entitled to a division of defence assets from existing UK capabilities and as highlighted above its early forces would have built upon these assets. However, the Scottish Government may have chosen to negotiate a deal with the UK Government that would ensure that rUK force capabilities were not unduly diminished by accepting some financial compensation in lieu of assets themselves—the benefit of which would be that Scotland could then procure capabilities that fit its own strategic interests rather than inherit capabilities that it did not require (Crawford and Marsh, 2012; Chalmers, 2013).

The Scottish Government placed a particular emphasis in cooperating with allies, including rUK and within NATO. The pro-independence campaign did not merely use NATO as an external security structure, it also emphasized Scotland's potential contribution to collective defence. It was particularly successful at drawing attention to defence gaps created by UK-wide defence cuts in the aftermath of the 2010 SDSR, especially the decision to scrap the replacement to the UK's ageing Maritime Patrol Aircraft, Nimrod. Its successor, MRA4 which was due to be delivered during the last parliament was cancelled, a decision which was heavily criticized at the time (House of Commons

Defence Committee, 2012), leaving significant capability gaps in maritime air surveillance and naval surface vessel capabilities in this region—capabilities which the Scottish Government underlined its commitment to fulfilling.[2]

The White Paper proposed a 'phased transition' of forces from those currently part of the British armed forces to an all-Scottish force. As a consequence, only certain elements of the SDF would be operational at the point of independence, with the full transition expected to take around ten years. During this period, the Scottish Government was committed to paying a financial contribution to cover UK-wide defence. Although there was some suggestion that more than ten years would be necessary, the transition period appears credible and could have provided defence and security continuity and allow Scotland and the rUK time to undertake detailed planning on future defence arrangements—including defence cooperation between Scotland and rUK. Like so many of the defence-related issues, whether or not the transition of forces was undertaken on time and with the full support of both governments rested on whether other issues were dealt with constructively; most importantly the nuclear question and the timeline on the removal of the UK deterrent from the Clyde.

Given that the UK Ministry of Defence was in the midst of significant downsizing as a result of its own Strategic Defence and Security Review (HM Government, 2010b), and was struggling to meet its targets to realign its regular and reserve forces in line with its future defence requirements, a phased transition might have been of benefit to both states (Dorman, 2012). Not least, there was a question over recruitment to a fledgling SDF and how long this would have taken. The White Paper left open the possibility that Scots could continue to join the UK armed forces and the UK's defence analysis paper highlighted, rightly or wrongly, that a career in the UK armed forces was more favourable to those wishing to embark on a military career.[3] Whether there would have been recruiting problems is a moot point, and the Scottish Government would have had to offer a good package to existing servicemen and women. If it did, however, it might have been expected that English personnel serving in Scotland may have chosen to enlist in the fledgling SDF.

The ability to start afresh and build a defence capability that would serve Scottish interests was critical to the Scottish Government's White Paper, but there were several voices which also called for Scotland to examine its defence requirements anew should it become independent. This was important so that Scotland did not start independence with legacy equipment from the UK defence

[2] Underlining the importance of MPA to the region, the UK government has since decided to procure nine Boeing P3 aircraft to fill this gap. (National Security Strategy and Strategic Defence and Security Review, 2015).

[3] The defence analysis paper's claim was set against newspaper reports that recruitment and the redevelopment of the UK forces were undergoing considerable problems.

inventory that it did not need and that would offer little or no strategic gain. Thus, while the Scottish Government indicated that its military headquarters would be at Faslane, there were some criticisms that this was too far away from the centre of power in Edinburgh. In the same vein, there were calls by some commentators that at the very least, the Scottish Government should not risk putting all its 'naval' eggs in one basket by designating Faslane as the sole Scottish naval base. It was a position that seems to have had some resonance in that the White Paper the Scottish Government makes clear that it will look 'into the feasibility of bringing Rosyth back into naval use' (Scottish Government, 2013f: 245).

Others argued that Scotland did not require the type of assets or order of battle it set out in the White Paper. If it had opted for Partnership for Peace (see section on NATO) as an alternative to full NATO membership, this could have reduced the amount it intended to spend on defence from the estimated £2.5 billion to £1.8 billion (Crawford and Marsh, 2012). In essence Scotland could offer territorial defence rather than opt for a more expensive, complex defence apparatus. That the Scottish Government chose NATO demonstrates its commitment to European defence on a regional basis, even if this was more to do with recognition as an independent state than it was about what it actually required as an armed military force.

NATO

Both the UK and Scottish Governments accepted the desirability of collective security in the form of NATO. Taking a small state perspective, Scotland would seek 'shelter' within wider defence structures such as NATO, the EU, and the Organization for Cooperation and Security in Europe (OSCE) (Robertson, 2013; Bailes, Thorhallsson, and Johnstone, 2013). By joining these organizations Scotland would be able to underpin its security in a way that it would not be possible if it remained neutral. This represented a change of strategy on the part of the SNP, which had long opposed NATO, largely on the grounds that it is a nuclear alliance. There had been moves to change this position and embrace collective security in the way the party had embraced Europe as a form of shelter essential for a small state. These, however, were overtaken by the Iraq War and only in 2012 did the party leadership return to the issue with a proposal to party conference. Although in recent years, the leadership has usually got its way, this issue caused the most serious rift in the party's ranks in recent years and was only narrowly accepted. Two MSPs resigned the party whip, followed later by a third. Defence spokesman, Angus Robertson (2013), put it this way:

> Security cooperation in our region functions primarily through NATO, which is regarded as the keystone defence organisation by Denmark, Norway, Iceland and

the United Kingdom. The SNP wishes Scotland to fulfil its responsibilities to neighbours and allies.

Whether Scotland could gain membership if it voted yes proved to be one of the most contentious issues in the whole defence debate. The No side consistently sought to sow doubts about whether Scotland would be admitted to NATO, similar to those created over membership of the European Union (see Chapter 6). Some of these concerned matters of principle and procedure but the most serious was that NATO membership requires acceptance of the Strategic Concept, including nuclear deterrence. SNP policy has long been to oppose the UK nuclear deterrent and also to prohibit the stationing of nuclear weapons in Scotland. Indeed, the ban on nuclear weapons was to be enshrined in the constitution of an independent Scotland. The Scottish Government's position was thus complicated. It was, in principle, willing to sign up to the alliance's Strategic Concept, thus implicitly accepting that NATO is a nuclear alliance, but to note that many members do not have nuclear weapons stationed on their territory or in their waters. Indeed, only three out of the current twenty-eight NATO members are nuclear states and, since the collapse of the Soviet Union, the alliance has had a policy of not basing nuclear weapons in the territory of new member states. This position was robustly challenged by the UK Coalition Government, the UK Ministry of Defence (MoD), and the broader No campaign, which argued that Scotland would be unable to join the North Atlantic alliance whilst it championed a non-nuclear policy.

The No side also linked the issue of NATO membership with that of the future of the Trident system. They argued that Scotland could not simultaneously join the Alliance but remove the UK's nuclear deterrent out of Scotland in a timescale that did not allow the UK government time to find suitable alternative sites to Faslane and Coulport. As Malcolm Chalmers put it (House of Commons Foreign Affairs Committee, 2013: 151):

> There would be little international sympathy, at least among the UK's traditional allies, were Scotland to insist that the UK's nuclear armed submarines leave its territory on a timescale that did not allow the rUK to construct alternative bases in England or Wales

For the SNP and Scottish Government this was presented as unproblematic, and in the main it rhetoric on the removal of the nuclear deterrent remained very consistent. As discussed below, how long it would take to relocate Trident to another site was a matter of debate, with some suggesting upwards of twenty years (Crawford and Marsh, 2012). If this issue was negotiated successfully by both sides, it would open the door to NATO membership and being anti-nuclear would not by itself preclude membership of the alliance if it agreed to sign, which it hinted it would do in the Scottish Government's White Paper.

Scotland's accession to membership of NATO would also have been strengthened its geostrategic importance to the Alliance. Although the United States and NATO hinted that they would prefer the status quo, if Scotland voted Yes it would have opened up a very different strategic environment and it would be better to have Scotland as a partner, with no interruptions to regional defence arrangements. Scotland's strategic interest married with a commitment to bring assets to regional defence, would have probably ensured it entered the alliance without too much fuss, as long as the Trident question was settled amicably (Fleming and Gebhard, 2014).

The SNP defence update (2012) also underlined an independent Scotland's desire to seek closer cooperation with its nearest neighbours, with particular emphasis being given to Scotland's 'domestic and regional security obligations' (Robertson, 2013). This would entail cooperation with rUK (Fleming, 2014) as well as neighbouring nations such as Denmark, Norway, and Iceland, with the goal of contributing to Northern European Defence through conducting joint maritime and air patrolling responsibilities in a NATO context (Robertson, 2013). However, Scotland would have had to provide assurances that it would be capable of contributing to both regional and international operations (Fleming and Gebhard, 2014; Fleming, 2014).

As with the EU, the mutual interest of all sides in not opening a gap in collective defence would suggest that an independent Scotland would have been admitted to NATO, albeit perhaps not unconditionally. This may have been be particularly the case in light of NATO's call for burden sharing, especially by its European members and deeper defence cooperation between Alliance members. The Alliance's 'open door' policy, enshrined in Article 10 of the Washington Treaty and reaffirmed along with NATO's Strategic Concept in 2010 underlines that any European state wishing to fulfil the Treaty obligations is open to apply for full membership. An independent Scotland would also have been in a slightly different position from other aspiring members. Already meeting the necessary democratic and economic criteria and with a long history as part of the alliance already, a future SDF would meet NATO criteria vis-à-vis equipment through its share of UK assets.

Questions remained, however, about the terms and about the sequence. Scotland would take around ten years or more to transition from being part of a UK defence to a fully independent defence force. NATO policy underlines that candidate members would be refused full membership if there is any ongoing dispute with other existing alliance members. Scotland's membership of NATO may thus be predicated on broader international recognition of its independence and in particular a negotiated agreement on defence and other issues with the rUK government. Consequently, if the Trident issue was not resolved satisfactorily between the two governments, it might be expected that Scotland's membership of NATO would have been refused. Under such circumstances, it may still have been possible to achieve continuity of effect and Scotland could have become an associate member as part of NATO's Partnership for Peace programme. This was established after the end of the Cold War to embrace countries in the NATO neighbourhood, without including them all within the Alliance itself. In includes former Soviet and Yugoslav republics as well as the neutral EU members and Switzerland, but it does not entail the common defence strategy or guarantees provided by NATO.

Trident

Since the 1960s, the UK's strategic deterrent has consisted of submarines based in the Firth of Clyde, most recently the Trident system. Until the early 1990s, the USA also kept nuclear-armed submarines in an adjacent loch. Both bases became a focus for anti-nuclear protests in the 1960s and again in the 1980s, inspired by the Campaign for Nuclear Disarmament. This gained wide support within the SNP and some prominent activists left the Labour Party to join the SNP more because of the nuclear question than because of the independence issue. Subsequently, the removal of Trident from the Clyde became, as John MacDonald (2014) observed, synonymous with the very idea of an independent Scotland. Nuclear disarmament has thus been a central issue within the SNP, as it also was for the Greens and the wider pro-independence left. During the time of the referendum, the UK Government was in the process of deciding on a renewal of Trident, which was supported by the Conservatives and the Labour leadership. There was a significant anti-Trident presence within the UK and Scottish Labour Party, while the Liberal Democrats equivocated, trying to find a form of slimmed-down deterrent that they could support. The Yes side were united on the proposition that Trident would have to be removed from an independent Scotland within an agreed time frame. This would have caused major problems for rUK, as there was nowhere obvious to relocate it and, even if somewhere were to be found, it would be very costly. There was thus a prospect that Scottish independence might mean the end of British nuclear weapons altogether (MacDonald, 2014).

The Scottish Government (2013f) White Paper noted that it would seek the quick and safe removal of the deterrent and would enter into negotiation with the UK Government on the issue. Although it indicated its preferred timetable for removal was by the end of the first parliament of an independent Scotland, it could well have taken longer, and with considerable expense. The UK defence analysis paper underlined the importance of this issue, not just in terms of the timescales for removal of the deterrent but also on Scotland's Accession to NATO. A Royal United Services Institute (RUSI) report (Chalmers and Chalmers, 2014) argued that the UK Government could find alternative basing arrangements at a lower cost than the latter had suggested, but doing so would still take time—perhaps as long as fourteen years after independence. For its part, the Scottish Government underlined that it was not its position to force nuclear disarmament on the rUK, noting simply that that decision rests with the government and people of the rUK. Meanwhile any deadlock on Trident could have held up negotiations on NATO membership, as well as other issues central to independence negotiations.

There were suggestions that a deal might have been done whereby the Scottish Government accepted that Trident could remain on the Clyde in a trade-off for the UK Government's acceptance of a sterling currency union. There might be a certain logic in this as a gaming strategy, but the two issues belonged in different arenas, with different constituencies. So the position of the Treasury and the Bank of England on sharing sterling would not easily be moved by considerations in another area, while the SNP activists for whom Trident was a touchstone issue would not be consoled by being allowed to keep the pound. Indeed, many of the left-wing independence supporters most opposed to Trident were also against monetary union.

The main problem facing the UK was not simply the removal of Faslane as its main operating base, it would also lose Coulport, the site at which the Trident weapons systems are transferred to the submarine. There was some suggestion that a replacement to Faslane may have been found; the difficulty was finding a replacement Coulport, where the warheads could be safely installed or removed from the submarines. Several sites in England and Wales were mooted, with Falmouth being the most obvious choice. However, the complexity involved with building two adjacent sites in a built environ-ment were colossal and would have involved years of planning before build-ing would be possible. It was this dilemma—finding the appropriate sites—that created the most serious uncertainty about the future of the UK as a nuclear armed state. The UK government would have required several years (perhaps as many as twenty years) to find then build suitable alternative bases. That it would be given such a lengthy stay of execution was a contested issue with different voices pursuing different agendas.

The Scottish Campaign for Nuclear Disarmament published a report stating that the nuclear warheads could be disabled within days and observed that it would take two years to remove the deterrent from Scottish waters. The Scottish government had initially backed this analysis and frequently called for the fastest safe removal of the nuclear fleet. It softened its view in the White Paper, partly, it seems, because of the NATO question, but also because Scotland required the cooperation of rUK in transitioning its defence forces. This is something that would have been significantly harder to do if they maintained a hard line on the nuclear issue. Thus, the Scottish Government tried, successfully in the main, to balance its anti-nuclear inclination against the practicalities of the evolving political situation. Whether it would have maintained its position if it had been a yes vote is an interesting question; it would certainly have found it difficult to keep its anti-nuclear supporters on side in the event of the type of grand bargain that would have been necessary for it to join NATO without lengthy delay.

Security Threats

Following the UK Government's defence analysis paper, its *Scotland Analysis: Security* (HM Government, 2013e) report set out to highlight the potential security risks for Scotland if it became an independent state. Like other UK reports before it the security analysis report underlined the warnings that Scotland would struggle as an independent state, arguing that it would result in critical security failures caused by the severing of British intelligence and security provision. Indeed, launching the report, Home Secretary Theresa May (2013) underlined her longstanding argument that Scotland would be a 'soft target' for terrorists, which the Scottish Government would be unable to manage with a diminished security apparatus (Chalmers, 2012).

The UK's access to information as a larger global player was thus pitted against the uncertainty of creating a new, much smaller security and intelligence apparatus. It was consistently argued that Scotland could not expect to be part of the 'five eyes' intelligence framework, comprising the UK, USA, Canada, Australia, and New Zealand. This was an argument that was hard for the Scottish Government to counter; as a new state it would not be guaranteed access to the club. If it was to join it would also have been likely that membership would not have been immediate. Scotland would have been required to demonstrate that it could handle shared intelligence with its partners before being permitted privileged information the UK could access through its existing networks. Like the UK's defence analysis paper, the security analysis document (HM Government, 2013e) strove to demonstrate the importance of size and its attendant capability through shared intelligence channels. The UK championed a large security apparatus and sought to generate uncertainty about the Scottish Government's plans for counter terrorism and security response, despite the ostensibly greater ability to hold a smaller department to account at a parliamentary level. Yet again, bigger was better.

Economic Arguments

An important point of criticism for the No side was the economic consequences of Scotland losing defence contracts. The unionist parties insisted that the UK Government would not commission warships from an independent Scotland, threatening industrial sector jobs including shipbuilding on the River Clyde in Glasgow. An independent Scotland could thus not guarantee the future of Scottish defence industries, whose sustainability, the UK Government insisted, 'would be a serious concern' (HM Government, 2013b: 67; Scotland Institute, 2013). The UK parties consistently highlighted that complex naval warships (such as the Queen Elizabeth Class aircraft carrier) and other items sensitive to national security would not be built in a foreign country. Further jobs losses would arise from the closure of the nuclear weapons facilities at Faslane and Coulport. The defence analysis report pointed out that the Ministry of Defence spent just under half of £20 million on manufacturing, securing 12,600 defence sector jobs in Scottish industry (HM Government, 2013b: 67). These would be put at risk if Scotland voted Yes, along with an important part of Scotland's broader industrial base.

The Scottish Government sought to reassure the public that it would remain competitive in defence industries—building its own naval assets and cooperating with UK projects. In addition, the Ministry of Defence regularly commissioned naval assets overseas. This is true, but it is discretionary and member states are not obliged to follow European Union procurement law when procuring assets of essential national security. Even if the SNP's proposed industrial cooperation within the defence industry could be negotiated in the short term (for those units already passed Main Gate), it could not expect to continue to have special access to the rUK's defence industry in the long term and would have to compete with rUK's own industrial base. Indeed, the White Paper had highlighted, in the same vein as the UK government, that the SNP would prioritize its own defence industry in its procurement process.

Conclusion

The defence and security debate was dominated over the question of the UK's nuclear deterrent and what its quick removal would mean for the UK's global role. Its importance was also indelibly linked to debates about whether or not Scotland would gain entry into NATO. Membership would have probably followed independence, but this is not to say that conditions would not apply. Chief among these would be what should be done about the removal of Trident from the Clyde. If Scotland insisted on a speedy removal this would certainly have slowed accession to the alliance. If it took a longer term view (something it seemed to suggest in the Scottish Government's White Paper) it would have eased concerns about UK power projection and Scottish intentions within the alliance.

The range of issues following from the defence and security debate was more diverse than simply these two issues, despite them taking up most column inches in the print media. The Scottish Government presented a credible defence blueprint, but because so much would have depended on negotiations if there had been a Yes vote, they were never able to present concrete plans. The No side used this to their advantage and successfully sowed uncertainty about the cost of independence, including defence sector job losses and loss of intelligence capability. Issues such as recruiting and maintaining the defence estate on budget were discussed, but these never really reached the public debate in any meaningful way. As in other fields, analysis of the issue is hampered by the lack of evidence and precedents and uncertainties about how the key actors would have responded in the case of a Yes vote and how far they would have been prepared to make concessions or find common ground.

8

The Constitution of an Independent Scotland

Popular Empowerment or Judicial Supremacy?

Stephen Tierney

Introduction

The referendum ended in a clear No vote. Questions which seemed so pressing in the Summer of 2014—What would an independent Scotland look like? What currency would it use? How easily would it accede to membership of the European Union? How would relations with the rest of the United Kingdom develop?—were each rendered redundant by the result. In the same way, speculation about how the constitution of an independent Scotland would have been drafted and what it would look like might well seem to be of only counter-factual interest today: it is a short trip from 'what if?' to 'so what?' There are, however, two ways in which the proposals put forward by the Scottish Government for both an interim and then a permanent constitution for an independent Scotland remained salient in the post-referendum landscape. The question of Scotland's constitutional status within the unwritten United Kingdom constitution, and deep uncertainty and dispute concerning that status, were provoked rather than settled by the referendum, particularly as the UK Government immediately embarked upon a fresh round of constitution-making that led to the Scotland Act 2016. For example, the provision in Section 1 of the 2016 Act that the Scottish Parliament and Scottish Government are each recognized as 'a permanent part of the United Kingdom's constitutional arrangements' provoked a debate about whether it is possible to embed constitutional guarantees within the UK constitutional system, which is defined by the unlimited legislative authority of Parliament (Elliott, 2015). But it is notable that during the referendum campaign the debate was about sovereignty as political power; there was little discussion, even among academics, about either the constitutional transition to independence which has proven to be so tricky in the independence of other British territories (Oliver, 2015), or the impact of Scottish independence upon the UK constitution itself. Secondly, the prospect of a permanent constitution for an independent Scotland, which would have replaced the interim constitution, remains interesting for the way in which it emerged at a time of renewed concern internationally with how constitutions are made and, in particular, in the role of citizens in constitution-making processes (House of Commons Political and Constitutional Reform Committee, 2015: 48, paras 14, 110). The proposal put forward by the Scottish Government was essentially concerned with process, namely the engagement of civil society in drafting the constitution. Again it is notable how little the constitutional future of Scotland was a focus in the referendum debate, perhaps because constitution-making was seen as a distant prospect which was overwhelmed by more immediate arguments.

In this chapter we revisit the proposals both for an interim constitution and for a process towards a permanent constitution, recognizing their continued significance. We then consider whether the trend towards ever more elaborate and detailed constitutions is in fact a healthy development in democratic terms. This is a huge question—whether the constitution should be an open political space or a foreclosed set of values, controlled by judges. The Scottish referendum encapsulated the spirit of vernacular politics—letting the people decide. It would seem odd, indeed somewhat ironic, if the ultimate outcome had been a move to a more formalized constitution in which the scope for active citizen engagement in major constitutional issues was to be inhibited rather than enhanced. Although this is a debate that did not feature in the referendum campaign, it will be argued in the final section of the chapter that it would surely have become a deeply contested issue in the event of a Yes vote.

Background

On 16 June 2014 the Scottish Government unveiled its Scottish Independence Bill ('the Bill') in an address by Nicola Sturgeon, Deputy First Minister of Scotland, to the Edinburgh Centre for Constitutional Law. The Bill, and the White Paper that accompanied it (Scottish Government, 2014c), set out the Government's two-stage plan for an interim and then a permanent constitution for an independent Scotland. This built upon the November 2013 White Paper, *Scotland's Future* (Scottish Government, 2013f)—which was the first document to formulate in detail the Scottish Government's plan for a written constitution (Tierney, 2013a). The intention was to replace Westminster parliamentary supremacy with the 'sovereignty of the people of Scotland' since, the Scottish Government claimed, popular sovereignty has historically been 'the central principle in the Scottish constitutional tradition' (Tierney, 2013b). The proposals were later largely replicated in the June 2014 White Paper which offered a three-stage process: from September 2014 until March 2016, negotiations would be completed with the UK Government on the transfer of powers to Scotland; from March 2016 until some undetermined date, an interim constitution would take effect in Scotland; and finally, after the Scottish elections of May 2016, a new permanent constitution for Scotland would be drafted. The June 2014 White Paper proposed that a permanent constitution should be written not by the government but by a constitutional convention, and that this process should be 'open, participative and inclusive' and 'designed by the people of Scotland, for the people of Scotland'.

The Proposed Interim Constitution

The Scottish Independence Bill contained a draft interim constitution which, it was intended, would be passed by the Scottish Parliament to take effect on Independence Day in 2016 (Scottish Government, 2014c: s. 1). This proposal, and the idea of a permanent constitution to follow, would have represented a dramatic break with the Westminster model, and yet neither led to much discussion by the campaigners, which is perhaps surprising given the potential significance of embedding particular constitutional values for a new state. The Scottish Government, with a majority in the Scottish Parliament and with the momentum of a referendum victory, would have had the authority to give effect to the interim constitution, and the UK Parliament, once the principle of independence had been conceded, would most likely have helped facilitate such a document. The interim constitution may also have had deeper significance than the term 'interim' might suggest. Evidence elsewhere has shown that in transitional situations, interim constitutions are often not replaced for a very long time, if ever, for a variety of reasons such as a failure to establish a drafting process for a permanent constitution, or a lack of political agreement on how to proceed (International IDEA, 2014). Additionally, a number of its provisions would probably have found their way into the final constitutional document; indeed the Scottish Government expressly anticipated this (Scottish Government, 2014c: Explanatory notes: 64).

That the interim constitution did not feature in the referendum campaign is particularly surprising given some of its more innovative provisions. There were standard matters which would ordinarily appear in a generic transitional constitutional document. The document provided that Scotland would be an 'independent, constitutional monarchy' and that the form of government in Scotland would be 'a parliamentary democracy' (Scottish Government, 2014c: s. 7). The Head of State would have been the Queen (Scottish Government, 2014c: s. 9). Legislative power would have continued to be vested in the Scottish Parliament (Scottish Government, 2014c: s. 10) and executive power in the Scottish Government (Scottish Government, 2014c: s. 11). The Court of Session and High Court of Judiciary, respectively Scotland's civil and criminal high courts, would have continued in existence and would together have constituted a Supreme Court (Scottish Government, 2014c: s. 14).

But the interim constitution would also enshrine a range of radical new provisions, including social and economic rights. There was of course a wider debate about social and economic rights as political values,[1] but this discussion did not generally extend to the issue of constitutional protection.[2] That the constitution would take account of these issues was first hinted at in the November 2013 White Paper where the Scottish Government offered a fairly extensive list of what it thought the constitution of an independent Scotland should contain (Scottish Government, 2013f). These continued to be central to its vision with a number appearing in the draft interim constitution contained in the Bill:

- equality of opportunity and entitlement to live free of discrimination and prejudice (this appeared in the 2013 White Paper and again in the draft Bill, s. 28, although there was no specific reference in s. 28 to prejudice);
- entitlement to public services and to a standard of living that, as a minimum, secures dignity and self-respect and provides the opportunity for people to realize their full potential both as individuals and as members of wider society (this was in the 2013 White Paper but not in the draft Bill);
- protection of the environment and the sustainable use of Scotland's natural resources to embed Scotland's commitment to sustainable development and tackling climate change (set out in 2013 and covered by the draft Bill ss. 32 and 33);
- a ban on nuclear weapons being based in Scotland (this was a controversial proposal in the 2013 White Paper and was watered down in the interim constitution proposal. The draft Bill s. 23 contained a commitment to 'pursue negotiations with a view to securing...the safe and expeditious removal from the territory of Scotland of nuclear weapons based there'[3]);
- controls on the use of military force and a role for an independent Scottish Parliament in approving and monitoring its use (there was no

---

[1] See Chapter 5.   [2] Although see Nolan (2014).
[3] This could well have been a stumbling block had the Scottish Government sought endorsement for the interim constitution by the Westminster Parliament.

specific reference in the draft Bill but s. 19, as well as committing Scotland to respecting international law, extends this commitment to promoting peace, justice and security);

- the existence and status of local government (did appear in the draft Bill, s. 17);
- rights in relation to health care, welfare, and pensions (various references to such issues appeared in the 2013 White Paper and the White Paper accompanying the interim constitution but were not in the draft Bill itself);
- children's rights (a duty on the Scottish Government to promote the well-being of children in Scotland was contained in the draft Bill, s. 29);
- rights concerning other social and economic matters, such as the right to education and a Youth Guarantee on employment, education, or training (again these were mentioned in both the 2013 and 2014 White Papers but did not appear in the draft Bill).

In the November 2013 White Paper there was no commitment that proposed constitutional rights, such as the opportunity of education, training, or employment and rights to welfare support and health care would be legally enforceable by courts, but rather a more open-ended suggestion that they will be 'questions of social justice at the forefront of the work of Scotland's Parliament, government and public institutions'. These rights did not find their way into the Bill at all, and it is unlikely they would have appeared in the interim constitution. Nonetheless, the issue of justiciability of social and economic rights remains an issue of international discussion, and it would have been interesting to see how debates around such values would have played out in debates over the interim and permanent constitutions, and what role would have been envisaged for the judges in implementing these rights.

Although the draft Bill also declared that Scotland is a 'constitutional monarchy' (s. 7) and 'the Queen is Head of State' (s. 9), this came in the context of a debate within the SNP about republicanism. This is of international interest as the 1999 referendum in Australia on the issue of the head of state demonstrates. In the White Paper of November 2013 it had already been stated that Scotland would remain a constitutional monarchy 'for as long as the people of Scotland wish us to be so'. Again this did not feature in the referendum campaign, and is perhaps another example of a deferred debate around popular sovereignty which would have been reopened in the process of drafting the permanent constitution.[4]

---

[4] The draft Scottish Independence Bill, s. 2 stated: 'In Scotland, the people are sovereign', and s. 3(2): 'All State power and authority accordingly derives from, and is subject to, the sovereign will of the people, and those exercising State power and authority are accountable for it to the people.'

Another issue that did not feature, perhaps due to its technical nature, was the possibility of a constitutional vacuum after independence until a permanent constitution was promulgated. The most logical conclusion is that the Scottish Parliament would have assumed the position of sovereign and that it would have been recognized by the courts as having, in effect, replaced Westminster as the ultimate source of constitutional authority. However, this was far from clear. The Bill itself sought to replace Westminster supremacy, under which the Scottish Parliament is clearly subordinate, with the supremacy of the interim constitution. Thereafter, the Scottish Parliament would operate through a regime of legislative restrictions in a limited number of areas. This raises the question of whether or not these restrictions would have been self-imposed, and therefore, subject to repeal by the Scottish Parliament. Would the interim constitution actually have been supreme, or would the Scottish Parliament have had the last say?

The Bill also sought to maintain the position contained in s. 29(2)(d) of the Scotland Act 1998 whereby the laws of the Scottish Parliament are to be struck down on the grounds of incompatibility with European Convention Rights (Scottish Government, 2014c: ss. 26 and 27). This contrasts with the approach taken in the Human Rights Act (HRA) 1998 to legislation passed by Westminster which can only be declared to be incompatible with Convention rights should the courts find there to be a conflict (HM Government, 1998). It was also anticipated that the Bill would 'sit alongside ... a refreshed and rewritten Scotland Act' (Scottish Government, 2014c: Explanatory Notes: 50), which would no doubt have reiterated the human rights restrictions in s. 29(2)(d) and perhaps even have integrated the HRA 1998 into the new regime through the principle of continuity of laws (Scottish Government, 2014c: s. 34). In the same way, the Bill would have reflected the pre-referendum position whereby the Scottish Parliament had no authority to pass law incompatible with that of the European Union. The June Bill was unequivocal in providing that 'Scots law is of no effect so far as it is inconsistent with EU law' (Scottish Government, 2014c: s. 24). Again this contrasts sharply with the UK position which asserts that EU law 'falls to be recognised and available in law in the United Kingdom only by virtue of' the European Communities Act (ECA) 1972 (HM Government, 2011: s. 18). We therefore have something of a paradox. On the one hand, the June 2014 Bill intended that Schedule 5 of the Scotland Act would be repealed, freeing the Scottish Parliament from the constraints of those matters currently reserved to the Westminster Parliament; but on the other, the Parliament, through its interim constitution, would re-impose restrictions on the competence of the parliament, from the inside as it were.

It seems that the intention was for the interim constitution to be a bridge from parliamentary supremacy to constitutional supremacy, which would finally be consolidated in the permanent constitution. But until the permanent constitution was promulgated, there would be a tension between the purported higher authority of the interim constitution and the authority of the Scottish Parliament by which it would presumably be passed, albeit possibly concurrently with legislation by Westminster. There is a certain irony here. If the authority of the interim constitution was deemed to stem from the Scottish Parliament then presumably it would be subject to that Parliament and hence amendable at will. If however it was deemed to stem from Westminster, then its supremacy over the Scottish Parliament would derive from the very source of authority which an independent Scotland was rejecting. This is a theoretical dilemma faced by other countries that have moved to independence from Britain (Oliver, 2015). Much then would depend upon where the authority for the interim constitution stemmed from and how it would be read by the courts. One scenario is that it would indeed have been passed by Westminster and would have been accepted as supreme by the courts. Another, however, is that once independence was achieved Westminster's former authority would be treated as at an end, and that it would then be necessary to find a Scottish source of authority, and the most obvious source would be the Scottish Parliament.

Although the Bill seemed to assert the higher authority of the interim constitution, there was no attempt to declare explicitly that its provisions were protected in any way from later repeal or amendment by the Scottish Parliament. The Explanatory Notes made clear that there would be no 'hard amendment formula' in the interim arrangements; in other words, its amendment would remain a matter for the Scottish Parliament by way of legislation (Scottish Government, 2014c: Explanatory Notes, p. 60).The status of the interim constitution would be preserved in part by a 'certification system' whereby a minister or MSP introducing a bill to the Parliament would declare if the new act would amend the existing interim constitution. But this implies clearly the power to amend the interim constitution and, in turn, no power on the part of the Scottish Supreme Court, which would also be created by the interim constitution, to declare such amendments to be unconstitutional. We therefore would have had an uneasy situation whereby Convention rights and EU law were accorded some form of supremacy, giving the courts the power to strike down the laws of the Scottish Parliament if incompatible with either of these, but the Scottish Parliament would retain the power to amend the interim constitution, and presumably even these provisions.

There is another scenario. The courts could accept that the source of authority for the interim constitution was the Scottish Parliament and not a pre-independence statute passed by Westminster, but also rule that it had, by this constitution, restricted its own power. This is a theoretical debate which also surrounds Westminster supremacy—is it possible for a sovereign parliament to limit its own power? The interim constitution proposal came at a time when the doctrine of Westminster supremacy was already under strain. Membership of the European Union, secured by the ECA 1972, had led to an uneasy accommodation between Westminster supremacy as recognized by the English courts and the supremacy of EU law as insisted upon by the European Court of Justice (Factortame case, 1992; HS2 case, 2014). In the same way the activism of the courts in interpreting the HRA 1998 consolidated the attitudes of those who, in claiming a common law role for the courts to protect the rule of law and fundamental rights, questioned whether, in the area of individual liberty, Parliament's power really was unlimited (Allan, 1994). The debates occasioned by these developments were in effect whether, through the passage of 'constitutional statutes' (Thoburn v Sunderland City Council, 2002; HS2 case, 2014), a slow transition was taking place whereby Westminster was embarking upon some forms of legislative self-limitation, accompanied by a more assertive attitude within the judiciary which would eventually articulate a new reality of Parliament's (self)-circumscription. The interim constitution proposed for Scotland lay within this murky theoretical terrain. The potential for judicial assertiveness was considerable. It is one thing to say that Westminster remains unlimited in its legislative competence both because it has long been recognized as such and because the ECA and HRA do not seek to relinquish its legislative power. It is arguably quite another to say that the Scottish Parliament, with no tradition of supremacy, would be treated as such by the courts when it attempted to amend an interim constitution which it had itself passed and in which it had, self-consciously, included terms which seemed designed to place powers beyond the reach of that very parliament. The Bill provided that the existing high courts, the Court of Session and High Court of Justiciary, would be in their respective areas of competence 'the Supreme Court of Scotland' (s. 14). After independence it would have been fascinating to observe what status the Supreme Court of Scotland would have accorded to the interim constitution and how it would have balanced this with the powers of the Scottish Parliament before a permanent constitution was drafted. But again this debate was not unpicked during the campaign as more pressing issues of substance dominated public discourse.

Towards a Permanent Constitution

In its 2013 White Paper, the Scottish Government expressed the view that the 'right time for a written constitution to be drafted is ... after independence, not before' (Scottish Government, 2013f: para 1.6). In fact, there was little in the proposals set out in either November 2013 or June 2014 to indicate what the content of a permanent constitution might be. I have noted that aspirations set out in the November White Paper such as the opportunity for education, training, or employment and rights to welfare support and health care would not have been legally enforceable by the courts. These did not appear in the June 2014 draft Bill but may have found their way into a permanent constitution. In such an event, enforceability would have been an issue, with a debate likely as to whether and how principles of this kind could be in any way legally guaranteed and potentially actionable.

The status and composition of the court system would also have been an issue. We have seen that the interim constitution would have led to the continuation of the existing higher courts in Scotland as 'the Supreme Court of Scotland' (Scottish Government, 2014c: s. 14). While there would have been some doubt as to the power of judges in the interim period to review acts of the Scottish Parliament, they would very probably have been given such a role explicitly in a permanent constitution, and this may well have extended to a wide range of constitutional provisions. In this case would the appellate and constitutional functions of the highest courts have been combined or separated? Would a new, specialist constitutional court be needed to deal with constitutional issues in a way different from final appeals? Would a new system of judicial appointments have been needed? Again these were debates which took place among lawyers (Edinburgh Centre for Constitutional Law, 2013), but did not reach the wider public.

Scotland may have been leaving the United Kingdom, but it has long been part of the tradition of parliamentary democracy. On this basis a move immediately to a strong model of judicial review was not an inevitable outcome. In a process of drafting a permanent constitution other options for constitutional review may have been considered, such as a review committee of the Scottish Parliament, which could advise that draft legislation might be counter to constitutional principles, the Parliament then retaining power to accept or reject this advice. The notion that judicial review of legislation is the automatic default option for constitutional review is accepted by many today but is in fact only one possible model of constitutional oversight. However, the international trend is towards an ever-stronger role for the judiciary and there is every reason think that this would have been the direction of travel for a permanent Scottish constitution. I will return to this later.

The White Paper did not offer much detail as to the design of the constitutional convention, except that it would be 'open, participative and inclusive' and that the new constitution 'should be designed by the people of Scotland, for the people of Scotland'. Again there was not much debate among referendum campaign groups or the general public. The whole idea probably seemed too distant and too abstract. For the Better Together campaign it was also surely preferable not to discuss in detail scenarios that presupposed a Yes victory. One initial question which would have been central to the debate following a Yes outcome is whether or not the convention would definitely have been convened. The duty to establish a convention was set out as a legally binding commitment within the draft Bill (s. 33). The Scottish Government indeed proposed some form of constitutional guarantee or entrenchment of the interim constitution. The proposal in November 2013 was that: 'The constitutional platform . . . will be the founding legislation of an independent Scotland and will not be subject to significant alteration pending the preparation of a permanent constitution by the constitutional convention'. Legislation would guarantee this. This again raises the question of whether the interim constitution would have been open to amendment or repeal, and the response of the courts would have been interesting were the Scottish Parliament to seek to remove the previous commitment to establish a constitutional convention. Again these debates would have played out at the interface of law and politics after a Yes vote.

In any case, given the political climate it does seem highly likely that a convention would have been established. This leaves us with questions about the nature of the convention itself since the Bill had little to say about this, proposing to leave both the membership of the convention and its operational rules for the Scottish Parliament to determine. In one passage the 2013 White Paper states:

> International best practice and the practical experience of other countries and territories should be considered and taken into account in advance of the determination of the process for the constitutional convention. In the last decade, citizen-led assemblies and constitutional conventions have been convened in British Columbia (2004), the Netherlands (2006), Ontario (2007) and Iceland (2010). Since 2012, Ireland has been holding a citizen-led constitutional convention to review various constitutional issues.
>
> (Scottish Government, 2013f: para 576)

From a number of these examples it is clear that citizens can be engaged directly and in meaningful ways in drafting important constitutional provisions (Tierney, 2012), but this passage is juxtaposed with the suggestion that the constitutional convention 'will ensure a participative and inclusive process where the people of Scotland, as well as politicians, civic society organisations, business interests, trade unions, local authorities and others, will have a direct role in shaping the constitution' (Scottish Government, 2013f: para 577).

It was unclear, therefore, whether the process really would have been a popular and meaningful engagement with citizens like the citizens' assembly processes in British Columbia and Ontario, or whether it would have been more of an elite-led event, like the Scottish Constitutional Convention from 1989 to 1995. Again this question is of ongoing relevance since there has been a renewed interest in the application of deliberative democracy to constitution-making in recent years.

A number of questions would have arisen in debate after a Yes vote not only about the constitution but about who could draft it. On the one hand, it is possible to advance a direct role in such a process for individuals or civil society organizations as a democratic good. But on the other, how representative would such people be? There has been something of a backlash in recent years against politicians but at least politicians are elected, act in a representative capacity and are ultimately accountable to the electorate. To whom are civil organizations accountable? Who would select members of these groups to sit on the convention, on what basis, and with what degree of decision-making power would they be vested? Or would their participation be self-selective? There is a risk in such processes that pressure groups with fixed agendas and a well-oiled activism machinery can hijack deliberative processes, arguing for the entrenchment in the new constitution of their own particular priorities, priorities which may not have the support of a plurality of citizens.

A further question is, what power would such a convention, whether popular or elite, have had? The June White Paper said it would 'prepare' the constitution. Does that mean it would have the authority to present a final version of the constitution for ratification? Or would its role be advisory only, subject to change by the Scottish Parliament? We do not know for sure, but it seems that the convention was intended to have determining power. The proposal suggested that the Scottish Government could only 'propose [certain matters] for consideration', which suggests that the convention would have had control over the inclusion or exclusion of all of the Government's goals outlined above, including the personality of the head of state. However, this power is not unqualified. According to the White Paper (Scottish Government, 2014c) the convention would itself be limited in its remit by at least one substantive precondition: 'Key equality and human rights principles, including the requirements of the European Convention on Human Rights (ECHR), would be embedded in the written constitution.' This seems to be a clear attempt to set substantive conditions even upon the constitutional convention, which it could not override. In other words, the convention would not be able to give effect to the ECHR in a way comparable to sections 3 and 4 of the HRA 1998, leaving the last word to the Scottish Parliament which is what Westminster currently enjoys. We have already seen the suggestion that legislation during the interim constitution period would have given the ECHR the same legal force for reserved matters as it already has for devolved matters. Of course it may have been that a constitutional convention or citizens' assembly would have come to the view that these matters should be constitutionally protected, and that the judges should have the power to override the will of the Scottish Parliament, but it seems odd that the Scottish Government intended to bind a constitutive constitutional convention before its work had even begun.

Another debate that would have emerged, and no doubt contentiously, is the question of how much influence the Scottish Government of the day would have been able to exert upon the drafting of a new constitution. Fresh from a successful referendum and with a majority in the Scottish Parliament, the Government would have had a lot of discretion in framing the interim constitution. I have suggested that the parties which constituted the Better Together campaign tended not to comment on the prospect of a post-independence constitution largely because they did not want to entertain publicly the prospect of a Yes vote. However, it is likely that all parties in Scotland would have developed their own constitutional agendas in the event that Scots had indeed voted for independence, and that this could have been an issue in the May 2016 Scottish elections, with the constitutional future of the country at stake.

Another issue is promulgation. The Bill proposed to leave to the Scottish Parliament 'the procedure by which the written constitution prepared by the Convention is to be agreed by or on behalf of the people' (Scottish Government, 2014c: s. 33). We do not know therefore how the permanent constitution would have been ratified. Would it have been done by a vote of the constitutional convention, by the Scottish Parliament, by a referendum, or by some combination of these? Given that a referendum is now such a strong feature of Scottish constitutional life, and that the legitimacy of independence itself would have stemmed from a popular vote, it does seem that there would have been very strong pressure for a new constitution to be ratified by a direct vote by the people.

One should be sceptical, of course, of the very idea of a 'permanent' constitution (Elkins, Ginsburg, and Melton, 2009). Whereas some countries do change constitutions frequently, in the post-war West constitutions have enjoyed more stability than in earlier times and in other parts of the world. We can assume then that a 'permanent' constitution for Scotland may indeed have been a document of considerable durability, particularly, as seems likely, after an elaborate drafting process, and if the constitution had concluded with a referendum for ratification. Despite this future of constitutional codification, the real debate on Scotland's future would have occurred, as perhaps is appropriate, after and not during the decision on independence itself.

Judicial Supremacy Not Popular Sovereignty?

Let us now turn critically to the very idea of a detailed written constitution for an independent Scotland, and in particular the Scottish Government's proposal to entrench within a permanent constitution so many issues which are in effect policy preferences. Although a written constitution was surely inevitable, the prospect of such an elaborate constitution would surely have provoked a debate about the dangers in elevating the judiciary to the position of overseers of detailed 'national' values.

Certainly a foundational document would be needed to replace the Scotland Acts of 1998 and 2012. The powers of the Scottish Parliament and Scottish Government would require to be defined, as would the court structure, its hierarchy and the limits of its jurisdiction. A proposal to make provision for local government (proposed by the White Paper) would also fit within this model of a limited, institution-framing constitution; all of which would serve as a democracy-facilitating, rather than a democracy-constraining, set of provisions. This raises the issue of whether it was necessary to go beyond such a minimal constitutional model, which would still leave policy choices to the new parliament. As we have seen, the June White Paper (Scottish Government, 2014c) anticipated a document that would collate a very broad range of principles and detailed policies. For example:

- entitlement to public services and to a minimum standard of living;
- protection of the environment and the sustainable use of Scotland's natural resources;
- a ban on nuclear weapons being based in Scotland;
- rights in relation to health care, welfare, and pensions;
- children's rights; and
- rights concerning other social and economic matters, such as the right to education and a Youth Guarantee on employment, education, or training.

It is reasonable to assume that this captures only a few of the policy preferences that would have been put on the table during any drafting process. Certainly all of these issues would have been for the constitutional convention drafting the constitution to determine, but the very fact that the White Paper considered such detailed policies to be appropriate for constitutional protection would serve to invite others to put forward their particular agendas and preferences, and these may well have found their way into a new constitution, no matter how specific, contingent and deeply contested they might have been.

Six key arguments which would have challenged such a detailed model of constitutional codification in any post-referendum debate on the constitution:

- legitimacy;
- judicial supremacy;
- rigidity;

- the stifling of political debate;
- a marginalization of the political power of citizens;
- the creation of a constitutional battleground.

First, it seems highly questionable from the perspective of democratic legitimacy that the first generation of post-independence Scots should have taken upon themselves the power to crystallize a broad range of current predilections—some of which may well have been issues of short-term interest or concern—as constitutional principles. A constitution of course constrains the decision-making capacity of successive generations of voters. But to do so from the beginning across a potentially vast array of policy issues would serve to hem in the democratic will of successive generations from the very beginning.

Second, by constitutionalizing specific values and policies, the constitution would significantly ramp up the powers of judges. We discussed above the assumption that a written constitution would bring with it strong judicial review. There is already a trend internationally whereby judges are becoming more and more influential in democratic politics (Hirschl, 2004; Choudhry, 2011). By placing so many detailed policy commitments in a constitution and then ensuring that acts of the Scottish Parliament could be struck down by courts, insofar as they are incompatible with these commitments, would serve to hand the authority to resolve disagreements which are currently matters of political deliberation to a small unelected group which is arguably both unsuited and, in democratic terms, unentitled to determine these issues. This could also put judges in an awkward position, asking them to settle deeply contentious policy issues which could undermine their own standing and constitutional legitimacy.

Third, such a constitutional arrangement would bring a radical transformation to the constitutional culture of the country itself. Scots would be leaving what is arguably the most flexible constitutional system in the world and creating potentially one of the least flexible. It is fashionable (mainly among academics) to criticize the UK constitutional system precisely because of its unwritten form and the concomitant privilege given to the Westminster Parliament as sovereign law-maker. Yet this model has worked very well over several centuries, allowing the UK body politic to adapt itself smoothly to new developments such as the creation and amendment of the devolution settlements for Scotland, Wales, and Northern Ireland since 1998, and the conclusion of the Edinburgh Agreement paving the way for the independence referendum. The principle underpinning parliamentary supremacy is a sound one: it is for Parliament, elected by the people, to debate and determine how law should manage competing political and moral values. If Parliament later changes its mind, this legislation is open to amendment or repeal by the same process. A written constitution replaces this with a form of rigidity which could lead to constitutional stasis. Furthermore, we also do not know how deeply entrenched the new Scottish constitution would have been because the convention which would have drafted the constitution would also have determined its amendment procedure. There is now a tendency around the world to make certain constitutional provisions virtually unamendable and there was a very real prospect that the permanent constitution for Scotland could have been very inflexible. At the very least, any issue given constitutional protection in a new Scottish state would be hard to change; that after all is the point of constitutional entrenchment. One mechanism which does serve to keep the people involved in constitutional deliberation is the referendum. It would have been interesting to see what role, if any, was intended for referendums in the process of constitutional amendment under any new arrangements. The Irish model of constitutional change is one where referendums are required for constitutional change, which gives citizens a significant say in the development of their system of government. A similar provision for Scotland would at least have gone some way to make good the notion of popular sovereignty set out in the November White Paper. These debates were perhaps too abstract to take place during the referendum, but they would surely have surfaced afterwards.

Beyond this, there is a danger that a highly detailed constitution can serve to supplant, and in so doing foreclose, political debate. Later attempts to amend issues which have been accorded constitutional protection will not only be difficult in practical terms but could be burdened with the stigma of illegitimacy. A constitution is not, after all, merely a regulatory device. It sets out the values of the state (particularly when it is a new state), and in doing so can help to shape the public identity of citizens. Once something is entrenched in a constitution it can become reified as a moral principle that transcends transient policy choices; extolled as a metaphysical value, the merits of which are rendered unimpeachable and to which citizens are called upon to plight unswerving allegiance. Those who later campaign to amend such principles can face not only opposing arguments but also charges of disloyalty to the constitution and the political system itself. Incidentally, another recent move is to suggest that all holders of public office must expressly pledge allegiance to the constitution and to its provisions: this is a particularly pernicious innovation, presenting the constitution as modern day Test Act, transforming dissent into heresy. This becomes all the more contentious the more detailed the constitution is, since it can contain policy commitments in relation to which reasonable disagreement might well attend. It is to be hoped that this form of intolerance would have been disavowed in any move towards a constitution for Scotland, but there is no guarantee that the debate on this point, and other issues of constitutional essentialism, would not have been deeply fractious.

This raises a fifth issue: why would so many issues need to be entrenched beyond the decision-making competence of ordinary citizens? If matters of wealth distribution, international responsibility and good environmental policy are the preference of a majority of right-thinking people, why not leave it to the Scottish Parliament to legislate in these areas? Would such a detailed constitution signal a failure of trust in the capacity of the people and/or the Parliament of an independent Scotland to make the right decisions? The rush to elevate so many issues beyond the realm of the political would certainly seem to demonstrate a lack of confidence in a new country. Should the first step after 'independence' really have been such a detailed circumscription of the areas over which the Scottish people could, from generation to generation, determine and re-determine their own policies, in order to 'protect' them from their own ignorance or poor judgement? If Scots were fit for self-government then surely they are sufficiently competent to build their future through the open debate of the political process.

A final danger is that if a signal had been sent that the constitution was intended to micro-manage political and moral values then the constitution-drafting process could well have become a battle for the soul of the country. The birth of the state could have led to a culture war resulting in a sharp delineation between victors and losers, and in turn leaving a large number of people feeling excluded from an elaborate, highly specific and deeply partial vision of national identity solidified in the constitution. Such a dispute could have been just as acute, or indeed more acute, than the referendum campaign itself. It is not hard to imagine that certain pressure groups would have been glad for the opportunity to see their own value preferences privileged within a constitution, placing these beyond the opposition of a simple (or large) majority of the people or their elected representatives. This, as I say, is a parlous game and a potentially undemocratic (as well as an entirely avoidable) one. It would risk the drafting process becoming heavily influenced by the most vocal and best-organized interest groups, including those that cast their opponents not only as wrong but as bad, thereby inhibiting future debate and claiming that the political victories which they manage to achieve at a particular juncture transform into morally unquestionable precepts. By this construction, it is not in reality the founding generation that gets to play for keeps, but rather activist elites within this generation, elites which may well be both unelected and unrepresentative.

All of these factors make the proposed process by which such a detailed constitution would have come about—and the debate which surrounded it—all the more important. Given that a highly detailed document was likely to emerge from the proposed constitutional convention, the composition of this body, who would decide on its composition, how it would deliberate and reach decisions would each have been a vital, and potentially deeply contentious, issue. The more detailed the constitution, in short, the more vital that the process towards it be properly democratic.

Conclusion

We live in an age where the written constitution is the default, for very good reasons. A framework is needed in any democratic system, establishing political institutions and demarcating their boundaries. Yet it has also become increasingly common today to fill out ever longer and more elaborate constitutions with what are, in effect, policy preferences. This can serve to curtail the democratic process, removing from the people and their democratic representatives the power to make decisions on these issues by way of ordinary legislation, and to adjust their positions in light of current circumstances and changing views.

It is perhaps symptomatic of the UK's unwritten system that the issue of what a Scottish constitution should look like and how it should be made did not feature in the referendum debate. But the substantive issues that would have been at stake—identity, rights, social protections, nuclear weapons— were central to the campaign. It is likely therefore that the constitutional debate was in fact simply being deferred until after the referendum itself. If a Yes vote had been secured there would have been a new challenge: the forging of a new state and of a new constitution which would give political identity to that state. At this point the process and substance of constitution-making would likely have emerged as one of the key issues facing Scots. We don't know what this debate would have looked like but it could have been a deeply contested one with the nature of Scottish democracy at stake.

9

The Small State Argument

Malcolm Harvey

Size in the Independence Debate

An independent Scotland would have been, in international comparison, a small state. The perception of being a 'small' nation was not challenged to any great degree during the referendum campaign. Former First Minister Jack McConnell's 2005 decision to market Scotland as 'the best small country in the world' was ridiculed as lacking in ambition—that aspiring only to be the best *small* country in the world was somewhat limited in objective—but few seriously challenged the notion that Scotland itself was a small country. Indeed, even Hugh MacDiarmid's famous verse—'Scotland small? Our multi-form, our infinite Scotland *small?*'—has more than a suggestion of irony. With a population of around 5 million and an area of around 17,000 km^2, there are twenty-two US states which have larger populations and no fewer than forty of the fifty which cover more area. Within the UK, Scotland's population is dwarfed by that of England's 53 million. In fixed population and territorial terms, Scotland could be considered small. However, size is a relative concept, and globally, compared to the approximately 250 states and non-sovereign territories, Scotland would rank around 116th—neither big nor small. In the European Union, Scotland's population would place it around eighteenth out of the twenty-eight member states: between Denmark and Finland—two countries which were often sought as comparators but which themselves are not especially small. The size comparison with England, however, became the dominant narrative, and Scotland was thus considered a 'small nation'.

Unionists have traditionally argued that Scotland's small size would be a disadvantage, pointing to the benefits of the larger union. In 2014, however, nationalists were able to point to a body of work to the effect that in a globalized world, small states have the advantage. There are several strands in this argument and not all of them are compatible with the SNP's core ideology of civic nationalism and social democracy. The Yes side therefore adopted them selectively. The important point of reference was the 'Nordic model', which was used both as an abstract vision and to illustrate the practical advantages of being small. There was, however, a tension between the aspiration to a Nordic, social democratic welfare state and the commitment not to raise taxation and even to reduce it.

Small States in the Modern World

The study of small states has been in vogue in recent years, and several studies have sought to provide evidence of a relationship between the size of a state, constitutional status, and policy outcomes (Baldersheim and Keating, 2015). It is not always easy to determine exactly what is meant by a small state. Population size is clearly relevant, but this in itself does not necessarily tell us about the viability and capacity of a state. International relations scholars such as Morgenthau (1970) and Neumann (1992) utilize the concept of power as a consideration as to whether a state can be considered small or large, though this is generally regarded to be military (and thus, 'hard') power. Keohane takes into account the state's own view of itself, arguing that if a state itself believes it cannot make a substantial impact on international politics, it should be considered small (1969). Geographic and population sizes prove problematic variables in considering the smallness of a state. Nigeria, for example, would be considered a large state in both area and population, yet it has limited impact upon global decision-making processes. The propensity for developing countries to have large populations also skews this variable. For Tilly (1990), the combination and interaction of economic and military factors contribute to how states—both large and small—develop. In turn, these factors serve to limit the choices available to states and, in some cases, constrain the development of states in particular ways or beyond a particular size. Thorhallsson (2006) developed this theme further by building a conceptual framework containing six categories to help define smallness: population and territorial size; effective sovereign size; political size; economic size; perceptual size; and preference size. This framework takes into account not only actual, fixed criteria (population, for example) but also state ambitions and perceptions about power. For Thorhallsson then, how the state views itself is also important in how it should be defined.

The main point is that small states cannot exercise the forms of power open to large states and must behave differently; there is less agreement on how this might be done. A widely shared argument is that, with international free trade and capital flows, it is no longer necessary for states to have large home markets, so making big states redundant. Some authors have assembled databases of states by size with a view to demonstrating that smaller ones are more prosperous and can actually cope better in global markets than their larger rivals (Skilling, 2012). This does not in itself tell us that size matters, since there may be other reasons for the success of these countries. Alesina and Spolaore (2005) claim that global free trade in itself encourages the emergence of small states. According to them, small units are ethnically homogeneous and the population will share policy preferences, allowing small states to deliver better public policy. However, evidence does not bear this out: small states are not necessarily more homogeneous than large states (Northern Ireland and Belgium, for example, are deeply divided). While Alesina and Spolaore's argument has persuaded some, most social scientists would see it as reductionist and argue that ethnicity is a difficult concept, which is contestable both on empirical and on normative grounds.

Most of the literature emphasizes, rather, institutions and the capacity of small states to respond rapidly to external shocks. Small size imposes vulnerabilities but also opens opportunities (Baldersheim and Keating, 2015). To manage these, they require an external shelter, in the form of transnational institutions such as NATO and the European Union, and also an internal buffer, in the form of mechanisms to adapt the global challenges, which they cannot resist, while maintaining autonomy and governing capacity. Short lines of communication allow for responsive policy communities and their smaller scale means policy experimentation can also be undertaken. Keating and Harvey (2014) distinguish two modes of adaptation. One is the market-liberal one in which small states submit to the exigencies of the global market, with low taxes and light regulation in order to attract mobile capital. The other is the social investment approach, which entails a larger public sector and more expenditure, to underpin development. This contrasts with Alesina and Spolaore's (2005) and Ohmae's (1995) neoliberal vision of adjustment to external imperatives by reducing the size of the public sector.

A lot of attention has been given to the Nordic states, generally seen as rather successful. While Norway, Denmark, Sweden, and Finland differ in important respects, they are generally seen as combining good economic performance with social cohesion. They have rather large public sectors and rather high taxes and are committed to social investment, and have maintained relatively low levels of social and economic inequality. They are also characterized by an ability to respond to external shocks through consensual and negotiated change. While the Nordic model has come under a lot of pressure as a result of global challenges and political change, it nevertheless remains a key point of reference in the debate.

External influence for small states comes through bilateral linkages and transnational institutions. Collective defence arrangements through NATO and the EU have limited the need for small European states (such as Denmark,

Norway, and the Republic of Ireland) to focus on security concerns and to spend vast sums on individual national defence strategies—though such shelter did come at the cost of ceding certain elements of sovereignty in joining those bodies. No one pretends small states have the same level of global influence as large states do. Cyprus and Germany, to take two EU examples, vary widely in their level of influence in EU decision-making. Yet one advantage that small states have in this area is their opportunity to focus their interests in specific niche areas and to become global leaders in one policy area in which they have a particular interest. Denmark has taken a lead on wind energy, climate change mitigation, and 'flexicurity' in labour markets. Sweden has been able to shape norms underpinning European defence and security policies (Jakobsen, 2009). Small states are often better positioned than larger states to force particular issues onto the EU agenda, given geopolitical positioning and their tendency to be more pro-EU than some of their larger counterparts (Arter, 1999). However, size plays a role in the EU decision-making processes, meaning larger states have more political power to shape EU law than small states do (Panke, 2010).

Small States in the Scottish Debate

References to other small nations achieving statehood have been a staple of SNP manifestos since the 1980s, with Norway, Austria, Denmark, the Netherlands, and the Republic of Ireland variously appearing as evidence that Scotland would be better off independent (Henderson, 2007). On the other hand, the party has carefully avoided the Alesina and Spolaore (2005) arguments about ethnic homogeneity. Rather, it has emphasized a civic and inclusive vision of the nation: pluralism and multiculturalism, and a welcome to immigrants. Since its conversion to membership of the European Union in the late 1980s, the SNP made a lot of the free trade argument, arguing that the way in which the EU provides access to a wider marketplace allows small states in Europe to become 'more economically successful than big ones' (Hepburn, 2010). Two points are important here. First, the argument that the EU provided a larger market for small states was a direct challenge to the historic case that big states are better because they have bigger markets. Second, the comparators utilized by the SNP here were, in the context of the EU, on the smaller end of the spectrum—a tacit acceptance of the smallness of Scotland. The status of small European states as constructive EU members, in common with other autonomist movements around Europe, helped to provide comparative examples for the SNP's argument for independence. The decision by the SNP in 2012 to accept NATO membership represented a further recognition of the need for small states to have an external shelter.

After his return as leader of the SNP in 2006, Alex Salmond made a speech in Edinburgh in which he referred to Scotland's neighbours as constituting an 'arc of prosperity':

> Scotland can change to a better future and be part of northern Europe's arc of prosperity. We have three countries – Ireland to our west, Iceland to our north and Norway to our east – all in the top six wealthiest countries in the world. In contrast devolved Scotland is in 18th place. We can join that arc of prosperity. By matching their success Scotland would be £4,000 a head better off. It's time we seized this opportunity.
>
> (SNP, 2006)

He continued by referring to the fact that 'distant London' was the barrier to Scotland achieving such prosperity, and that only with independence could Scotland join 'Europe's small, powerhouse economies'. With independence, he argued, Scotland could deliver 'the right pro-Scottish business policies, *lower taxes*, support for innovators and improvements to [our] national infrastructure' that would set Scotland on a similar path (SNP, 2006; emphasis mine). Expanding on this theme at a speech to Harvard University in March 2008—after he became First Minister—Salmond argued that the flexibility of small states allowed them to adapt more quickly to changing economic circumstances. Further, he emphasized that the ability of Scotland to grow its economy was hampered by the limited powers it controlled under the devolved settlement. Here, he suggested that control over corporation tax, among the other powers that independence would bring, would help to encourage foreign direct investment in Scotland—effectively providing a competitive environment for businesses to operate in. The Harvard speech—titled 'Free to Prosper: Creating the Celtic Lion economy'—focused again on the 'arc of prosperity', asking why it was that Scotland's small neighbours were proving successful. Salmond's answer was that the opportunities created for small nations by globalization and the establishment of supranational institutions such as the EU was at the root of this success. He also elaborated upon his 'arc of prosperity' theme, arguing that the UN Human Development Index's placement of Iceland, Norway, and the Republic of Ireland among the top five states in the world provided evidence in support of their success. He conceded that those states were affected by the 'global forces' of the time (then simply referred to as 'the credit crunch') 'just like their larger neighbours', but that those small states were likely to 'rebound quickest and strongest from current difficulties' (Salmond, 2008). Indeed, he went further, arguing that 'the smaller economies of Europe are just as well equipped as the larger economies—if not better—to provide the skills, the incentives and the regulatory environment that big business needs to succeed' (Salmond, 2008).

The subsequent global financial crisis led to substantive economic contraction—and some of the small states that Salmond identified as constituting the 'arc of prosperity' were hit particularly hard. The Republic of Ireland fell deep into recession, which led to a bailout by the European Union in early 2011, with the fall of its government a further consequence. Iceland's banks defaulted, and with no one to bail them out, collapsed, leaving the Icelandic economy in ruins. Even Norway, with its oil reserve fund, was not immune to the crisis, though it did recover significantly quicker than most, while Denmark, Finland, and Sweden were not far behind. The successful small independent nations around Scotland, for so long a central component of the SNP's argument for independence, became a millstone around their neck. The First Minister's so-called 'arc of prosperity' was soon re-characterized as the 'arc of insolvency' by opponents who relished the party's difficulty to answer the tough financial questions posed by the economic collapse of formerly wealthy neighbours (Sunday Herald, 2008). As a result, Norway became a more favoured comparator for the SNP (and later, the Yes Scotland campaign), while allusions to Iceland and Ireland were quietly dropped.

In an interview with the BBC's Jon Sopel in October 2008, the point was put to Salmond that his 'arc of prosperity' was now an 'arc of insolvency'. Salmond skipped over Iceland as having 'a population half the size of Glasgow', ignored Ireland entirely, and focused exclusively on Norway as the comparator of choice. Challenged by Sopel that these 'small independent countries [who] are now struggling because of their size', Salmond responded that size was not the issue, that the focus on size was 'misplaced' and that Norway was 'doing extremely well in extremely difficult economic circumstances' (BBC Sunday Politics, 12 October 2008). Here, Salmond was trying to regain the initiative on the small state argument by once again pointing to the Norwegian sovereign oil fund and the ability that Norway had to manage its own natural resources.

As the independence proposals were elaborated, more focus was placed on the Nordic model of success. This had several advantages. It distinguished the Nordic states (which had come through the global crisis relatively well) from the rest of the old 'arc of prosperity'. It provided a more precise explanation of success, rooted in social investment and cohesion. Finally, it put an emphasis on social welfare in line with the Yes side's strategy of emphasizing welfare and combatting the arguments of their opponents that only the union could secure the welfare state. This was critical in extending the support base for independence to the left and into the working class, a critical factor in the eventual result.

Small States Good

The White Paper on independence (Scottish Government, 2013f) made both general and specific references to small independent nations. From a simplistic perspective, the white paper argued that:

... similar countries to Scotland have seen higher levels of economic growth over the past generation. That is because they have the bonus of being independent and are able to make the right choices for their nation and economy.

(Scottish Government, 2013f: 23, emphasis mine)

Later, in the section titled 'The Case for Independence', the argument was repeated:

Nations that are similar to Scotland—such as Norway, Finland, Denmark and Sweden—sit at the top of the world wealth and well-being league tables. Unlike Scotland, they are independent and are able to take decisions in the best interests of their own economies.

(Scottish Government, 2013f: 43)

The descriptor 'similar to Scotland' was not expanded upon, although in this context it is likely to refer to size, geographical location, and political orientation. The size element featured in the section on 'Finance and the Economy' in the White Paper, which pointed out that of the top fifteen economies measured by the OECD, nine of them were of similar size to Scotland, while a majority of the top twenty positions in the UN Human Development Index were filled by small countries (Scottish Government, 2013f: 91). This was evidence, they argued, that 'the performance of many small countries demonstrates the advantage of having a policy framework appropriate to local circumstances' (Scottish Government, 2013f: 91). The argument was clear: small states could prosper in the world, but they could only do so when they had the freedom to pursue their own economic interests. In other words, the economic outlook of small states was linked to their constitutional status.

This central argument is that small states have better mechanisms for internal adjustment. Katzenstein (1985) argued that the secret in his cases lay in corporatism. This provides one means of adaptation for small states: utilizing tripartite bargaining in order to cope with external shocks and deliver mutually beneficial outcomes for government, businesses, and trade unions. Full-blown corporatism has gone out of fashion and is, arguably, impossible in a global economy in which capital can freely locate to escape such obligations. Many countries, however, brought it back in a lighter and more flexible form as social partnership or concerted action (Keating and Harvey, 2014). These included Ireland, where it was credited with some of the success of the 'Celtic Tiger' before being abandoned in the financial crash. It is also argued that the shorter lines of communication and the small policy communities mean that it is easier in small states to 'get the usual suspects together' to discuss public policy—in other words, in seeking to make adjustments to the internal structure of the state, smallness can be an advantage (Keating and Harvey, 2014). Attempts to emulate the 'Nordic Model' of social investment were clearly articulated within the White Paper. *Scotland's Future* emphasized a social investment approach in an attempt to 'develop more targeted labour market policies' (Scottish Government, 2013f). The social investment model was seen as a means to foster:

> . . . a culture in society that is more inclusive, more respectful and more equal. It also places the cash transfers that people traditionally think of as welfare—such as out of work benefits and tax credits—in a wider, more cost-effective and socially beneficial context when viewed over the longer-term.
>
> (Scottish Government, 2013f)

The social investment approach, it was argued, would provide an 'opportunity to invest in the supply of services, rather than subsidizing demand'; a change in focus which moved the emphasis from outputs to inputs (Scottish Government, 2013f). The Nordic states were referenced extensively as examples of best practice as to how the social investment model could operate in Scotland. There were also some references to social partnership. In the White Paper, the Scottish Government pointed out the importance of partnership when dealing with challenges to the labour market, and cited their own work in this area at the time. Beyond a commitment to 'continue that approach after independence' and mention of increasing childcare provision, however, there was limited detail on how this would be achieved, nor the mechanisms by which such a partnership could be institutionalized.

Another weak point in the argument was an unwillingness to face up to the implications of the Nordic model for taxation. In the interest of international competitiveness, the SNP promised to cut corporation tax and air passenger duty, and to keep taxes generally in line with the rest of the UK. It also appeared to ignore how a similar strategy had played out in the Republic of Ireland, whose government had tried to combine the high cost and low tax models. This was the Scottish Government hedging its bets a little: appealing to the social democratic electorate with plans for a social investment strategy, while at the same time trying not to alienate more centre-right votes by limiting the discussion on increased taxation—in fact, actively pledging to keep the majority of taxes the same or reducing them (Harvey, 2015).

Outside the official 'Yes' campaign, The Jimmy Reid Foundation, the Common Weal project, Labour for Independence, along with the left-of-centre grassroots movements, also drew inspiration from small independent states, in particular the Nordics. While there was recognition of the economic challenges of being a small state in the global economy—with lessons from the Nordics in the 1990s, and again after the global financial crisis in 2008 particularly instructive—there remained an admiration about the different way in which these small states were organized. The Common Weal focused particularly on the social democratic, social investment model of adaptation apparent in the Nordic states, promoting:

> ...a balanced and creative economy, with emphasis on cooperatives and social enterprises; a more progressive taxation system, including a welfare system based on active labour market policies; nationalisation of industry, in particular public transport services; and a revitalisation of democracy through more local government.
>
> (Jimmy Reid Foundation, 2013)

Smallness, in this instance, was seen as advantageous to enhancing the levels of social solidarity apparent in the Nordic states: a key component in the development of the universal welfare systems which were much admired. The Scottish Government's proposals were criticized for a desire to have their cake and eat it: that they wanted Nordic levels of public services without Nordic levels of taxation. By contrast, the proposals from the Common Weal readily accepted the substantive cost of instituting a social investment system and actively advocated a radical overhaul of the tax system to make it more progressive.

Big States Better

In contrast to *Scotland's Future*, the UK Government's 'Scotland Analysis' series emphasized the difficulties that small states encountered on the global stage. Although repeating David Cameron's 2013 assertion that, of course 'an independent Scottish state could, like other small states, be a successful player on the international stage' the command paper stressed that the 'important question is whether it would be more successful in promoting the interests of people and businesses in Scotland internationally than the UK currently is' (HM Government, 2014b: 13). However, it was in the realm of domestic policy where the series of command papers sought to attack the Scottish Government's characterization of small states more substantially. In particular, the Scottish Government's continued references to the higher levels of public spending in the Nordic states came under scrutiny. The issue, rather predictably, was the Scottish Government's desire to deliver Nordic levels of spending without Nordic levels of taxation. The *Scotland Analysis* series pointed out that:

> ...tax revenues in Norway, Denmark, Finland and Sweden average 46 per cent of GDP, which is substantially higher than the 38 per cent of GDP that Scotland currently generates.
>
> (HM Government, 2014c: 20)

This was partly due to the higher tax rates in the Nordic states. In contrast to the UK's VAT and Corporation Tax rates (set at the time at 20 per cent),

Norway's rates were the highest of the Nordic states at 25 per cent and 27 per cent, with each of the others significantly higher than the UK. In addition, it was noted that a wider range of goods and services were taxed in the Nordic states while the UK allows a zero-rate of VAT on selected items (most foods and children's clothes, for example). Here, the command paper noted that, far from proposing an increased level of taxation or a widening of the tax base, *Scotland's Future* had actually indicated that the Scottish Government intended to reduce both Corporation Tax and Air Passenger Duty (HM Government, 2014c: 21). The command paper dealing with work and pensions cited the ageing population and other changing demographics which almost all states face and argued that, though the UK would also be challenged by these issues, economies of scale meant that it would be better equipped to deal with the uncertainties arising from fluctuations in demographics and migration. The argument was made here that migration *within* the UK would have no overall impact on social security across the UK, since the overall UK population (and tax base) would remain the same—however, if Scotland was independent, any movement between Scotland and the remainder of the UK would impact upon both states' social security provisions (HM Government, 2014d: 38). Economies of scale were also cited in relation to the administration and payment of social security, and how to deliver broadly similar systems and outcomes on a dramatically reduced scale (HM Government, 2014d: 66). There was a strong emphasis on the risk entailed in assuming responsibility for welfare without a large population and wide tax base. The evidence from the global financial crisis appeared to point to the fact that smaller states were more at risk to fluctuations in the market than larger states, with Iceland and Ireland cited as key supporting arguments.

While the Scottish Government and the Yes Scotland campaign were rather united on the main political questions, the Better Together campaign and the UK Government were represented by a wider spread of the political spectrum. Better Together was led by Scottish Labour, a party which was not in government in either Scotland or at UK level. Given the lack of Conservative support in Scotland and the decline in support for the Liberal Democrats after they entered coalition government in 2010, the proposal for a Labour-led campaign was entirely pragmatic. What this meant was that the campaign could attempt to distance itself from the 'official' UK Government position in some cases, while at the same time it did not have to adhere to formal agreements or levels of decorum expected of governments. In short, the campaign could be a bit more outspoken on some issues—and this was clearly the case with regards to the small state argument. In addition, they played upon the stereotypically Scottish national pastime—going to the pub—by pointing to the cost of a pint of beer in some of the Nordic states, which they claimed to be in the region of £10. This focus was not unreasonable: the price of a pint was one which resonated with much of the Scottish population, as evidenced by the tendency for tabloid newspapers, in the wake of the Chancellor's annual budget statement, to lead with the changes to the cost of alcohol.

Yet the broader issue could also divide the No camp as Labour was accusing the Conservative–Liberal Democrat UK Government of undermining the welfare state. The Conservatives could dismiss the Nordic countries as highly taxed, highly regulated, anti-business states; for Labour to do so would give the SNP the mantle of social democracy. Labour's argument that the United Kingdom was a 'sharing union' was an effort to address this problem, based both on the notion of a large state that could pool risk, and the concept of British solidarity. The No side also sought to combat the argument that international bodies could provide Scotland with security and market access, so making the UK redundant. This underlay the recurrent doubts they sowed about whether Scotland would be allowed into NATO and the European Union (see Chapters 6 and 7).

However, while tactically this message was useful—much like the Scottish Government's proposals for social investment—neither side provided much in the way of sophisticated analysis as to *why* the Nordic states had opted for such models nor did they appreciate the differences between the economic policies within Ireland, Iceland, Sweden, Denmark, Norway, and Finland, preferring instead to caricature the cases in order to further their own constitutional preferences. Better Together's argument that a 'No' vote in the referendum would provide the 'best of both worlds' for Scotland tapped into the concerns over the risks associated with smallness and emphasized the advantages of large states—in particular economies of scale in relation to changing demographics and the welfare system. They argued that the benefits of smallness—adaptability, distinct public policy, short lines of communication—could be achieved within the Union, with none of the disadvantages (vulnerability to external shocks) associated with being a small state.

Balancing the Arguments

On the whole, the small state argument drew less upon the constitutional powers or the global influence of small states and more upon the internal structures and policy choices those states undertook. The referendum question was a dichotomous choice between an independent future for Scotland or continuing membership of the UK. However, the reality of the constitutional question in Scotland is much more complex, and the political economy choices available to Scotland are largely independent of the constitutional options. The case of Quebec demonstrates this point clearly: twice the province rejected independence from Canada, yet it has still delivered distinctive public policy which is, by and large, markedly different from its neighbouring provinces. There are clearly a range of powers that substate entities can obtain and utilize in different ways to deliver different policy outcomes—in some cases, policy outcomes which are markedly different from the centre (and which, potentially, the centre would prefer they did not pursue). The small state argument conflated the two, inferring that the political economy of small states and their successes and failures was a consequence of their constitutional status as well as their size. Thus the archetypal social investment states of the Nordic countries were portrayed as examples of how small states could thrive on a global stage while providing substantive social security for their populations. Post-crash, they were cited as a warning for proponents of independence; the lack of any financial assistance for Iceland after its entire banking system collapsed a stark reminder of the risks small independent states face in global markets.

However, in neither case was a cohesive strategy apparent. The Nordic model was lauded for its ability to combine social assistance with economic growth, but there was no consideration of the cost of implementing such a system. The financially devastating outcome in Iceland was oft-cited to show that small states could not manage their banks, but critics did not examine the lack of regulation of the financial sector there. This was the hallmark of the small state argument: selective examples. Both campaigns utilized a 'pick and mix' approach to supporting evidence, utilizing those elements of the case studies which best articulated their own constitutional preference, ignoring equally important counter-arguments or structural features which explained why this was the case. For this reason, the argument appeared rather import-ant in the early phases of the debate. In particular, small states as comparators featured heavily during the SNP Government's 'National Conversation' which occurred during the party's first term in (minority) government: a substantive three-year consultation incorporating public meetings, speeches, online blogs, and government information papers. Established with the intention of being the precursor to an independence referendum during the 2007–11 Scottish parliamentary term, it was useful for the party to utilize successful small states as examples when citing the benefits of independence. For if other small states could be successful, why not Scotland? What was it about Scotland that was so uniquely unsuitable to independence? If Scotland was independent, with the powers that entailed and the opportunities it provided, it could emulate these successful small states. So went the argument. Then the financial crisis provided the counter-argument: independence is a risk, small states have suffered disproportionately, they have been unable to adapt to the market, and this is what could happen to Scotland.

The small state argument was perhaps too complex to have changed the campaign and often consisted of assertions and counter-assertions. Yet it did allow both sides to bring in concrete examples to supplement abstract arguments and speculations. It also left a legacy in that it did raise issues about the relationship among constitutional arrangements: institutions for policy-making and policy choices. As the argument after the referendum moved onto to what new powers Scotland could gain and how it might use them, especially in the fields of welfare and taxation, some of the issues ventilated in the campaign were brought back. Independent or not, Scotland remains a small country embedded in a complex of relationships with the UK, Europe and the world. While divided on the issue of independence, the main parties are quite close to each other on matters of social and economic policy and the aspiration to the celebrated Nordic model remains.

10

Voters' Response to the Campaign

Evidence from the Survey

Robert Liñeira, Ailsa Henderson, and Liam Delaney

Introduction

The previous chapters have shown that the referendum campaign focused not only on particular constitutional options such as independence but also on broader issues about the type of society and type of state to which people aspire. All aspects of Scottish and UK political and economic life were part of this debate and it engaged public opinion in an unprecedented fashion, leading eventually to voter turnout rates far exceeding those observed in UK elections in recent decades. This chapter examines public opinion on the Scottish referendum in the run-up to and after the vote.

Within the Centre on Constitutional Change (CCC), we conducted both pre- and post-referendum surveys to explore the broad themes that influenced public opinion through the independence debate. These included the relative influence of different blocks of variables: socio-demographics, political predispositions, issue evaluations, and risks perceptions and attitudes. The survey data were collected by ICM Research three months before and three months after the referendum using a panel design. In order to track changes during the campaign, we focus here on those who replied to both our pre- and our post-referendum surveys as well as a separate post-referendum survey examining preferences for policy options in the context of the Smith Commission report. We identify these as: CCC pre-referendum survey; CCC post-referendum survey; and Smith Commission survey. We also draw on the Scottish Social Attitudes Survey and the findings reported on the *What Scotland Thinks* site (http://whatscotlandthinks.org).

These provide us with an array of data on voter attitudes to both constitutional change and substantive policy issues, and about perceptions of, and aversion to, risk. We take the main themes from the chapters above, including the economy, currency, welfare, and defence, and trace voters' attitudes on these and whether they changed over the course of the referendum campaign and its aftermath. We also identify particular groups such as younger people, women, and those born outside Scotland to see whether they have views that set them apart. We identify those issues that were associated with support for each of the constitutional options in the referendum. We then assess the role that such views play in structuring support for the constitutional options now open to Scotland following the No vote and the proposals for further devolution.

It should be said at the outset that, due to their relative infrequency, our knowledge of the determinants of attitudes to different options in referendum campaigns is sketchier than that of election campaigns (LeDuc, 2003; de Vreese, 2007; de Vreese and Semetko, 2004). On the one hand, voters are expected to reach decisions in referendum campaigns similar to the way that they would in election campaigns, with their choices influenced by a variety of demographic and attitudinal predictors of support. So we should expect traditional models employing demographic and political identity factors to help to structure referendum attitudes, with a mix of core values and campaign reactions influencing eventual vote choice (Clarke, Kornberg, and Stewart, 2004). On the other hand, referendums may provide environments in which typical decision-making determinants are less influential. This includes lower levels of awareness and knowledge of referendum issues, as well as the absence of cues and other heuristic devices that allow voters to cut through a lot of contradictory information (Bowler and Donovan, 2000; Lupia, 1994). In the absence of cues—or more realistically, in the absence of consistent cues—voters might find it difficult to translate campaign information into the knowledge sufficient to make an informed referendum choice.

In certain key ways, the decision-making process for voters in referendums may differ from that facing voters in election campaigns. In referendum campaigns voters may be unfamiliar with the referendum issue, parties may be divided and supporting opposing sides, or otherwise rival parties may campaign together (LeDuc, 2002). This may lead to changing or inconsistent attitudes among the electorate, late decisions, and vote-switching. Yet referendum campaigns on independence are in some ways not typical of the low-salient and low-information contexts that characterize other types of referendums (Clarke, Kornberg, and Stewart, 2004; Nadeau, Martin, and Blais, 1999). The issue of independence is a salient and emotive one, with preferences set long before the formal referendum campaign begins (Martin,

1994). However, the infrequency with which territories within states achieve independence and the necessarily future-oriented nature of much of the debate in which campaign teams portray different visions of the future for a polity make it difficult for voters to evaluate the real consequences of either referendum choice. This suggests that vote choices might well be structured by prior attitudes such as national and party identification; but the uncertainty of the choice makes attitudes to risk, and not merely the evaluations of different proposals and claims made by the campaign teams, a factor that may influence vote choice (see Chapter 2).

The rest of this chapter is structured as follows. First we examine broad preferences for constitutional change, in particular looking at the extent to which voters were in favour of independence, retaining the status quo, or moving towards more fully devolved powers for Scotland. Next, we explore the influence of socio-demographic factors and political predispositions (identification with national groups and political parties) on constitutional preferences. In the following section, we move to the main issues of the campaign, particularly, the economy and welfare services. Here we will examine the electorate's judgement about the main claims by the two campaigns, how risky the different scenarios were perceived to be, and the role of risk attitudes on individuals' vote choice. Finally, we look at preferences for constitutional options after the referendum.

Status Quo, Independence, or Further Devolution?

While the final referendum question asked citizens to choose between independence or remaining within the UK, it is clear that the options were more complex in practice (see Chapter 1). Although proposals to include a three-way referendum question asking voters to choose between the status quo, independence, and a third option involving full devolution ('devo-max') were rejected, this third option continued implicitly to hold an important influence on the attitudes of voters and in the public debate.

Eliciting preferences for territorial power distributions is complex (McCrone and Paterson, 2002); as with most attitudinal questions on surveys, how the different alternatives are presented to survey respondents may affect people's answers (Schuman and Presser, 1996). Fortunately, the picture we get from people's constitutional preferences is fairly consistent across measures. Figure 10.1, taken from the Scottish Social Attitudes Survey, displays the first and second ranked preferences of individuals for the different constitutional options in January 2013, around the time that the Yes and the No campaigns were designing their strategies. The option 'the Scottish Parliament should make all decisions'—which we could equate to independence—gathered

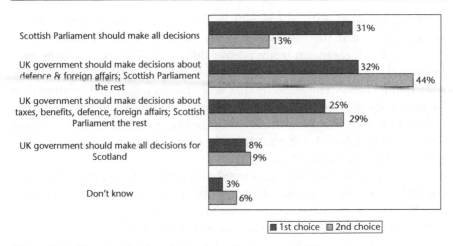

Figure 10.1. Constitutional preferences
Source: Scottish Social Attitudes Survey, January 2013

31 per cent of support, whereas the view that the Scottish Parliament should make all decisions with the exception of defence and foreign affairs—which we could relate to 'devo-max' proposals—was chosen by 32 per cent of the respondents. The other alternatives were less supported: the UK Government in charge of defence, foreign policy, taxes, and benefits—similar to the status quo of 2013—was chosen by 25 per cent of the people, whereas removing all jurisdiction from the Scottish Parliament was supported by the remaining 8 per cent.

This distribution of preferences helped campaigns to set their strategies. If we focus on respondents' first preferences, it becomes evident that the median voter was a devo-max supporter. It was essential for both the Yes and the No campaigns to attract this voter in order to reach a majority and win the referendum. This picture is reinforced when respondents were asked about their second preference, should their first one fail. The devo-max option was clearly the most successful in attracting these strategic second-preferences, with some pro-independence and some pro-status quo voters converging on it. In contrast, the pro-independence option only gathered 13 per cent of second preferences. This state of affairs clearly influenced the proposals presented by the rival campaigns, both of which sought to secure the middle ground. The Yes side campaigned on a platform that could effectively be characterized as 'independence-light', with independence meaning the break-up of the parliamentary union with the rest of the UK, but with retention of other unions like the currency or the monarchy. Similarly, the No side promised that a No vote would not be synonymous with supporting the status quo, but rather would trigger a constitutional reform that would grant

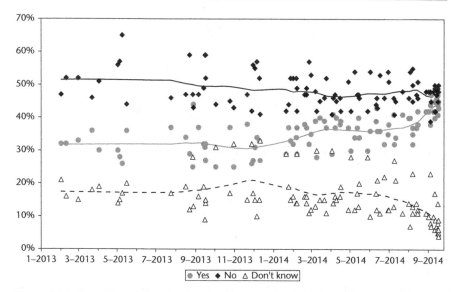

Figure 10.2. Scottish independence referendum voting intentions

Source: http://whatscotlandthinks.org. The figure gathers the answers to the exact question 'Should Scotland be an independent country?' on any representative survey of Scotland's population conducted by polling companies that belong to the British Polling Council (n=99). The trend lines are estimated using local polynomial regression, locally estimated scatterplot smoothing (LOESS)

more powers to the Scottish Parliament, a position that was reinforced during the last week of the campaign (see Chapter 1).

There is strong evidence to suggest that the later stage of the referendum campaign influenced preferences and encouraged some voters to change their views on the independence question. Figure 10.2 gathers the voting intentions produced by the 99 polls that were conducted since the moment when the exact wording of the referendum question became known. The figure shows that the campaign produced no substantial changes for the whole of 2013 and the first quarter of 2014. During this entire period, the No side had a substantial lead over the Yes side, while the undecided remained around the 15 per cent mark. This resulted in a dominant media perception that for most voters the independence question was so embedded in their identities and core values that few were likely to change sides as a result of the debate and the campaigns. By the spring of 2014, the gap between the two options had closed marginally, but it was in the last weeks of the campaign that major changes occurred.

In early August, the first debate between the two campaign leaders—Alistair Darling and Alex Salmond—drew people's attention to two main campaign propositions. By the time of the second and final leaders' debate on 26 August, the campaign had intensified and the Scottish debate reached the front pages of the international media. As shown in Figure 10.2, it was precisely when the

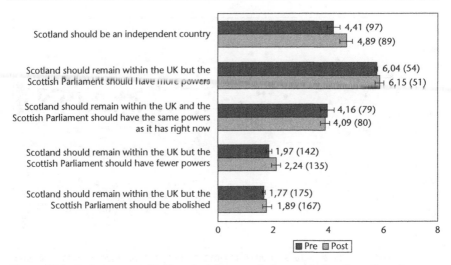

Figure 10.3. Scales on constitutional preferences before and after the referendum

Source: CCC pre- and post-referendum surveys. Numbers are the result of a paired t-test between the pre- and the post-referendum measure. They show the mean and the coefficient of variation (in parentheses). The thin bars show the standard error at the 95 per cent confidence level

campaign became more intense and the voting day got closer that the major changes in voting intention were reflected in the opinion polls. During the last two weeks of the campaign there was a decrease in the number of undecided voters, and the gap between the No and Yes sides closed.

Our own pre- and post-referendum surveys identify these shifts. Figures 10.3 and 10.4 show two different measures of these preferences and how they changed. Although the options offered to respondents in both indicators are the same, the preferences are measured differently: in Figure 10.3 respondents are asked to assess the appeal of each option on a 0 to 10 scale, whereas in Figure 10.4 they are demanded to choose their preferred alternative. According to our first measure (see Figure 10.3), the option of devolving more powers to the Scottish Parliament, while remaining within the UK, continued to be the most popular one. It was also the least controversial of the options: it has the smallest coefficient of variation, which means that the ratings in our 0 to 10 scale are less spread for this option than for any of the others. Independence was the second most popular option: it got a mean rating of 4.41 (out of 10) before the referendum, but its popularity reached the 4.89 level, a statistically significant increase. There was no change in the level of support for maintaining the constitutional status quo before and after the referendum (around 4.1 out of 10), whereas diminishing the powers granted to the Scottish Parliament or abolishing it got very low levels of popularity in both waves of the survey. In summary,

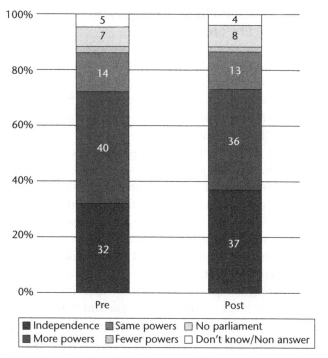

Figure 10.4. Constitutional preferences before and after the referendum
Source: CCC pre- and post-referendum surveys

throughout the campaign voters continued to express high degrees of support for retaining the Union but with increased powers for Scotland. The campaign did appear to generate increased preference for independence, but this remained a less popular choice among voters.

We get a similar picture if we focus on our second measure of preferences, among five alternatives ranging from no parliament to independence. Before the referendum, a parliament with more powers was the most popular option, with 40 per cent of support, but this has diminished to 36 per cent after the referendum. Support for independence increased from 32 per cent to 37 per cent before and after the referendum—still less than the actual vote for independence (45 per cent) in the referendum when, as we have noted, voters were given only two options. However, the combined support of the independence and more powers options did not change much: both options got 72 per cent of the support in the pre-referendum survey and 73 per cent in the post-referendum survey. This makes it evident that the pro-independence side enlarged its support during the campaign by attracting former devo-max supporters. In summary, the 'more powers' supporters were, and could still be, the key to the independence question.

Demographic Factors, Political Predispositions, and Constitutional Preferences

In this section, we focus on the referendum vote and the constitutional preferences of different groups. The 'panel' element of our main survey means that we were able to interview the same voters before and after the referendum. We take advantage of this to contrast the voting intention (before the referendum) and the vote recall (after it) of different groups.

Figure 10.5 below illustrates the voting percentages—before and after the referendum—broken down by gender, age, origin, and social class. In order to facilitate accurate comparisons we have removed those undecided and those that did not reply to vote questions. The figures then reflect the net swing between the Yes and No sides. The top-left panel compares the vote of women and men before and after the referendum. Differences are not huge, but the data reveal that women leant more toward the No side than men, but both groups swung from the No to the Yes side in similar proportions. Variations in the voting of different age groups are more remarkable. First, the top-right figure reveals that the relationship between age and vote is not a linear one. Older groups show a stronger likelihood of voting No than young groups, but the youngest of them all (those between sixteen and twenty-four) break the pattern and show a vote profile which leans more towards the union side than those between twenty-five and thirty-four, which our data suggest is the most pro-independence of all age groups. The youngest group also reveals a second interesting pattern: although all groups show a swing from No to Yes, the swing of the youngest is the greatest. This potentially demonstrates the more volatile opinions of the group with least electoral experience, which contrasts with the stability in the opinions of the most-experienced over-sixty-five group.

Social class also seems to be the source of some differences: the middle class appears as more pro-union than the working class.[1] However, the middle class shows a greater swing from No to Yes during the course of the campaign. Finally, the final chart shows the vote differences by origin. These are divided into three groups: those born in Scotland; those born elsewhere in the UK; and those born outside the UK. This last group includes European and Commonwealth citizens living in Scotland, who had the right to vote in the referendum. Unsurprisingly, those born in the rest of the UK are more pro-union than those born in Scotland, although there is by no means a perfect correlation between origin and vote. In our survey, the No vote was the majority choice for all origin

---

[1] We use the classification maintained by the Market Research Society to measure social class, an objective measure based on occupation. We have collapsed the original six categories into two: the middle class (which includes the original upper-middle, middle, and lower-middle classes) and the working class (collapsing the original skilled working class, working class, and non-working categories into a single one).

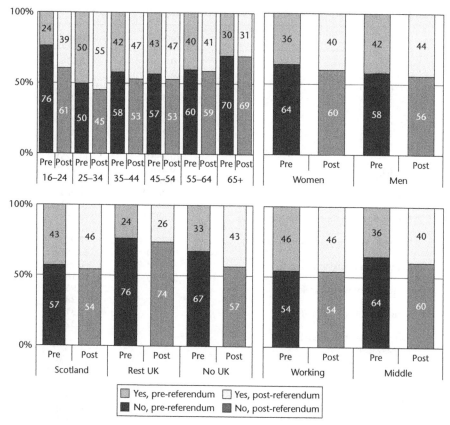

Figure 10.5. Independence voting by socio-demographics
Source: CCC pre- and post-referendum surveys

groups while a quarter of those born elsewhere in the UK voted Yes. Perhaps more surprisingly, support for independence among those born overseas was closer to the Scots-born than to those born elsewhere in the UK, which constitutes the origin group most opposed to independence.

To what extent did socio-demographic characteristics condition referendum vote choice? Table 10.1 shows the results of two regression models that allow us to examine the effects of the different demographic factors while holding each of the other factors constant. The first model shows the effect of socio-demographics variables on voting Yes (or No) at the referendum; that is, to what extent gender, age, origin, education, and class made a difference on vote choice. The second model adds two types of identification variables: the voters' level of identification with Scotland and Britain, and the voters' party identification. The strategy of introducing first the socio-demographics and later the attitudes is related to the sequence in which these variables affect the

Table 10.1. Predictors of voting Yes at the referendum (Ref. category: No vote)

	Model 1	Model 2
Men (women)	0.126	0.138
	(0.131)	(0.179)
Age (16–24)		
(25–34)	0.340	−0.011
	(0.257)	(0.316)
(35–44)	0.077	−0.276
	(0.250)	(0.313)
(45–54)	−0.110	−0.260
	(0.258)	(0.325)
(55–64)	−0.376	−0.824*
	(0.266)	(0.355)
(+65)	−0.766**	−1.025**
	(0.256)	(0.341)
Born in Scotland (born outside Scotland)	0.637***	−0.769**
	(0.151)	(0.270)
University degree (no university degree)	−0.003	0.024
	(0.133)	(0.180)
Middle class (working class)	−0.294*	−0.044
	(0.131)	(0.180)
Scottish identity (0–1 scale)		1.956***
		(0.385)
British identity (0–1 scale)		−3.315***
		(0.328)
Party identification (none)		
Conservative		−1.767***
		(0.383)
Labour		−0.837***
		(0.229)
Liberal-Democrats		−0.742
		(0.455)
SNP		2.574***
		(0.309)
Other		0.661
		(0.383)
DK		−0.037
		(0.290)
Constant	−0.300	1.508***
	(0.265)	(0.446)
x^2	62.46	640.9
Pseudo R^2	0.039	0.410
N	1,238	1,229

*** p<0.001, ** p<0.01, * p<0.05. Logit coefficients. Standard errors in parentheses. The outcome is taken from our post-referendum survey asking respondents how they voted in the referendum. All the predictors were elicited at the pre-referendum measure. Base categories for categorical independent variables are placed in parentheses.

Source: CCC pre- and post-referendum surveys

vote; whereas the socio-demographic characteristics of an individual may affect his or her political predispositions, the latter may not affect the former.

From the point of view of socio-demographics, model 1 provides evidence of important differences: being over sixty-five, born outside Scotland, and a member of the middle class is related to voting No. However, model 2 makes it clear that most of these effects were mediated by political attitudes, making socio-demographics irrelevant once voters' identification with the political parties and the Scottish and British communities are introduced into the model.

Age is the only factor that remains significant even after taking political attitudes into account; the oldest group voted No more than any other age group. In contrast, the effect of social class disappears once national and, specially, party identification are entered into the analysis.[2] The mechanism that links both national and party identification to constitutional preferences is a similar one: they both summarize socialization and past experiences, conditioning voters' attitudes and reactions towards certain political issues (Blais and Nadeau, 1992). Party identifications may also influence the vote choice because the parties' stances and arguments during the campaign offer oriented information from sources they trust to those who identify with a particular party (Clarke, Kornberg, and Stewart, 2004).

Attitudes reveal a strong predictive power on vote choice. On the one hand, national identification confirms its relationship with independence choice. Whereas a strong identification with Scotland is related to voting Yes, a strong identification with Britain is related to voting No. The latter association is the stronger, although the numbers are smaller. As has long been the case, most Scots identify as Scottish whether they are pro-independence or not. Finally, party identification and, especially, the levels of identification with the SNP and the Conservatives respectively, show the expected relationship with the vote.

Issues and Risk Perceptions

Socio-demographics and political predispositions are not the only determinants of secession preferences. The economy and the currency arrangement of an independent Scotland were probably the most debated issues during the campaign. These issues were attacked by the No side as the main risks and inconveniences of independence, whereas the Yes side tried to counterbalance these arguments by emphasizing the possibilities that independence would create to implement progressive welfare policies. These and other claims may have influenced vote choice, but because they were contested by the two sides, voters lacked the sufficient information to judge their validity. The high level of uncertainty that characterizes independence referendums

[2] Scottish origin shows a surprising negative effect (those born in Scotland would be more likely to vote No), but this is just the consequence of controlling for identity, i.e. the coefficient shows the effect of origin holding Scottish and British identity constants. Given that origin is strongly correlated to both Scottish and British identities, this is informing us of a very small subgroup of voters.

heightens the voters' perception of risks so that risk tolerance and aversion become drivers of the ballot choice.

The Economy

The literature has devoted extensive attention to the relationship between the economy and independence and, in particular, to how the perceived economic benefits and costs of independence influence the support to secession in different contexts (Bélanger and Perrella, 2008; Blais, Martin, and Nadeau, 1995; Blais and Nadeau, 1992; Curtice, 2015b; Howe, 1998; Mendelsohn, 2003; Muñoz and Tormos, 2015). However, these analyses do not agree on the causal effect of economic attitudes. Voters' expectations about the economic consequences of independence might well be a rationalization of individuals' pre-existing preferences; when asked about their economic expectations voters might be expressing a view congruent with their own preferences so that those in favour of secession might overestimate the benefits and those against might overestimate the costs.[3]

Irrespective of the causal status of the economic arguments on the vote decision, the economy was a very salient issue during the referendum campaign in Scotland. Aware that economic attitudes were more susceptible to change than core values and political orientations such as national identification, both campaigns tried to convince the undecideds and those with less-firm preferences that their option was safe and their opponents' one was not. The Yes side underlined the benefits of an economic policy best suited to Scotland's interests and a stronger priority for welfare in the event of independence, while the No side insisted on the advantages of pooling risks with the rest of the UK and not introducing any barriers to trade.

Both campaigns scored some successes presenting their views. Figure 10.6 gathers data on how plausible the public perceived different scenarios debated

[3] There are two feasible strategies to address the endogeneity problem that arises from the use of observational data analysis. On the one hand, an instrument variable estimation as proposed by Howe (1998) to analyse the Quebec case, which might deal with the 'reverse causation' problem if a suitable instrument (an exogenous factor correlated to people's perceptions on the economic consequences of independence) is identified. Failing to do so, the available evidence leads Howe to conclude that rationalization of existing preferences is the main mechanism that links economic expectations to independence preferences. On the other hand, one may use an experimental setup in which respondents are presented with different economic scenarios to see how they affect their independence preferences. This is done by Muñoz and Tormos (2015) who found a modest impact of economic expectations on the vote in the context of Catalonia. However, as they discuss, their method might be underestimating the effect of economic arguments on independence preferences because experimental setups have difficulties dealing with 'real-world pre-treatments' (Gaines and Kuklinski, 2011), i.e. the fact that the public may already be familiar with any credible economic argument used as treatment in a context in which the independence debate is a very salient one.

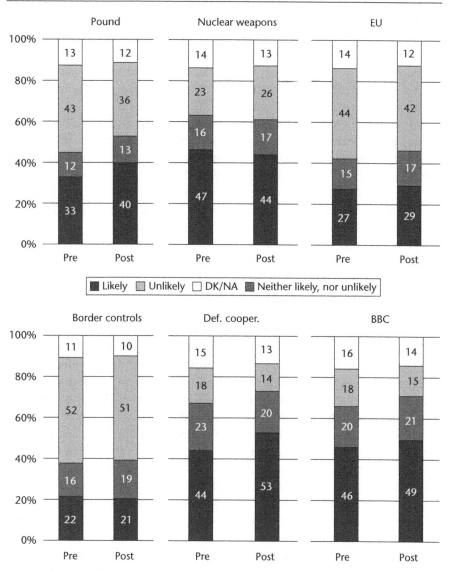

Figure 10.6. Popular perception of different scenarios in the event of independence

Responses to the question: 'If Scotland becomes (would have become) independent, how likely is that [different scenarios]: 1. The UK government would allow Scotland to keep the pound; 2. The UK government would move nuclear weapons out of Scotland; 3. Scotland would be able to retain membership of the EU on the same terms as the UK; 4. There would be passport and border controls between Scotland and England; 5. Scotland and the UK would arrange a defence cooperation; 6. Scotland would continue to contribute to and access services of the BBC'

Source: CCC pre- and post-referendum surveys

during the campaign in the event of independence to be, both before and after the referendum. The evidence shows that most of the potential risks related to independence were not perceived as such by the whole electorate. Only a fifth of respondents believed it likely that a Yes vote would lead to passport and border controls between Scotland and England; only a sixth believed it unlikely that Scotland and the rest of the UK would not cooperate on security issues; and less than a fifth judged as unlikely that Scotland would have access to the BBC. In short, there were more voters that perceived that border controls, defence cooperation, or access to the BBC were not at stake in the event of independence than voters who believed the opposite. Finally, the removal of nuclear weapons from Scotland—a position framed as a gain by the Scottish Government (see Chapter 7)—was perceived as likely by almost half of the voters in the event of independence.

By contrast, Scotland's membership of the EU and the access to the Bank of England were perceived at risk. Regarding the EU (Chapter 6), 44 per cent of the voters perceived as unlikely that Scotland would be able to retain membership of the EU on the same terms as the UK, whereas only 27 per cent perceived this as likely. It was, however, the currency and monetary policy arrangements debate that was the most vociferous during the campaign (Chapter 4). The Chancellor of the Exchequer, Shadow Chancellor, and the Liberal Democrats' Chief Secretary to the Treasury all claimed that an independent Scotland would not be permitted to remain within the existing structures and that it would need to establish a separate currency and separate Central Bank. Given the potential implications of this for security of pensions, deposits, and other important financial aspects of household life, it is not surprising that it gained a high degree of prominence in the debate. As can be seen in Figure 10.6, only a minority of respondents to our pre-referendum survey believed it likely that Scotland could remain within the existing currency arrangement. However, it must be noted that this is the only issue on which the Yes side argument made progress; despite the No side being categorical about the impossibility of a currency agreement, there are more voters in our post-referendum measure that found the agreement likely (40 per cent) than the opposite (36 per cent).

In contrast, the possible risks and costs related to Scotland remaining within the UK had less salience during the campaign. The SNP tried to link the notions of risk and cost also to the No choice, and some of their claims achieved resonance among the public. According to data gathered in Figure 10.7, the financial resources available for financing the public services and, paradoxically, Scotland's membership of the EU were the two main risks that the public related to a No victory. Specifically, there were more voters who thought that within the UK, Scotland would experience cuts in available spending for public service (38 per cent) than voters who perceived this as unlikely

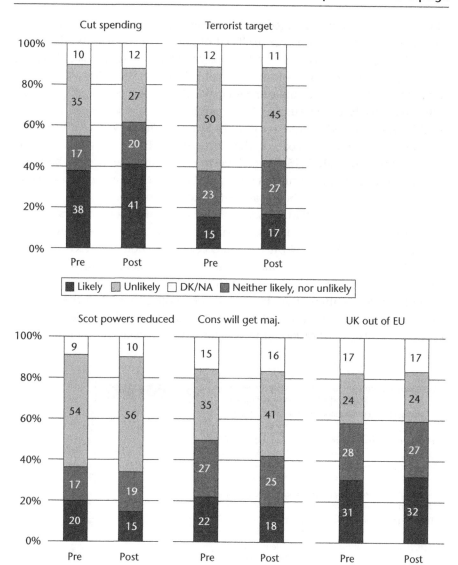

Figure 10.7. Popular perception of different scenarios in the event of remaining in the Union

Responses to the question: 'If Scotland remains within the UK, how likely is that [different scenarios]: 1. A UK government would cut spending available for Scottish public services; 2. UK foreign policy would make Scotland a target for terrorist attacks; 3. The powers of the Scottish Parliament will be reduced; 4. The Conservative Party will win a majority government in the 2015 UK General Election; 5. The UK will vote itself out of Europe in a membership referendum'

Source: CCC pre- and post-referendum surveys

(35 per cent), a gap that enlarged after the referendum. Our data also show that the claim that the 'UK will vote itself out of Europe in the membership referendum' was perceived as likely by 31 per cent of the voters and as unlikely by only 24 per cent. However, other potential risks associated with a No victory occupied much less of the public imagination. More voters perceived as unlikely rather than likely claims such as 'the foreign policy of the United Kingdom would make Scotland a target for terrorist attacks', 'the powers of the Scottish Parliament would be reduced', or 'the Conservative Party will win a majority government in the UK 2015 General Election'. In any case, it must be noted that the campaign did not make significant differences for any of these claims which show similar values before and after the referendum.

Not all of these issues had the same potential in influencing voters' choice. Figure 10.8, from the pre-referendum survey, shows how more likely people would be to vote Yes or No if they had certainty about these contentious issues. The data make evident that uncertainty was particularly pre-eminent in the event of secession because most of the contested scenarios were related to the independence alternative. It must also be noted that all of them would have benefited the Yes score in the event of certainty, with the sole exception of the imposition of border controls. The latter is precisely the one which

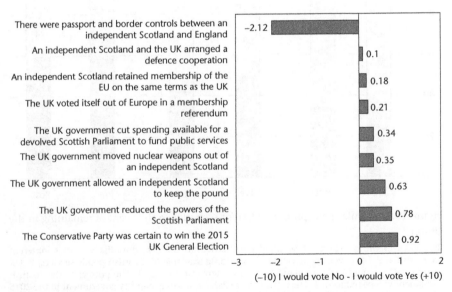

Figure 10.8. The effect of different scenarios on the vote

Responses to the question: 'Some people are more likely to vote Yes or No under specific circumstances. What about you? If each of the following occurred would this make you more or less likely to vote for independence?'

Source: CCC pre-referendum survey

shows a bigger potential effect on vote choice but, as we have seen, most people did not believe that this would happen. Defence and Europe were less important and were only intermittently stressed during the campaign. The currency, on the other hand, comes out as an issue that did affect voter choice in the pre-referendum survey, working strongly against the Yes side.

The post-referendum data confirm that the currency uncertainty was the major obstacle for voting Yes. Figure 10.9 reflects how people would have voted under different scenarios. According to this evidence, a currency agreement would have been the most beneficial issue for the pro-independence side, followed by certainty that Scotland would have not faced any obstacle to become an EU member state. However, it is the currency agreement that gives a clearer lead to the Yes side and is the main one which could potentially have become a referendum winner for the pro-independence side. Nonetheless, we must bear in mind that 21 per cent of our sample could not make up their minds under such a scenario, so a currency agreement might not have been enough to guarantee a Yes victory. It would still require a more general certainty about the benefit (or, at least, the lack of harm) of independence for the Scottish economy (Liñeira, Henderson, and Delaney, 2015).

Finally, the importance of economic uncertainty in the referendum outcome is reinforced by the results displayed in Figure 10.10, which shows the

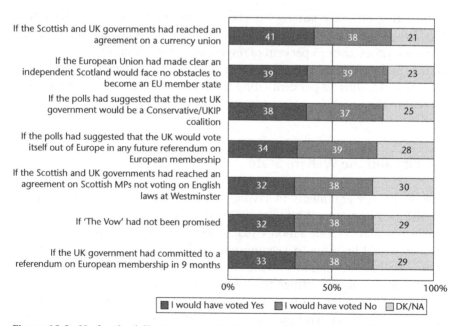

Figure 10.9. Under the following scenarios, how would you have voted?
Source: CCC post-referendum survey

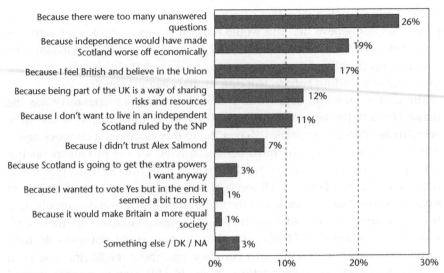

The figure show the responses of those who recalled to vote No in the post-referendum survey.

Figure 10.10. Single most important reason for voting No

The figure shows the responses of those who recalled to vote No in the post-referendum survey

Source: CCC post-referendum survey.

main voting rationale among No voters according to our post-referendum data. While national identity and political party issues feature prominently in the responses, over 25 per cent of respondents cited 'unanswered questions' as their main rationale and 19 per cent cited Scotland being made worse off economically, with 12 per cent citing the risk-sharing advantages of remaining within the union.

Equality and the Welfare State

One of the key arguments in favour of independence put forward in the Scottish Government's White Paper (2013) on independence is that it would enable Scotland to create a more equal society; a change that the Government believes would be more in keeping with the country's values. Figure 10.11 tracks the public's opinion about the consequences of independence on inequality. The figure gathers the respondents' opinion from January 2012 to January 2014, taking us from months after the SNP's victory in 2011 to the early stages of the referendum campaign. In 2012 there was almost a majority that thought that neither independence nor the union would make any difference on the inequality issue. Twenty per cent believed that independence

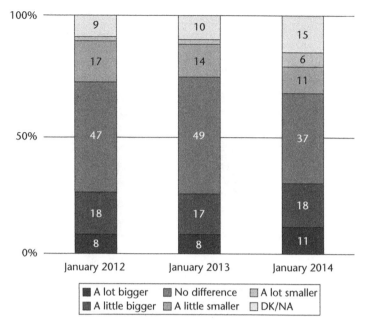

Figure 10.11. Independence and the gap between the rich and the poor

Responses to the question: 'If Scotland were to become independent, would gap between rich and poor be bigger, smaller or no difference?'

Source: Scottish Social Attitudes Survey

would make things worse ('a lot bigger' or 'a little bigger' differences between the rich and the poor), whereas 19 per cent believed that independence would shrink the gap. The following two years do not show relevant changes on the support for these three options. Although these data do not cover the most intense period of the campaign, they show no evidence that the Yes side was successful on their case that independence would lead to a different outcome on equality.

The White Paper also argued that independence would allow Scotland to build a stronger welfare state. This would be one of the tools to achieve a more equal society, with better pensions, stronger public health and social care services. Figure 10.12 focuses on the latter and shows the opinion of the public on the provision of social care three months after the referendum. A third of respondents believed that independence would have meant better provision of childcare and better services for older and disabled people; about a quarter thought that neither independence nor the union would make a difference; and a little more than a fifth judged that the union would be the best option for the provision of these services (either with the same or with more powers for the Scottish Parliament). Independence therefore seemed the preferred choice for social care provision.

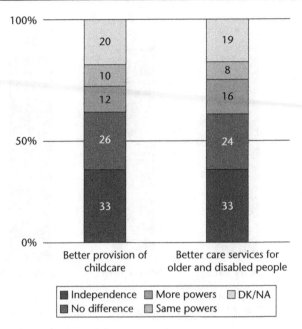

Figure 10.12. Independence and the care services
Source: CCC post-referendum survey

However, this is just a relative triumph for the Yes side. First, almost a half of the respondents did not show an opinion or believed that independence would make any difference on the issue. Second, only a third of respondents shared the Yes side's optimism, which is below the level of those who support independence. Although our narrow evidence limits our capacity to extract firm conclusions, we found no proof that the pro-independence side was successful neither with their purpose of relating constitutional choices to welfare policies, nor with their case that independence is the best guarantee for a strong welfare state. All this limits the capacity of the welfare case as a driver to vote Yes.

The Role of Risk Attitudes

We have seen that the public went to the polls with high levels of uncertainty about the consequences of independence for the economy, the currency arrangement, or Scotland's membership in the EU. These uncertainties made very difficult any estimation of the prospective economy (or the position of Scotland with regard to the EU) in the event of independence. The lack of certainty muddles any cost-benefit calculation on the independence choice

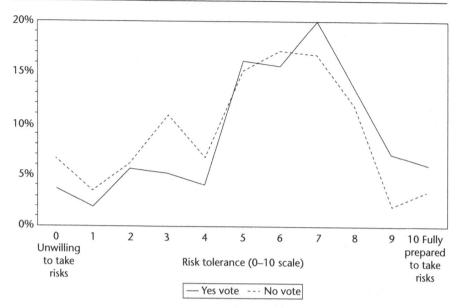

Figure 10.13. General risk attitudes and independence vote choice
Source: CCC pre- and post-referendum surveys

and it is the reason why voters' aversion or tolerance to make risky decisions may also influence their vote choice (Bell, Delaney, and McGoldrick, 2014; Liñeira, Henderson, and Delaney, 2015; Nadeau, Martin, and Blais, 1999).

Voters can never be sure about the consequences of their choice, but independence is a particularly uncertain one. Referendums on self-determination are rare among stable democracies, so the electorate can barely rely on any precedent to obtain knowledge about the consequences of independence. Additionally, the specific settlement of independence in the event of a Yes vote usually depends on post-referendum bargains which involve (at least) the government of the future sovereign state and the government of the state from which it secedes. It should not be assumed, however, that the alternative to independence is free from uncertainties. It is unlikely that the status quo can be maintained after an independence referendum, even if the independence option is defeated (Hobolt, 2009); the Better Together campaign in Scotland promised, for instance, further powers to the Scottish Parliament in the event of a No victory. However, the choice is asymmetrical from the point of view of uncertainties and the unknowns related to a union vote pale in comparison to the ones related to an independence one.

We should then expect that there is a relationship between voters' attitudes towards risk and referendum vote choice. Figure 10.13 shows the distribution of respondents' attitudes to risks in general for those who recall to have voted Yes or No.[4] The figure shows that Yes voters are more risk tolerant than those who voted No. The relationship between risk attitudes and independence vote choice is robust and stands after holding constant for any other variable that may affect independence vote choice (Liñeira, Henderson, and Delaney, 2015). In fact, risk aversion is the causal mechanism that would explain the so-called status quo bias: the electorate's tendency to vote against change proposals in referendums (Christin, Hug, and Sciarini, 2002). It is because a portion of the electorate tends to avoid uncertainty that electorates tend to prefer well-known alternatives, which creates an advantage for the status quo (Berger, Munger, and Potthoff, 2000). This fact may be crucial particularly in close races.

What Next for Scotland?

Immediately after the referendum, the terms of the debate shifted quickly to focus on enhanced devolution for the Scotland. Given the nature of the referendum campaign, the focus of public debate was on the relative merits of independence versus the status quo. Very quickly afterwards, both options were set aside for a very quick evaluation of what enhancements could be made. The public that had engaged with the referendum issues was now witness to an elite-dominated exploration of new issues. It was in this context that we conducted a second post-referendum survey (the Smith survey) to see if similar predictors structure attitudes to enhanced devolution.

What we find is, again, a general preference for more powers over independence. We asked also about the types of policy areas that should be devolved. Figure 10.14 shows that for all policy areas there is a plurality of respondents who cannot make up their minds and choose a jurisdiction. However, among those who have an institutional preference, we see a clear distinction between policy areas where there are more respondents who support Scottish Parliament control, such as health, education, and agriculture, and policy areas such as defence, foreign affairs, and pensions with a strong support for control to remain at Westminster. By contrast, opinion is particularly divided in policy areas such as taxation and welfare in which a quarter of our respondents choose the Scottish Parliament and a quarter choose Westminster.

Previous research has shown that support for strengthening devolved powers does not necessarily translate into support for introducing policy change or policy variation with regard to the rest of the UK (Henderson,

---

[4] For the sake of simplicity, we use here a very simple survey question to measure general risk attitudes: 'How willing you are to take risks in general', where 0 indicates 'unwilling to take risks' and 10 indicates 'fully prepared to take risks'. The answers to the risk question correspond to the pre-referendum survey, whereas the vote is measured using the post-referendum.

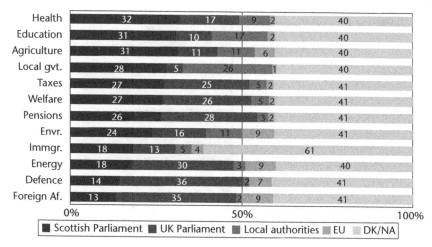

Figure 10.14. Support for devolution of powers
Source: Smith Survey 2014

Jeffery, and Wincott, 2013). To test if this is still the case, we measure here whether respondents wanted levels of taxation or benefit provision to be the same as in the rest of the UK, higher, or lower. According to Figure 10.15, for all but tax on North Sea oil and gas revenues and corporation tax, there is majority support for uniform policy across the UK. This is in keeping with the findings of Bell and Eiser (2015) who, analysing data from our June 2014 survey described above, find that there is considerable support for further decentralization of powers in Scotland, but far less support for changes to the rates of the main categories of taxation and benefits. For those supporting varying levels, the general trend is for lower taxes, lower VAT, income tax, and corporation tax, for example, and higher benefits, such as state pension and disability.

Scots also hold a general preference for pooling resources for policy options (see Figure 10.16). While 44 per cent prefer Scottish public services such as health and education—currently devolved policy areas—to be funded internally, there is plurality or majority preference for funding pensions and welfare benefits across the UK as a whole. While voters appear to want greater Scottish Parliament control over policy areas, they would like policy uniformity and policies to be funded across the UK (Henderson, Jeffery, Liñeira, 2015).

Conclusion

Did the referendum campaign make a difference? On the one hand, there is strong evidence that the level of support for independence rose and, by the

Robert Liñeira, Ailsa Henderson, and Liam Delaney

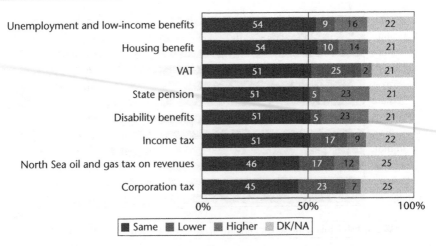

Figure 10.15. What should the Scottish Parliament do with the following taxation powers?
Source: Smith Survey 2014

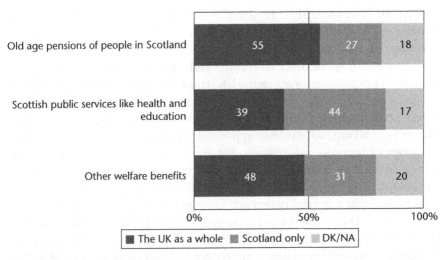

Figure 10.16. How should services be financed?
Source: Smith Survey 2014

end of the campaign, more voters were supporting independence than at the beginning. In fact, support for secession seems higher than ever. On the other hand, we did not find evidence that this upsurge in independence support brought along change in the socio-demographics of independence and union voters; the older, women, those born in the rest of the UK, and the middle class have consistently shown less support for independence.

Why did independence support surge? The most obvious possibility is that voters thought differently about the relative merits of independence or the problems of staying in the Union as a result of the debate. Our tracking of public opinion before and after the most intense period of the campaign shows some change in voters' perceptions. The most important difference is related to the fall in the risk perception of an independent Scotland not having access to the Bank of England. This may account for some of the Yes vote surge given the huge consideration that the electorate gave to this issue, but it is a change too small to reflect and account for the wider movement in voting intention.

It could also be the case that some changes occurred before the first wave of our panel in June 2014. After all, it had been a long campaign which, in contrast to the sixteen-week regulated period, arguably began when an agreement was reached on the question wording of the ballot paper in February 2013. The voting intention data show some surge on the Yes vote in the spring of 2014, but they also show that support for independence experienced a significant boost in the last weeks of the campaign. Some of the change therefore occurred or crystallized during the short campaign.

Change in perceptions is not the only possible explanation of the rise in independence support. Alternatively, the trend may result from a more consistent relationship between perceptions and preferences; that is, people's views of the consequences of independence and their willingness to support the idea would become more closely aligned during the course of the campaign. Curtice (2015a) presents evidence in favour of this argument, as do we. In our pre-referendum survey only 65 per cent of those who judged likely that an independent Scotland could maintain access to the Bank of England were in favour of independence; the percentage rose to 80 per cent in the post-referendum survey. Some other items also show change congruent with stronger consistency.

The campaign would have then helped some voters to reach a more consistent decision (Gelman and King, 1993). The fact that most of the campaign arguments were about independence rather than on the merits or otherwise of the Union raised independence considerations to the front of the voter's mind. In consequence it was people's views about independence that took centre stage in their referendum decision-making. In the context of a very salient debate which involved and engaged the electorate as never before, some voters who have always had sympathy for independence convinced themselves that the whole project was feasible. The result has been a change that has broken the mould of Scottish politics.

By contrast, independence was too uncertain for some other people. The unpredictability around many of the core outcomes led more risk-averse voters who may have seen some appeal in an independent Scotland to not vote for it. In particular, the uncertainty around the existing currency relationships and the whole economy implications in the event of a Yes seem to have been crucial for the choice of these voters.

11

Beyond the Referendum

Nicola McEwen and Michael Keating

Lessons of the Referendum

The unique Scottish experience provides many insights into the difficulties of conducting an independence referendum. Matters are so complex and the future so difficult to predict that providing an objective base of evidence is challenging. This gives ample opportunity for the two sides to offer reassurance or evoke uncertainty and risk. The issues themselves evolved during the campaign in response to polling and focus groups, as the two sides got the measure of the electorate's preoccupations. The aftermath was critically shaped by events during the campaign, notably the last-minute pledge by the No side rapidly to deliver more devolution if they won. It was a premise of our research project that there is a not a stark, binary distinction between independence and union but rather a whole range of positions on a series of issues, including macroeconomic policy, the currency, welfare, and shared institutions. The campaign and its aftermath fully vindicate this judgement. One issue was settled, in that the Yes side did not obtain a mandate for independence; but many of the other critical issues raised during the campaign have remained in contention in the post-referendum negotiations on further constitutional change. The United Kingdom remains an instructive example of state transformation and rescaling, as it continues to debate both its internal constitution and its external relationships with Europe and the world.

Dominant Campaign Themes

Reflecting on the different dimensions and issues of the referendum debate, some cross-cutting themes come to the fore. Prominent among them is the inherent uncertainty of the choice voters were asked to make. Any electoral contest brings with it an element of uncertainty. Parties compete on the basis of a set of manifesto commitments, policy priorities or—increasingly—their general competence to govern, but there are no guarantees that they will be able to deliver on these promises once confronted with the challenges of office. The prospect of a territory's secession from one state and the creation of a new independent state involves a level of uncertainty on an altogether different scale. As several of the chapters observe, there is no precedent for a territory within an advanced democratic state acceding to independence. As a result, there was scant comparative evidence upon which to draw. Even if there were, the context within which an independent Scotland would emerge could not be known in advance because it would be subject to the outcome of negotiations between the Scottish and UK governments, as well as the behaviour of citizens, businesses, investors, and the European and international community.

The Yes campaign attempted to mask the uncertainty by offering reassurances about the kind of Scotland that independence would create: an economically prosperous country with the resources and commitment to deliver progressive social justice; one where trade and people would cross the border freely, sharing a currency, a common market, and a variety of public institutions; a country that maintained a cooperative 'partnership of equals' with the rest of the UK while making the seamless transition to independent EU membership; and one that would be rid of nuclear weapons but remain a constructive member of the NATO alliance. As all of these scenarios were contingent upon the outcome of negotiations, the nature of the independence settlement, and the short- and medium-term reactions within and beyond Scotland, alleviating the sense of risk and uncertainty was always going to be difficult.

Also prominent is the contested nature of evidence across all campaign debates. As several of our contributors note, the documents emerging from each government were intended to support 'their' side in the debate. The Scottish Government's White Paper was designed to convince a mass audience of the merits of independence. The Scotland Analysis papers coordinated by the UK Treasury, while apparently presenting a fact-based, detailed analysis, were less accessible in style but no less partial. Officials of the European Union, who normally do not intervene in domestic political issues, gave contentious interpretations of the rules of entry of new member states, where there was in fact no law or precedent for the accession of part of an existing member state. Dispassionate voices attempted to intervene in the debate, but their evidence was often selectively presented by campaigns and the media. As Bell and Eiser note (Chapter 3), these analyses also suffered from the lack of available, accurate data on, for example, trade, indirect taxes, and

GNP. This was compounded by the intrinsic difficulty in producing reliable economic models for the future, given the often unreliable projections of demographic change or economic revenues and performance (not least the highly volatile price of oil). However, the unqualified campaign messages left no room for doubt about the future they desired or dreaded, creating a credibility gap from a voter perspective. Even some of the authoritative interventions from impartial bodies were less qualified than they might have been since they did not always acknowledge the inherent problems of futurology.

In addition to this inherent uncertainty we must recognize the tactical interest of those campaigning against independence or major constitutional change in generating the feeling that such a change would be a leap in the dark and fraught with difficulty. With one notable exception (on the currency), the leading No protagonists and the UK Government in particular were careful to avoid rejecting as impossible the propositions put forward by the SNP government; they were conscious of the danger of appearing to suggest that the Scots could not run their own affairs. The tactic was, rather, to point to the unknowns. They did not say that there could not be a common travel area between Scotland and the rest of the UK, but stressed that it would involve difficult negotiations and likely constraints on visa and immigration policy. They did not assert that an independent Scotland would be impoverished or face economic turmoil, but instead talked up the difficulties created by its relatively ageing population and diminishing and economically volatile natural resources. They did not insist that an independent Scotland could not become a member-state of the European Union or of NATO, but pointed to the obstacles that meant these outcomes would not be assured, and certainly not on the terms suggested by the Scottish Government. Only on the issue of a sterling currency union did the UK Government reject outright the position advanced by the Scottish Government, but even here, there remained doubt about the credibility of the claim. In this case, however, the Scottish Government itself created a sense of risk by its reluctance to offer a clear alternative (Plan B) should full currency union prove impossible.

Did the Campaign Matter?

The referendum campaign saw a massive mobilization of activists and a huge interest on the part of voters. It galvanized electors in a way that is unusual in modern politics. The turnout, at 85 per cent, with 97 per of eligible voters registering, was the highest on record. As a democratic experiment, it can be judged a success, irrespective of one's views on the merits of the main question.

In referendums, as in elections, vote choice is influenced to varying degrees by a mix of enduring sociological factors, party and territorial identification, and perceptions of the costs and benefits of the alternative outcomes. It is beyond the scope of this book to explore fully the reasons why people voted yes or no, but the analysis by Liñeira et al. (Chapter 10) does help to identify some patterns in referendum voting, and in particular the effects of the referendum campaign. In general, support for independence was strongest among men, younger and middle-aged voters, and those born in Scotland. National identity appears to be a strong influence, but is itself a complicated matter. Traditionally, SNP voters, independence supporters, and those identifying as Scottish were three groups, which overlapped but were not identical (Bond, 2000; Keating, 2009). The largest group of independence supporters was sometimes to be found among Labour voters (since, prior to 2011, there were many more of these). While Scottish identity has not intensified, it has become more politicized; there is now closer correlation between those identifying as strongly Scottish, those supporting independence, and those voting for the SNP.

The campaign did appear to make a difference, with a notable drift across most groups from No to Yes. This suggests that, in some respects at least, the Yes campaign's framing of the issues resonated more with the electorate than the core messages of their opponents. In the wake of the campaign, the surveys suggested that more were persuaded that an independent Scotland would be able to retain the pound and arrange a system of defence cooperation than believed so at an earlier period in the campaign, while in other matters such as the continued absence of border controls, and continued access to the BBC, most were already more closely aligned with the Yes than with the No side, and remained so even after the period of intense campaigning. Conversely, the dominant themes of risk and uncertainty that permeated the discourse of the No side also struck a chord with the electorate, especially those who were already more inclined to be risk averse (Henderson et al., 2014).

Any referendum which includes only two opposing options is likely to become polarized, especially one on as emotive an issue as political independence. That was certainly the case in the Scottish independence campaign with respect to the main protagonists in either camp. But the evidence from our surveys suggests strongly that the Scottish electorate is far less polarized than political debate and commentary would suggest. Electors appear to crowd into the middle ground, where the distinctions between a maximalist version of devolution within the union and a soft version of independence become very fine indeed. Both campaigns were acutely aware of this need to appeal to the median voter, influencing both the strategy, content, and perhaps especially the presentation of their respective constitutional offers. The term 'independence-lite' was never used by its protagonists, but the independence vision proffered by leading forces within the Yes movement was intended to appeal to those who favoured continued associations with the rest of the UK. The promise of 'nothing less than a modern form of Scottish Home Rule', as Gordon Brown put it ten days before the vote, had similar intentions of appealing to the middle ground.

Winners and Losers in the Referendum Debate

The Scottish independence referendum was never only about winning or losing. There was always the prospect that both sides could win—the No side securing its majority but the Yes side securing a sufficient level of support to bring pressure to bear on the UK Government and the UK parties to make further concessions to Scottish self-government. Understood in this way, it helps to explain why the SNP government embarked on an independence referendum gamble despite there being no obvious increase in support for independence among the electorate. Of course, they aimed to win the vote when it was held, by convincing a majority of Scots that independence offered the best prospects for their country. In the process, they initiated a campaign which gave birth to a movement that spread beyond the confines of the Scottish National Party and achieved a level of support for independence which reached an historic high.

That the referendum was a victory of sorts for the Yes campaign and the SNP in particular is evident in the party's success in the year that followed. At the time of the referendum, the party had just over 25,000 members—by some distance the largest of Scotland's political parties. Within six months, membership figures were in excess of 100,000. Its new leader, Nicola Sturgeon, built upon the profile she had secured in the referendum campaign, as well as her years as a minister, to become not only the most popular politician in Scotland but, according to one poll (TNS), the most popular politician across Britain (Settle, 2015), and, in another, the most popular and widely appreciated living person among Scots! (YouGov, 2015) That popularity was evident in the UK General Election, where the SNP gained all but three of the seats in Scotland, and 50 per cent of the popular vote. The scale of the SNP's achievement in the election is evident in Table 11.1. The party increased its share of the vote by 30 percentage points, gaining fifty seats compared to its previous General Election performance. That the party gained from the referendum was not a surprise, but the extent to which it has done so, at least in the short term, has been staggering.

The referendum, then, produced more than one winner. More surprising, perhaps, is the extent to which the parties on the winning side failed to capitalize on their victory. For some parties within Better Together, the

Table 11.1. Result of 2015 General Election in Scotland

	SNP	Labour	Cons	Lib Dem	Greens	UKIP
% vote share	50	24.3	14.9	7.6	1.3	1.6
+/– since 2010	+30	−17.7	−1.8	−11.3	+0.7	+0.9
No. of seats	56	1	1	1	–	–
+/– since 2010	+50	−40	–	10	–	–
Deposits lost	0	3	2	47	28	41

referendum victory appeared to come at a cost. The Conservatives, already unpopular in Scotland, suffered their worst electoral performance in a UK election in Scotland. The Scottish Liberal Democrats had already paid an electoral price in the 2011 Scottish parliamentary election for the UK party's governing alliance with Conservatives. It was reduced to just five (out of 129) MSPs in 2011, and sunk to similar depths in the 2015 UK election. The Labour Party suffered the most dramatic decline. Long the dominant force in Scottish politics, the party's representation in the House of Commons was reduced to a single seat in 2015 and its share of the vote collapsed. Its failure in Scotland confirms the unprecedented fragmentation of UK party politics and representation. In effect, there is no longer a British party system but a differentiated pattern of party competition, in which Scottish politics may become more self-referential and British[1] parties find it difficult to assemble majorities across the country.

The spatial and temporal context of this debate had a significant effect on the way it developed. The Cold War had ended a quarter of a century earlier, so that issues of defence and security were less salient than they might have been in an earlier era. For forty years, the United Kingdom had been a member of the European Communities/Union, based on ideas of shared sovereignty and open economic borders; neither side sought to challenge the desirability of this order, which does represent a new form of overarching authority or union. Had the UK decided to join the euro, then the Yes side would have had a clearer answer on what an independent Scotland's currency would be. On the other hand, the travails of the eurozone focused academic and political attention on the difficulties of operating a currency union without a political union, casting doubt on the proposal to keep the pound. The Yes side's economic calculations, at least in the short term, depended on an oil price of over $100 a barrel, which is about where they were. A year and a half later, the value of oil had plummeted. Of course, it was recognized that oil prices fluctuate, but independence would have been a harder sell with the price

---

[1] We say British because the party system in Northern Ireland has always been distinct.

under $30. The debate also coincided with a programme for reforming the welfare state which became intricately bound up with the question of independence. It occurred before the May 2015 General Election, which produced a Conservative majority government in the UK, despite continuing low levels of Conservative support in Scotland. This government in turn introduced a referendum on British membership of the European Union, which was addressed quite differently in Scotland and brought back the question of Scotland's place in Europe. These contextual conditions are continuing to evolve as does the domestic political balance within Scotland.

This all underlines the fact that the referendum on independence did not settle the issue of Scotland's future. The Union, and Scotland's place within it, will continue to be a key debate in Scottish politics and the key fault-line in party political debate. The Prime Minister declared frequently that the devolution reforms in the Scotland Bill 2015 would ensure a settlement that is 'built to last'. This is unlikely. Political developments and electoral dynamics, as well as the institutional complexities and interdependencies associated with the proposed new competences, point to the prospect of at least a further revision of devolution sooner rather than later.

A second independence referendum is not out of the question, but nor is it inevitable. The SNP faces challenges as a government and party in a difficult fiscal environment. The long-term popularity of the party and its leader cannot be taken for granted. Moreover, the party leadership will not push for another referendum unless it is confident that it can win it—losing one referendum may be a victory of sorts; losing two, however narrowly, could be devastating to the still deeply held ambition to ensure Scotland becomes an independent country.

When No Means More

The intergovernmental Edinburgh Agreement that paved the way for the transfer of legal competence to the Scottish Parliament to hold the referendum ensured that the electorate would only be given a binary choice for or against independence. Yet voting Yes (according to the SNP) meant supporting a particular, attenuated form of independence, while voting No did not mean maintenance of the status quo. Further confusion was introduced by the now infamous 'vow' made by the three UK party leaders two days prior to the referendum vote, following publication of an opinion poll suggesting a majority might vote Yes. Published on the front page of a Labour-supporting tabloid newspaper on mock parchment, the vow promised a 'permanent' Scottish Parliament with 'extensive new powers', continuity of the Barnett formula, and 'faster, safer, better change than separation' (*Daily Record*, 16 September

2015). In the run-up to the referendum, all three main UK parties had conducted internal inquiries resulting in the offer of further devolution, focused principally on varying degrees of fiscal autonomy. Because of the wording of the referendum question, however, none of the proposals were subject to scrutiny in the campaign—the original intention was for them to become manifesto commitments ahead of the 2015 UK election.

Instead, the Smith Commission, a closed cross-party brokering process initiated by the Prime Minister on the morning after the referendum, was instructed to produce proposals for further devolution by St Andrew's Day (30 November) with a commitment to draft legislative clauses by Burns' Day (25 January). Although both Yes and No parties (SNP, Green, Conservative, Labour, and Liberal Democrat) were represented, there was scarce time for a considered review of devolution and the haste of the process attracted considerable criticism. Draft clauses were indeed produced before the 2015 General Election and a Scotland Bill was the first piece of legislation introduced to the new Parliament. The new devolution settlement will herald a significant transfer of constitutional competences from Westminster to the Scottish Parliament, most notably in tax and welfare, but the 'fiscal framework', which determines the overall funding available to Scotland, remained a matter of intergovernmental negotiation conducted behind closed doors. After the massive public engagement during the referendum campaign, the secretive and elite-led nature of this process generated considerable disillusionment.

It is telling that many of the uncertainties which surrounded debates on tax, welfare, and the economy in the referendum campaign remain relevant to the context of reforming devolution, although neither government seems keen to draw attention to these. The UK Government and Better Together talked up the complexities of disentangling a highly integrated social security system during a transition to independence, and the costs of setting up new Scottish welfare bureaucracies, but the same challenges face government in the context of further devolution. Indeed, a partial devolution of social security is arguably even more complex. The interdependence between entitlements to reserved benefits and those to be devolved heightens the prospect of policy decisions at one level having spill-over effects at the other. The Scottish Government will have power to introduce new benefits, top-up reserved benefits, and shape the newly devolved welfare benefits. Yet if it exercises these powers in ways that diverge from UK policy, it might be necessary to set up separate Scottish delivery agencies. Conversely, if the two governments share a welfare bureaucracy (as had been intended for the early post-independence years), this would mean the Scottish Government paying the UK Government to deliver services on its behalf, and would carry the additional cost of limiting the scope for policy deviation. The Smith Commission introduced the principle of 'no detriment', according to which if one government takes action that imposes costs upon the other then compensation may be due, but there was no detail on how this such a principle could be upheld and implemented.

The impact of tax devolution on the economy and on the Scottish Government's capacity to raise revenue is hampered by the same lack of available, accurate data that beset economic modelling in the referendum campaign, as has been highlighted in both UK and Scottish parliaments and within the academic community. The new settlement is set to transfer 100 per cent of taxes on earned income. So Scots will no longer pay income tax to the UK Government and the Scottish Government will set the rates and thresholds for Scottish tax payers. The personal allowance, taxes on savings and dividends, capital gains tax, and national insurance—all of which interact very closely with income tax on earnings—will remain reserved and, consequently, Scottish tax autonomy will be shaped by UK policy decisions over which it will have no control. The new settlement will leave the Scottish Government heavily reliant on revenues from one tax and a very small group of high-earning tax payers[2] without giving it control over those other areas of tax, economic, and employment policy that contribute to the health of the economy (McEwen, 2016; Bell, 2015). As Bell and Eiser point out (Chapter 3), we know too little about the attitudes and likely behaviours of those high earners contributing the bulk of Scottish tax revenues to anticipate how they would respond, either to independence or to tax policy changes under enhanced devolution. In light of constitutional and financial constraints, and the ongoing pressures of UK fiscal consolidation, the Scottish Government may find it difficult to maintain existing levels of public provision without increasing taxes, before even considering whether to exercise new powers such as the power to 'top-up' UK welfare benefits.

Far from resolving uncertainties, then, the outcome of the referendum has been to generate further doubts about the future of taxes and public services in Scotland. In contrast to the referendum campaign, which generated such unprecedented public engagement and debate, the process of constitutional change conducted in the wake of the referendum has largely excluded the public. The crisis engulfing the unionist parties in the wake of the referendum has also narrowed the scope of political debate in Scotland. With the SNP still committed to independence and the unionist parties seriously debilitated following the referendum and the General Election, nobody really owns the emerging model of enhanced devolution.

---

[2] As Bell (2015) identified, 10 per cent of earners contribute more than 50 per cent of all Scottish income tax revenues and the top 5 per cent (around 130,000 people) contribute 40 per cent of revenues.

Beyond the Scottish Case

The Scottish experience in 2014 was followed closely around the world and especially in Europe, where many feared that the Scottish precedent could have a destabilizing influence, encouraging other nationalist movements to demand their own referendums. The same year saw a massive mobilization in Catalonia, where support for independence had been rising for some years, to equal or surpass the traditional Catalan preference for home rule. The Spanish constitution clearly prohibits secession, although it is debatable whether it prohibits a consultative referendum. Independence supporters made much use of the Scottish precedent and, when an official referendum was refused, the Catalan Government organized an unofficial one in November (boycotted by most unionists) followed by 'plebiscitary elections', which also produced an ambivalent outcome. Neither side accepted the legitimacy of the other's position and the Spanish Government explicitly rejected the Scottish precedent on the grounds that Spain has a written constitution that affirms the unity of Spain.

Yet the Scottish example has shown that, in the right conditions, a potentially polarizing question can be addressed through public debate and resolved with an agreed procedure and a democratic vote that is accepted by both sides. It shows that constitutions can be interpreted in a flexible manner. This is not inherent in the constitutional practice of the United Kingdom. In the late nineteenth century, Conservative and Unionist governments persistently refused to allow even home rule for Ireland. When, in the early twentieth century, the Liberal government proposed Irish home rule, the Conservative leadership even countenanced armed resistance among the Ulster Protestants. Only after a violent conflict did the British Parliament accept Irish independence and that was initially within the framework of the Empire and monarchy. During the 1980s and 1990s, Conservative governments refused devolution for Scotland in the face of manifest demands. The Edinburgh Agreement must therefore be seen as part of a new approach to the politics of national accommodation.

In this it resembles the judgment of the Supreme Court of Canada (1998), which followed a reference by the Canadian Government, anxious to block another independence referendum in Quebec. The Court found that the Constitution did not grant self-determination to Quebec. On the other hand, it should be interpreted in a democratic mode, in which case a clear decision on secession by a clear majority would create a duty on the part of Canada to negotiate. Although Canada and Quebec have never agreed on how to interpret this judgment in practice, it has changed thinking about self-determination around the world.

Fears that the Scottish case would provoke a chain-reaction around Europe have not materialized, although matters could have been different had the Yes side won. The circumstances of each case are quite different. The Basque Nationalist Party, even faced with competition from more radical nationalists, has explicitly chosen not to follow the Catalan road but is seeking a new form of accommodation within a plurinational Spain; this represents a moderation of its previous position. In Flanders, the New Flemish Alliance in principle supports independence, but, faced with the lack of popular support, it has chosen a long road. Ironically, after the 2014 elections, in which it came first and subsequently joined the Belgian government, there was, for the first time in many years, no commitment to further transfer of powers to the regions and communities. A referendum on independence was held in March 2014 in the Italian region of Veneto, generating a large Yes majority, but this was a piece of political theatre. The poll was online, there were many questions about the identity of voters, and it was safe to vote Yes, knowing that there were no consequences. There is no sign that the major European states are about to disintegrate, but there are still independence-seeking movements, and from time to time they will be in a position to pose the question.

This is an issue that international and European institutions are poorly equipped to address. The suggestion by some EU officials that an independent Scotland, however democratically achieved, could be excluded from EU membership appears at odds with the European commitment to self-determination and democracy. It is likely that the EU may have to confront at some point the prospect of a territory of an existing member state seceding and seeking to remain an EU member. There has long been a commitment to enlargement of the EU to encompass the whole of Europe and, since the Lisbon Treaty, there is provision for the negotiated secession from the EU of an existing member state. There may now be a case for a provision on 'internal enlargement' or rules for the accommodation of new states emerging within the existing union.

We have emphasized the forced nature of the choice between independence and union and how it simplified the issues at stake, with both sides presenting more nuanced visions; indeed each side was able to deploy the language both of self-government and of union. This, too, has broader implications for a Europe in which political authority is rescaling at multiple levels and across multiple dimensions. The United Kingdom's flexible constitution has allowed it to experiment with new forms of territorial government without worrying about constitutional restrictions or doctrines of unity and symmetry. We might even say (tongue in cheek) that it has made the transition from a premodern polity (mocked by Tom Nairn as an *ancien régime*) to a post-modern order without being caught in the rigid form of the modern nation-state (Keating, 2009). This, too, has lessons for other plurinational states, especially within the European Union.

The European issue did not play a big part in the referendum campaign and largely focused on the question of whether an independent Scotland could become a member. Yet the European question is now intrinsically linked to the internal constitutional question in the United Kingdom, as its component parts adjust in different ways to the result of the 2016 Brexit referendum. It may be time to revisit the role that regions and stateless nations can play within European institutions, offering a role short of full membership where that is the choice of its citizens. The European state system is still based on a conventional view of the sovereign nation-state out of touch with the reality of a complex and multi-scalar order which European integration has itself helped to generate.

In this book, we have treated the independence question as a constitutional one, focused on sovereignty, but our particular contribution has been to link constitutional issues to public policy questions, to ask exactly what Scotland could do under different constitutional dispensations and in particular to examine the debate about the status and policy capacities of Scotland as an independent country. This, too, has wider resonance as other European states decentralize and federalize and difficult policy questions are addressed at new scales. Our next book, from the same project, will use Scotland to ask what a small jurisdiction, possessed of substantial powers but not formal sovereignty, can do to address big and long-term issues of sustainable growth and social cohesion.

Bibliography

Acemoglu, D. and Robinson, J. A. (2012) *Why Nations Fail: The Origins of Power, Prosperity and Poverty*. London: Profile Books Ltd.

Aghion, P. and Howitt, P. (2009) *The Economics of Growth*. Cambridge, MA: MIT Press.

Alesina, A. and Barro, R. (2001) Dollarization. *American Economic Review*. Vol. 91(2), pp. 381–5.

Alesina, A. and Spolaore, E. (2005) *The Size of Nations*. Cambridge, MA: MIT Press.

Allan, T. R. S. (1994) *Law, Liberty, and Justice: The Legal Foundations of British Constitutionalism*. Oxford: Clarendon Press.

Allen, A. D. (2012) Buying Votes, Building Identities: Federal Social Policy Responses to Sub-State Nationalism in Québec. *American Review of Canadian Studies*. Vol. 42(2), pp. 210–35.

Amior, M., Crawford, R., and Tetlow, G. (2013) Fiscal Sustainability of an Independent Scotland. Institute for Fiscal Studies. November. Available at: http://www.ifs.org.uk/comms/r88.pdf (accessed 8 Aug 2016).

Anderson, J. E. and van Wincoop, E. (2003) Gravity with Gravitas: A Solution to the Border Puzzle. *The American Economic Review*. Vol. 93, pp. 170–92.

The Andrew Marr Show (2014a) BBC. 7 September.

The Andrew Marr Show (2014b) BBC. 14 September.

Armstrong, A. and Ebell, M. (2013) *Scotland's Currency Options*. London: National Institute of Economic and Social Research, NIESR Discussion Paper 415.

Armstrong, A. and Ebell, M. (2014a) *Sterling currency zone would not include a Fiscal Compact or Banking Union and resemble 'dollarization'*. London: National Institute of Economic and Social Research.

Armstrong, A. and Ebell, M. (2014b) *Assets and Liabilities and Scottish Independence* (No. 11820). National Institute of Economic and Social Research.

Arter, D. (1999) *Scandinavian Politics Today*. Manchester: Manchester University Press.

Avery, G. (2014a) *Could an independent Scotland join the European Union?* Policy Brief. Brussels: European Policy Centre.

Avery, G. (2014b) *Independentism and the European Union*. Policy Brief. Brussels: European Policy Centre.

Bailes, A., Thorhallsson, B., and Johnstone, R. (2013) Scotland as an independent small state: where would it seek shelter? *Fræðigreinar—Icelandic review of politics and administration*. Vol. 9(1), pp. 1–20.

Baldersheim, H. and Keating, M. (eds) (2015) *Small States in the Modern World*. Cheltenham: Edward Elgar.

Bibliography

Banting, K. G. (1995) The welfare state as statecraft: territorial politics and Canadian social policy, in Leibfried, S. and Pierson, P. (eds) *European Social Policy—Between Fragmentation and Integration*. Washington, DC: The Brookings Institute, pp. 269–300.

Banting, K. G. (2005) Canada: nation-building in a federal welfare state, in Obinger, H. et al. (eds) *Federalism and the Welfare State*. Cambridge: Cambridge University Press.

BBC Sunday Politics (2008) *Jon Sopel interview with Alex Salmond*. 12 October 2008. Available at: http://news.bbc.co.uk/1/hi/programmes/politics_show/7665915.stm (accessed 8 Aug 2016).

BBC Trust (2015) *Scotland Annual Review 2014–15*. Available at: http://www.bbc.co.uk/bbctrust/who_we_are/audience_councils/scotland/annual_review.html (accessed 8 Aug 2016).

Bechhofer, F. and McCrone, D. (2009) *National Identity, Nationalism and Constitutional Change*. Basingstoke: Palgrave.

Béland, D. and Lecours, A. (2008) *Nationalism and Social Policy*. Oxford: Oxford University Press.

Bélanger, É. and Perrella, A. (2008) Facteurs d'appui à la souveraineté du Québec chez les jeunes: Une comparaison entre francophones, anglophones et allophones. *Politique et Sociétés*. Vol. 27(3), pp. 13–40.

Bell, D. (2015) *A Year On . . . A Report for the Hunter Foundation*. Available at: http://www.thehunterfoundation.co.uk/wp-content/uploads/2016/03/a-year-on.pdf (accessed 8 Aug 2016).

Bell, D., Comerford, D., and Eiser, D. (2014) State pensions and independence: assessing the views of the Scottish and UK Governments. *Centre on Constitutional Change blog*. Available at: http://www.centreonconstitutionalchange.ac.uk/blog/state-pensions-independence-assessing-views-scottish-uk-governments (accessed 8 Aug 2016).

Bell, D., Delaney, L., and McGoldrick, M. (2014) *Citizen Preferences for Constitutional Change in Scotland*. Edinburgh: Centre on Constitutional Change. Available at: http://www.centreonconstitutionalchange.ac.uk/sites/default/files/papers/Citizen%20Preferences%20for%20Constitutional%20Change%20in%20Scotland.pdf (accessed 8 Aug 2016).

Bell, D. and Eiser, D. (2015) The Economic Case for Further Fiscal Decentralisation to Scotland: Theoretical and Empirical Perspectives. *National Institute Economic and Social Review*. Vol. 233, R27–R36.

Bell, D. N. F. and McGoldrick, M. (2014) Business Attitudes to Constitutional Change. Available at: http://www.scottishchambers.org.uk/userfiles/files/SCC%20Constitutional%20Survey.pdf (accessed 8 Aug 2016).

Benford, R. D. and Snow, D. A. (2000) Framing processes and social movements: an overview and assessment. *Annual Review of Sociology*. Vol. 26, pp. 11–39.

Berger, M., Munger, M. and Potthoff, R. (2000) The Downsian Model Predicts Divergence. *Journal of Theoretical Politics*. Vol. 12(2), pp. 228–40.

Better Together (2014a) *A Sharing Union: Our case on Social Security*. Edinburgh: Better Together.

Better Together (2014b) *Scotland in the UK: The case for our NHS*. Edinburgh: Better Together.

Billig, M. (1995) *Banal Nationalism*. London: Sage.

Blackhurst, C. (2014) John Swinney interview on Scottish independence: Can we go it alone and pay our way. Of course we can. *The Independent*. 23 June.

Blais, A., Martin, P., and Nadeau, R. (1995) Attentes économiques et linguistiques et appui à la souveraineté du Québec: Une analyse prospective et comparative. *Canadian Journal of Political Science/Revue canadienne de science politique*. Vol. 28(4), pp. 637–57.

Blais, A. and Nadeau, R. (1992) To Be or Not to Be Sovereignist: Quebeckers' Perennial Dilemma. *Canadian Public Policy/Analyse de Politiques*. Vol. 18(1), pp. 89–103.

Boardman, A., Greenberg, D., Vining, A., and Weimer, D. (1996) *Cost-Benefit Analysis: Concepts and Practice*. Upper Saddle River, NJ: Prentice Hall.

Bond, R. (2000) Squaring the Circles: Demonstrating and Explaining the Political 'Non-Alignment' of Scottish National Identity. *Scottish Affairs*, Vol. 32, pp. 15–35.

Bonoli, G. (2000) *The Politics of Pension Reform: Institutions and Policy Change in Western Europe*. Cambridge: Cambridge University Press.

Bowler, S. and Donovan, T. (2000) *Demanding Choices*. Ann Arbor: Michigan University Press.

Briggs, A. (2000) The welfare state in historical perspective, in Pierson, C. and Castle F. G. (eds) *The Welfare State: A Reader*. Cambridge: Polity Press.

Brown, G. (2012) *Pro-Union speech*. Kirkcaldy. 3 November. Available at: http://www.scotsman.com/news/politics/gordon-brown-s-pro-union-speech-in-full-1-2613258 (accessed 8 Aug 2016).

Brown, G. (2014a) *My Scotland, Our Britain: A Future Worth Sharing*. London: Simon and Schuster.

Brown, G. (2014b) *Silent no more*. Better Together Love Scotland Vote No rally, Maryhill. 17 September.

Brown, G. and Alexander, D. (1999) *New Scotland, New Britain*. Speech to the Smith Institute conference on Britishness. 15 April.

Buchanan, R. (2013) Scottish Independence: Yes chairman Canavan backs Scots currency. BBC News. 30 April.

Burns, H. (2014) Harry Burns: UK faces increasing NHS privatisation and there is little Scotland can do if we remain in union. *Sunday Herald*. 14 September.

Carney, M. (2014) The economics of currency unions. Edinburgh, 29 January.

Carrell, S. and Brooks, L. (2014) Scottish debate: Salmond and Darling in angry clash over independence. *The Guardian*. 6 August.

Cellan-Jones, R. (2014) Who has won the social referendum? *BBC News Technology*. Available at: http://www.bbc.co.uk/news/technology-29235876 (accessed 8 Aug 2016).

Centre for Macroeconomics (2014) Economic Consequences of an Independent Scotland. Available at: http://cfmsurvey.org/surveys/economic-consequences-independent-scotland-june-2014 (accessed 8 Aug 2016).

Centre for Public Policy for Regions (2014) CPPR Briefing Note—Fiscal Implications for an independent Scotland when assuming that it takes on a low, or zero, share of existing debt.

Chalmers, H. and Chalmers, M. (2014) Relocation, Relocation, Relocation: Could the UK's Nuclear Force be Moved after Scottish Independence? *Occasional Paper*. London: RUSI.

Chalmers, M. (2012) Kingdom's end? *RUSI journal*. Vol. 157(3), pp. 6–11.

Chalmers, M. (2013) Scotland's cooperative option—could post-independence defence costs be reduced through a 'special relationship' with the UK? *Glasgow Global Security Network Conference: Global Security, National Defence, and the Future of Scotland*. Glasgow University, 8 and 9 November 2013.

Choudhry, S. (ed.) (2011) *The Migration of Constitutional Ideas*. Cambridge: Cambridge University Press.

Christie, A. and Swales, J. K. (2010) The Barnett allocation mechanism: Formula plus influence. *Regional Studies*. Vol. 44, pp. 761–75.

Christin, T., Hug, S., and Sciarini, P. (2002) Interests and Information in Referendum Voting: An Analysis of Swiss Voters. *European Journal of Political Research*. Vol. 41(6), pp. 759–76.

Clarke, H., Kornberg, A., and Stewart, M. (2004) Referendum Voting as Political Choice: The Case of Quebec. *British Journal of Political Science*. Vol. 34(2), pp. 345–55.

Clegg, N. (2010) Fair Shares. *The Northern Echo*. 29 June.

Colls, R. (2002) *Identity of England*. Oxford: Oxford University Press.

Colquhoun, R. (2014) *Social Media: #YesBecause*. Available at: http://www.rosscolquhoun.com/journal/2015/8/23/hashtag-yesbecause (accessed 8 Aug 2016).

Comerford, D. and Rodriguez Mora, J. V. (2015) The Gains from Economic Integration. *Discussion Paper, Department of Economics*. University of Edinburgh.

Commission on Scottish Devolution (2009) *Serving Scotland Better: Scotland and the United Kingdom in the 21st Century*. Final Report. June. Available at: http://www.scottishconstitutionalfutures.org/Resources/UsefulPublications/OfficialPublications/tabid/1778/Default.aspx (accessed 8 Aug 2016).

Coughlin, C. C. and Novy, D. (2011) Is the International Border Effect Larger than the Domestic Border Effect? Evidence from U.S. Trade. *Federal Reserve Bank of St. Louis Research Division, Working Paper 2009–057C*.

Crawford, J. and Boyle, A. (2013) Referendum on the Independence of Scotland International Law Aspects. *Annex to the UK Government's Report on 'Devolution and the Implications of Scottish Independence'*. UK Government, Cm 8554.

Crawford, S. and Marsh, R. (2012) A' The Blue Bonnets: Defending an Independent Scotland. *Whitehall Report* 3–12. Royal United Services Institute.

Curtice, J. (2015a) *Has the Referendum Campaign Made a Difference?* Edinburgh: ScotCen. Available at: http://www.centreonconstitutionalchange.ac.uk/sites/default/files/papers/SSA%202014%20Launch%20JC%20Briefing%20FINAL.pdf (accessed 8 Aug 2016).

Curtice, J. (2015b) *How Scotland Voted: Economic Perceptions in the Scottish Independence Referendum*. Glasgow: International Public Policy Institute Policy. Available at: http://strathprints.strath.ac.uk/53562/1/CurticeJ_IPPI_2015_How_Scotland_voted_economic_perceptions_in_the_Scottish_independence_referendum.pdf (accessed 8 Aug 2016).

Curtice, J. (2015c) Scotland 'one year on': the legacy of the independence referendum. *IPPI Occasional Paper*. University of Strathclyde.

Cuthbert, J. and Cuthbert, M. (2014) The IFS 'observation' on funding Scotland's NHS ignores the key risk to the NHS within the UK. Available at: http://bellacaledonia.org.uk/2014/09/12/the-ifs-observation-on-funding-scotlands-nhs-ignores-the-key-risk-to-the-nhs-within-the-uk/ (accessed 8 Aug 2016).

Dicey, A. V. (1912) *A Leap in the Dark. A Criticism of the Principles of Home Rule as Illustrated by the Bill of 1893*, 3rd edn. London: John Murray.

Dicey, A. V. and Rait, R. (1920) *Thoughts on the Union between England and Scotland.* London: Macmillan.

Dion, S. (1991) Le nationalisme dans la convergence culturelle. Le Québec contemporain et le paradoxe de Tocqueville, in Hudon, R. and Pelletier, R. (eds) *L'engagement intellectuel. Mélanges en l'honneur de Léon Dion.* Sainte-Foy: Presses de l'Université de Laval.

Dorman, A. (2012) Written evidence: defence impact of Scottish independence. House of Commons Defence Committee: *Defence implications of possible Scottish independence.* HC.483, session 2012–13.

Douglas-Scott, S. (2014) *(How easily) Could an Independent Scotland Join the EU?* University of Oxford Legal Research Paper Series.

Edinburgh Centre for Constitutional Law (2013) Beyond the Referendum: A Supreme Court for Scotland? *Edinburgh Centre for Constitutional Law and Scottish Public Law Group seminar.* March.

Edward, D. (2012) *Scotland and the European Union.* Scottish Constitutional Futures Forum. Available at: http://www.scottishconstitutionalfutures.org (accessed 8 Aug 2016).

Edward, D. (2014) Agenda: Let me explain why I am a Unionist and will vote No in the referendum. *The Herald.* 12 July.

El Economista (2015) No habrá independencia de Cataluña: Rajoy. 19 August.

Electoral Commission (2013) *Referendum on independence for Scotland. Advice of the Electoral Commission on the proposed referendum question.* Available at: http://www. electoralcommission.org.uk/__data/assets/pdf_file/0007/153691/Referendum-on-independence-for-Scotland-our-advice-on-referendum-question.pdf (accessed 8 Aug 2016).

Electoral Commission (2015) *Scottish Independence Referendum Report on the regulation of campaigners at the independence referendum held on 18 September 2014.* Available at: http://www.electoralcommission.org.uk/__data/assets/pdf_file/0018/190521/Casework-and-spending-report.pdf (accessed 8 Aug 2016).

Elkins, Z., Ginsburg, T., and Melton, J. (2009) *The Endurance of National Constitutions.* Cambridge: Cambridge University Press.

Elliott, M. (2015) The Draft Scotland Bill and the sovereignty of the UK Parliament. *Public Law for Everyone blog.* 22 January. Available at: http://publiclawforeveryone. com/2015/01/22/the-draft-scotland-bill-and-the-sovereignty-of-the-uk-parliament/ (8 Aug 2016).

Entman, R. M. (1993) Framing: Toward Clarification of a Fractured Paradigm. *Journal of Communication.* Vol. 43, pp. 51–8.

Expert Working Group on Welfare (2013) *First Report.* Edinburgh: Scottish Government.

Expert Working Group on Welfare and Constitutional Reform (2014) *Re-thinking Welfare: Fair, Personal and Simple.* Edinburgh: Scottish Government.

Finlay, R. (1997) *A Partnership for Good? Scottish Politics and the Union since 1880.* Edinburgh: John Donald.

Fiscal Commission Working Group (2013) *First Report—Macroeconomic Framework.* Scottish Government.

Fleming, C. (2014) After independence? The challenges and benefits of Scottish—UK defence cooperation. *International Affairs*. Vol. 90(4), pp. 761–71.

Fleming, C. and Gebhard, C. (2014) Scotland, NATO, and transatlantic security. *European Security*. Vol. 23(3), pp. 307–25.

Foley, J. and Ramand, P, (2014) *Yes: The Radical Case for Scottish Independence*. London: Pluto.

Foreign Affairs Committee of Session (2013) *Foreign Policy Considerations for the UK and Scotland in the Event of Scotland Becoming an Independent Country*, in *Response from the Secretary of State for Foreign and Commonwealth Affairs*. Sixth report. London: HM Government.

Friedman, M. (1953) The Methodology of Positive Economics, in *Essays in Positive Economics*. Chicago: Chicago University Press.

Gaines, B. and Kuklinski, J. (2011) Treatment Effects, in Druckman, J. N., Green, D. P., Kuklinski, J. H., and Lupia, A. (eds) *Cambridge Handbook of Experimental Political Science*. Cambridge and New York: Cambridge University Press.

Gall, G. (2013) *Scotland the Brave? Independence and Radical Social Change*. Biggar: Scottish Left Review.

Gardiner, B., Martin, R., Sunley, P., and Tyler, P. (2013) Spatially Unbalanced Growth in the British Economy. *Journal of Economic Geography*. Vol. 13, pp. 889–928.

Garea, F. (2014) Rajoy advierte que consultas en Escocia y Cataluña provocan 'pobreza y recesión'. *Política*. 27 September.

Gelman, A. and King, G. (1993) Why Are American Presidential Election Campaign Polls So Variable When Votes Are So Predictable? *British Journal of Political Science*. Vol. 23(4), pp. 409–51.

Gibbons, R. (1992) *A Primer in Game Theory*. Harlow: Prentice Hall.

Gitlin, T. (1980) *The Whole World is Watching: Mass Media in the Making & Unmaking of the News*. Berkeley: University of California Press.

Goudie, A. (ed.) (2013) *Scotland's Future: The Economics of Constitutional Change*. Dundee: Dundee University Press.

Gulde, A. M. and Tsangarides, C. (2008) *The CFA Franc Zone: Common Currency, Uncommon Challenges*. New York: International Monetary Fund.

Hallahan, K. (2011) Political public relations and strategic framing, in Stromback, J. and Kiousis, S. (eds) *Political Public Relations: Principles and Applications*. New York: Taylor & Francis.

Harvey, M. (2015) A Social Democratic Future? Political and Institutional Hurdles in Scotland. *The Political Quarterly*. Vol. 86(2), pp. 249–56.

Hazell, R. and O'Leary, B. (1999) A rolling programme of devolution, slippery slope or safeguard of the Union?, in Hazell, R. (ed.) *Constitutional Futures. A History of the Next Ten Years*. Oxford: Oxford University Press.

Hearn, J. (2000) *Claiming Scotland. National Identity and Liberal Culture*. Edinburgh: Polygon.

Helleiner, E. (1998) Historicizing Territorial Currencies: Monetary Space and the Nation-State in North America. *Political Geography*. Vol. 18, pp. 309–39.

Helleiner, E. (2003) *The Making of National Money: Territorial Currencies in Historical Perspective*. Cornell: Cornell University Press.

Helleiner, E. (2007) *Towards North American Monetary Union? The Politics and History of Canada's Exchange Rate Regime*. Montreal: McGill-Queen's University Press.

Helpman, E. (2008) *Institutions and Economic Performance*. Cambridge, MA: Harvard University Press.

Henderson, A. (2007) *Hierarchies of Belonging: National Identity and Political Culture in Scotland and Quebec*. Montreal: McGill-Queen's University Press.

Henderson, A., Delaney, L., and Liñeira, R. (2014) Risk and Attitudes to Constitutional Change. Available at: http://www.centreonconstitutionalchange.ac.uk/publications/research-briefings/risk-and-attitudes-constitutional-change (accessed 18 Aug 2016).

Henderson, A., Jeffery, C., and Liñeira, R. (2015) National Identity or National Interest? Scottish, English and Welsh Attitudes to the Constitutional Debate. *Political Quarterly*, Vol. 86(2), pp. 265–74.

Henderson, A., Jeffery, C., and Wincott, D. (eds) (2013) *Citizenship after the Nation State. Regionalism, Nationalism and Public Attitudes in Europe*. Basingstoke: Palgrave Macmillan.

Hepburn, E. (2010) *Using Europe. Territorial Party Strategies in a Multi-level System*. Manchester: Manchester University Press.

Hildreth, P. and Bailey, D. (2013) The Economics Behind the Move to 'Localism' in England. *Cambridge Journal of Regions, Economy and Society*. Vol. 6, pp. 233–49.

Hirschl, R. (2004) *Towards Juristocracy: The Origins and Consequences of the New Constitutionalism*. Cambridge and London: Harvard University Press.

HM Government (1998) Human Rights Act. London: HMSO.

HM Government (2010a) *Local Growth: Realising Every Place's Potential*. Cm 7961.

HM Government (2010b) *Securing Britain in an age of uncertainty: The strategic defence and security review*. October. Cm 7948.

HM Government (2011) European Union Act. London: HMSO.

HM Government (2013a) *Scotland Analysis: Currency and monetary policy*.

HM Government (2013b) *Scotland Analysis: Defence*.

HM Government (2013c) *Scotland Analysis: Devolution and the implications of Scottish independence*. Cm 8554. London: HMSO.

HM Government (2013d) *Scotland Analysis: Macroeconomic and fiscal performance*. Cm 8694. London: TSO.

HM Government (2013e) *Scotland Analysis: Security*.

HM Government (2013f) *The Green Book, Appraisal and Evaluation in Central Government*. London: TSO.

HM Government (2014a) *Scotland Analysis: Assessment of a sterling currency union*.

HM Government (2014b) *Scotland Analysis: EU and international issues*. Cmnd. 8765. London: HMSO.

HM Government (2014c) *Scotland Analysis: Fiscal Policy and Sustainability*. Cm 8854. London: HMSO.

HM Government (2014d) *Scotland analysis: work and pensions*. Cmnd. 8849. London: HMSO.

HM Government (2014e) *UK debt and the Scotland independence referendum*. 13 January.

HM Government (2014f) *United Kingdom, United Future*.

HM Government (2014g) Scottish people will be £1,400 better off as part of the UK analysis shows. May. Available at: http://www.gov.uk/government/news/scottish-people-will-be-1400-better-off-as-part-of-the-uk-analysis-show (accessed 9 Aug 2016).

Hobolt, S. (2009) *Europe in Question. Referendums on European Integration*. Oxford: Oxford University Press.

House of Commons Defence Committee (2012) *Future Maritime Surveillance*. Fifth Report of Session 2012–13. HC 110.

House of Commons Defence Committee (2013) *The Defence Implications of Possible Scottish Independence – Volume 1*. Sixth Report of Session 2013. HC198.

House of Commons Foreign Affairs Committee (2013) *Foreign Policy considerations for UK and Scotland in the event of Scotland becoming an Independent Country*. Sixth Report of Session 2012–13. HC 643.

House of Commons Political and Constitutional Reform Committee (2015) *Eleventh Report of Session 2014–15*. HC 700. 29 March. Conclusions and Recommendations.

House of Commons Public Administration Committee (2015) *Lessons for Civil Service impartiality from the Scottish independence referendum*. Fifth Report of Session. Available at: http://www.publications.parliament.uk/pa/cm201415/cmselect/cmpubadm/111/11102.htm (accessed 9 Aug 2016).

House of Commons Scottish Affairs Committee (2012) *The referendum on separation for Scotland: terminating Trident—days or decades?* Fourth Report of Session 2012–13. HC 676.

House of Commons Scottish Affairs Committee (2013) *The Referendum on Separation for Scotland: How would separation affect jobs in the Scottish Defence Industry*. Eighth Report of Session 2013. HC 957.

House of Commons Scottish Affairs Committee (2014) *The Referendum on Separation for Scotland: no doubt-no currency union*. Third report of Session 2014–15.

House of Lords (2009) Select Committee on the Barnett Formula. *1st Report of Session 2008–09, The Barnett Formula: Report with Evidence. HL Paper 139*. London: TSO.

Howe, P. (1998) Rationality and Sovereignty Support in Quebec. *Canadian Journal of Political Science/Revue canadienne de science politique*. Vol. 31(1), pp. 31–59.

Hughes Hallett, A. (2014) Why assessments of Scotland's economy under independence are often misleading. *Royal Economic Society Newsletter*. Available at: http://www.res.org.uk/view/art6Jul14Features.html (accessed 9 Aug 2016).

ICAS (2013) Scotland's Pensions Future: What Pensions Arrangements Would Scotland Need? April.

ICAS (2014) Scotland's Pensions Future: Have Our Questions Been Answered? February.

International IDEA (2014) Interim Constitutions in Post-Conflict Settings. *Discussion Report*. 4–5 December 2014. International IDEA and the Edinburgh Centre for Constitutional Law, Edinburgh.

Ipsos Mori (2015) *Ipsos Mori Almanac*. London: Ipsos Mori.

Jakobsen, P. V. (2009) Small States, Big Influence: The Overlooked Nordic Influence on the Civilian ESDP. *Journal of Common Market Studies*. Vol. 47(1), pp. 81–102.

James, P. and Lusztig, M. (2002) Say Goodbye to the Dream of One Canada: The Failure of the Welfare State to Buy National Unity, in Telford, H. and Lazar, H. (eds) *Canada: The State of the Federation 2000/01*. Montreal: McGill-Queen's University Press.

Jeffery, C. (2002) Uniformity and diversity in policy provision: insights from the US, Germany and Canada, in Adams, J. and Robinson, P. (eds) *Devolution in Practice: public policy differences within the UK*. London: IPPR.

Jeffery, C. and Perman, R. (eds) (2014) *Scotland's Decision. 16 Questions to think about before the referendum on 18 September*. Edinburgh: Birlinn.

Jimmy Reid Foundation (2013) *The Common Weal: A Model for Economic and Social Development in Scotland*. Glasgow: Jimmy Reid Foundation.

Johnson, P. and Phillips, D. (2014) The Scottish NHS—more financially secure outside the UK? *Institute for Fiscal Studies*. Available at: http://www.ifs.org.uk/publications/7366 (accessed 9 Aug 2016).

Kahneman, D. (2011) *Thinking, Fast and Slow*. London: Penguin Books.

Katzenstein, P. J. (1985) *Small States in World Markets: Industrial Policy in Europe*. Ithaca: Cornell University Press.

Keating, M. (2001) *Plurinational Democracy. Stateless Nations in a Post-Sovereignty Era*. Oxford: Oxford University Press.

Keating, M. (2009) *The Independence of Scotland*. Oxford: Oxford University Press.

Keating, M. (2013) *Rescaling the European State*. Oxford: Oxford University Press.

Keating, M. and Harvey, M. (2014) *Small Nations in a Big World. What Scotland Can Learn*. Edinburgh: Luath Press.

Keating, M. and McGarry, J. (eds) (2001) *Minority Nationalism and the Changing International Order*. Oxford: Oxford University Press.

Keohane, R. O. (1969) Lilliputians' Dilemmas: Small States in International Politics. *International Organizations*. Vol. 23(2), pp. 291–310.

Keynes, J. M. (1936) *The General Theory of Employment, Interest and Money*. Basingstoke: Palgrave Macmillan.

Kidd, C. (2008) *Union and Unionisms*. Cambridge: Cambridge University Press.

Korovilas, J. (2002) The Economic Sustainability of Post-conflict Kosovo. *Post-Communist Economies*, Vol. 14(1), pp. 109–21.

La Vanguardia (2013) España dice que su postura ante independencia Escocia dependerá de la de Londres. 16 December. Available at: http://www.lavanguardia.com/politica/20131216/54398273307/espana-dice-su-postura-ante-independencia-escocia-dependera-de-la-de-londres.html (accessed 9 Aug 2016).

Lecca, P., McGregor, P., and Swales, J. K. (2015a) The Impact of Enhanced Regional Fiscal Autonomy: Towards a Scandinavian Model for Scotland? *IPPI Occasional Paper*. Glasgow: University of Strathclyde, Department of Economics.

Lecca, P., McGregor, P., and Swales, J. K. (2015b) The Interregional Impact of a Balanced Budget Fiscal Expansion: No Detriment, No Danger. *IPPI Occasional Paper*. Glasgow: University of Strathclyde, Department of Economics.

LeDuc, L. (2002) Opinion Change and Voting Behaviour in Referendums. *European Journal of Political Research*. Vol. 41(6), pp. 711–32.

LeDuc, L. (2003) *The Politics of Direct Democracy: Referendums in Global Perspective*. Peterborough, Ont.: Broadview Press.

Lees, C. (2006) Regional Disparities and Growth in Europe. *Mimeo*. London: HM Treasury.

Liñeira, R., Henderson, A., and Delaney, L. (2015) Risk and Support to Independence in Scotland. *Conference of Europeanists*, Paris, 8–10 July.

LSE Growth Commission (2013) Investing for Prosperity. *Report of the LSE Growth Commission*. Available at: http://www.lse.ac.uk/researchAndExpertise/units/growth-Commission/home.aspx (accessed 9 Aug 2016)

Lupia, A. (1994) Shortcuts Versus Encyclopedias: Information and Voting Behavior in California Insurance Reform Elections. *The American Political Science Review*. Vol. 88(1), pp. 63–76.

Lynch, P. (1996) *Minority Nationalism and European Integration.* Cardiff: University of Wales Press.

MacAskill, K. (2004) *Building a Nation: Post Devolution Nationalism in Scotland.* Edinburgh: Luath Press.

McCallum, J. (1995) National borders matter: Canada–US regional trade patterns. *The American Economic Review.* Vol. 85, pp. 615–23.

MacCormick, N. (1999) *Questioning Sovereignty. Law, State and Nation in the European Commonwealth.* Oxford: Oxford University Press.

McCrone, D. (1992) Understanding Scotland: the Sociology of a Stateless Nation. London and New York: Routledge.

McCrone, D. and Bechhofer, F. (2015) *Understanding National Identity.* Cambridge: Cambridge University Press.

McCrone, D. and Paterson, L. (2002) The Conundrum of Scottish Independence. *Scottish Affairs.* Vol. 40(1), pp. 54–75.

MacDonald, J. (2014) A blessing in disguise? Scottish independence and the end of the UK nuclear posture. *European Security.* Vol. 23(3), pp. 326–43.

MacDonald, R. (2014a) *An Independent Scotland's Currency Options Redux: Assessing the Costs and Benefits of Currency Choice.* (No. 4952) Munich: CESifo Group.

MacDonald, R. (2014b) *The Economics of Scotland's Currency Choices.* Edinburgh: Centre on Constitutional Change. Available at: http://www.centreonconstitutionalchange. ac.uk/blog/economics-scotlands-currency-choices (accessed 9 Aug 2016).

McEwen, N. (2006) *Nationalism and the State: Welfare and Identity in Scotland and Quebec.* Regionalism and Federalism Book Series. Brussels: Presses interuniversitaires européennes/Peter Lang.

McEwen, N. (2013) Embedded Independence: Between Autonomy and Interdependence in the Scottish Constitutional Debate. *Paper presented to a workshop in the University of Konstanz.* June 2013.

McEwen, N. (2016) A Constitution in Flux: the Dynamics of Constitutional Change after the Referendum, in McHarg, A., Mullen, T., Page, A., and Walker, N. (eds) *The Scottish Independence Referendum: Constitutional and Political Implications.* Oxford: Oxford University Press.

McEwen, N. and Moreno L. (eds) (2005) *The Territorial Politics of Welfare.* London: Routledge.

McGarry, J. and Keating, M. (eds) (2006) *European Integration and the Nationalities Question.* London: Routledge.

McGarry, N. (2013) *Women and Independence: Natalie McGarry's Glasgow Uni Referendum Speech.* Delivered as a representative of Women for Independence at an event on Gender and Independence. University of Glasgow. 21 February. Available at: http:// nationalcollective.com/2013/02/07/women-and-independence-natalie-mcgarrys-glasgow-uni-referendum-speech/ (accessed 9 Aug 2016).

Mackay, B. (2014) Business decision-making in conditions of constitutional and political uncertainty in the UK and Scotland: evidence from business final report, Future of UK and Scotland programme. Available at: http://www.centreonconstitutionalchange.ac.uk/sites/default/files/papers/Evidence%20from%20Business%20Summary%20Report%20Final.pdf (accessed 18 Aug 2016).

McLaren, J. and Armstrong, J. (2014) Agreeing a post-independence currency union: Are there fiscal rules that Scotland can follow to satisfy UK concerns? *Fiscal Affairs Scotland*, AP/2014/002.

Macpherson, N. (2014) Scotland and a Currency Union. HM Treasury. 11 February.

Macpherson, N. (2015) The Treasury and the Union. Speech by the Permanent Secretary to the Treasury delivered to the Strand Group, King's College London. 19 January 2015. Available at: https://www.kcl.ac.uk/sspp/policy-institute/events/assets/Speech-macpherson190115.pdf (accessed 18 Aug 2016).

Major, J. (1993) Foreword by the Prime Minister, in Secretary of State for Scotland, *Scotland in the Union: A Partnership for Good*. Edinburgh: HMSO.

Marshall, T. H. (1950) *Citizenship and Social Class*. Cambridge: Cambridge University Press.

Martin, P. (1994) Générations politiques, rationalité économique et appui à la souveraineté au Québec. *Canadian Journal of Political Science/Revue canadienne de science politique*. Vol. 27(2), pp. 345–59.

Matas, J., Gonzalez, A., Jaria, J., and Roman, L. (2011) *The Internal Enlargement of the European Union. Analysis of the Legal and Political Consequences for the European Union in the case of member state's secession or dissolution*. Brussels: Centre Maurits Coppieters.

Mendelsohn, M. (2003) Rational Choice and Socio-Psychological Explanation for Opinion on Quebec Sovereignty. *Canadian Journal of Political Science/Revue canadienne de science politique*. Vol. 36(3), pp. 511–37.

Milward, A. (2000) *The European Rescue of the Nation-State*, 2nd edn. London: Routledge.

Mishra, R. (1999) *Globalization and the Welfare State*. Cheltenham: Edward Elgar.

Mitchell, J. (2014) *The Scottish Question*. Oxford: Oxford University Press.

Moore, M. (2013) Cited in: Foreign Secretary Statement on Foreign Policy Implications of an Independent Scotland. London: HM Government.

Morgenthau, H. J. (1970) *Truth and Power: Essays of a Decade 1960–1970*. Greenwood: Praeger Publishers.

Morton, R. (2011) Class in a 'Classless' Society: The Paradox of Scottish Egalitarianism. *Scottish Affairs*. Vol. 75(1), pp. 83–99.

Muñoz, J. and Tormos, R. (2015) Economic Expectations and Support for Secession in Catalonia: Between Causality and Rationalization. *European Political Science Review*. Vol. 7(2), pp. 315–41.

N-56 (2014) Scotland's set for oil bonanza that heralds a new golden age for the North Sea lasting for another century. Available at: http://n-56.org/updates/scotland-set-oil-bonanza-heralds-new-golden-age-north-sea-lasting-another-century (accessed 9 Aug 2016).

Nadeau, R., Martin, P., and Blais, A. (1999) Attitude Towards Risk-Taking and Individual Choice in the Quebec Referendum on Sovereignty. *British Journal of Political Science*. Vol. 29(3), pp. 523–39.

National Security Strategy and Strategic Defence and Security Review (2015) A secure and Prosperous United Kingdom. Cm 9161.

Neumann, I. B. (ed.) (1992) *Regional Great Powers in International Politics*. Basingstoke: St Martin's Press.

Nolan, A. (2014) Protecting Economic and Social Rights in Scotland's Future. Lecture to Edinburgh Centre for Constitutional Law. 11 December 2014.

Ohmae. K. (1995) The End of the Nation State. The Rise of Regional Economies. New York: Free Press.

Oliver, P. (2015) *The Constitution of Independence: The Development of Constitutional Theory in Australia, Canada, and New Zealand*. Oxford: Oxford University Press.

Osborne, G. (2014) On the prospect of a currency union with an independent Scotland. Edinburgh. 13 February. Available at: https://www.gov.uk/government/speeches/chancellor-on-the-prospect-of-a-currency-union-with-an-independent-scotland (accessed 15 Nov 2015).

Oxford Economics (2014) The Potential Implications for Business of Scottish Independence. May. Accessed at: http://www.oxfordeconomics.com/my-oxford/projects/266799 (accessed 9 Aug 2016).

Panelbase (2014) Survey for Sunday Times and Real Radio. 6 February 2014. Available at: What Scotland Thinks, http://whatscotlandthinks.org/search?query=currency (accessed 9 Aug 2016).

Panke, D. (2010) *Small States in the European Union: Coping with Structural Disadvantages*. Farnham: Ashgate.

Parry, R. (2014) Pensions and benefits in the referendum debate: neutralising a major policy area? *Centre on Constitutional Change blog*. Available at: http://www.centreonconstitutionalchange.ac.uk/blog/pensions-and-benefits-referendum-debate-neutralising-major-policy-area (accessed 9 Aug 2016).

Paterson, L., Bechhofer, F., and McCrone, D. (2004) *Living in Scotland. Social and Economic Change since 1980*. Edinburgh: Edinburgh University Press.

Pike, J. (2015) *Project Fear. How an Unlikely Alliance Left a Kingdom United but a Country Divided*. London: Biteback.

Política (2013) Margallo, convencido de que Escocia votará 'no' a la secesión del Reino Unido, 6 March.

R (Factortame Ltd) v Secretary of State for Transport (No 2) [1992] 1 AC 603; *R (HS2 Action Alliance Ltd) v Secretary of State for Transport* [2014] UKSC 3; and see European Union Act 2011, s. 18.

Radical Independence Campaign (2013) *Radical Independence Declaration*, read by David Hayman. Available at: http://www.youtube.com/watch?v=4T_whGSREd8 (accessed 9 Aug 2016).

Radical Independence Campaign (2014) Our Message to the Victims of Austerity, *Sunday Herald*. 23 February.

Reicher, S. and Hopkins, N. (2001) *Self and Nation*. London: Sage.

Riley-Smith, B. (2014) 'Entirely possible' Scotland won't share pound after independence, Alex Salmond's top economist admits. *The Telegraph*. 19 August 2014. Available at: http://www.telegraph.co.uk/news/uknews/scottish-independence/11044798/Entirely-possible-Scotland-wont-share-pound-after-independence-Alex-Salmonds-top-economist-admits.html (accessed 15 Nov 2015).

Robertson, A. (2013) *The Geopolitics of an Independent Scotland*. Copenhagen: Centre for Military Studies.

Rokkan, S. (1999) *State Formation, Nation-Building and Mass Politics in Europe. The Theory of Stein Rokkan*, Flora, P., Kuhnle, S., and Urwin, D. (eds). Oxford: Oxford University Press.

Rosie, M. and Bond, R. (2007) Social Democratic Scotland?, in Keating, M. (ed.), *Scottish Social Democracy*. Brussels: Presses interuniversitaires européennes/Peter Lang.

RSE and BA (2014) Royal Society of Edinburgh and British Academy. *Enlightening the Constitutional Debate*. Edinburgh: RSE.

Salmond, A. (2008) *Free to Prosper: Creating the Celtic Lion Economy*. Speech to Harvard University. 31 March. Available at: http://www.gov.scot/News/Speeches/Speeches/First-Minister/harvard-university (accessed 9 Aug 2016).

Salmond, A. (2012) *Scotland's Place in the World*. Hugo Young Lecture Guardian's Kings Cross office, London. 24 January.

Salmond, A. (2013) *The Currency Union*. Speech on 16 July, Isle of Man. Available at: http://news.scotland.gov.uk/Speeches-Briefings/The-Currency-Union-523.aspx (accessed 15 Nov 2015).

Salmond, A. (2014) *First Minister Speech*. Edinburgh. 17 February. Available at: http://news.scotland.gov.uk/Speeches-Briefings/First-Minister-speech-February-17-2014-95a.aspx (accessed 15 Nov 2015).

Salmond, A. (2015) *The Dream Shall Never Die. 100 Days that Changed Scotland Forever*. London: Collins.

Schuman, H. and Presser, S. (1996) *Questions and Answers in Attitude Surveys: Experiments on Question Form, Wording, and Context*. Thousand Oaks: Sage.

Schwab, J. (1892) The Finances of the Confederate States. *Political Science Quarterly*. Vol. 7(1), pp. 38–56.

Scotland Institute (2013) *Defence and Security in an Independent Scotland*.

Scott, D. (2012) *An Independent Scotland Could Not be Required to Adopt the Euro as its Currency*. Scottish Constitutional Futures Forum. Available from: http://www.scottishconstitutionalfutures.org/OpinionandAnalysis/ViewBlogPost/tabid/1767/articleType/ArticleView/articleId/480/Drew-Scott-An-Independent-Scotland-Could-Not-be-Required-to-Adopt-the-Euro-as-its-Currency.aspx (accessed 9 Aug 2016).

Scottish Government (2009) *Your Scotland, Your Voice: A National Conversation*.

Scottish Government (2011) *Devolving Corporation Tax in the Scotland Bill*. September. Available at: http://www.gov.scot/resource/doc/919/0120770.pdf (accessed 9 Aug 2016).

Scottish Government (2012) *An Oil Fund for Scotland*. Available at: http://www.gov.scot/resource/0043/00435599.pdf (accessed 9 Aug 2016).

Scottish Government (2013a) *Currency Choices for an Independent Scotland*: Response to the Fiscal Commission Working Group.

Scottish Government (2013b) *Economic and Competition Regulation in an Independent Scotland*. February. Available at: http://www.gov.scot/Publications/2013/02/1911 (accessed 9 Aug 2016).

Scottish Government (2013c) *Fiscal Commission Working Group: Fiscal Rules and Fiscal Commissions*. November. Available at: http://www.gov.scot/resource/0043/00434977.pdf (accessed 9 Aug 2016).

Scottish Government (2013d) *Fiscal Commission Working Group: Principles for a Modern and Efficient Tax System in an Independent Scotland.* November. Available at: http://www.gov.scot/resource/0043/00434977.pdf (accessed 9 Aug 2016).

Scottish Government (2013e) *Pensions in an Independent Scotland.* September. Available at: http://www.gov.scot/resource/0043/00434502.pdf (accessed 9 Aug 2016).

Scottish Government (2013f) *Scotland's Future: Your Guide to an Independent Scotland.* Edinburgh: Scottish Government.

Scottish Government (2014a) *Outlook for Scotland's Public Finances and the Opportunities of Independence.* Edinburgh: Scottish Government.

Scottish Government (2014b) *Scotland in the European Union.* Edinburgh: Scottish Government.

Scottish Government (2014c) *The Scottish Independence Bill: A Consultation on an Interim Constitution for Scotland.* Edinburgh: The Scottish Government.

Scottish Greens (2014a) Independent Economy Needs Independent Currency. *Scottish Greens.* 29 January.

Scottish Greens (2014b) Osborne currency threat 'bluster'. *Scottish Greens.* 12 February.

Scottish Labour Party (2014) *Powers for a Purpose.* Glasgow: Scottish Labour Party.

Scottish Parliament (2014) *Economy and Finance.* Available at: http://www.parliament.scot/parliamentarybusiness/67690.aspx (accessed 9 Aug 2016).

Scottish Parliament European and External Affairs Committee (2014) *Report on the Scottish Government's proposals for an independent Scotland: Membership of the European Union.* Second Report, Session 4 2014. Edinburgh: Scottish Parliament.

Settle, M. (2015) Poll shows Sturgeon is now the most popular politician across Britain. *The Herald,* 29 April. Available at: http://www.heraldscotland.com/news/13211668.Poll_shows_Sturgeon_is_now_the_most_popular_politician_across_Britain/ (accessed 9 Aug 2016).

Sillars, J. (2014) The cost of currency union is far too high. *Edinburgh Evening News.* 4 February.

Skilling, D. (2012) *In Uncertain Seas: Positioning small countries to succeed in a changing world.* Singapore: Landfall Strategy Group.

SNP (1977) Aims and Policy of the SNP.

SNP (1997) YES WE CAN Win the Best for Scotland.

SNP (2001) We Stand for Scotland.

SNP (2006) Scotland can Join Europe's Arc of Prosperity. Press release. Friday, 11 August.

SNP (2010) Elect a Local Champion.

SSAS (1999–2014) *Scottish Social Attitudes Survey.* Edinburgh: Scottish Centre for Social Research.

Stockwell, S. (1998) Instilling the 'sterling tradition': Decolonization and the creation of a Central Bank in Ghana. *The Journal of Imperial and Commonwealth History.* Vol. 26 (2), pp. 100–19.

Sturgeon, N. (2012) *Bringing the powers home to build a better nation.* Speech delivered at Strathclyde University. 3 December. Available at: http://www.gov.scot/News/Speeches/better-nation-031212 (accessed 9 Aug 2016).

Sturgeon, N. (2013) *Child Poverty*. Speech delivered at Child Poverty Action Group annual conference. 14 June. Available at: http://www.gov.scot/News/Speeches/child-proverty-14-06-2013 (accessed 9 Aug 2016).

Sturgeon, N. (2014a) *Addressing Scotland's 5 Key Challenges*. Speech delivered at Scottish Council for Development and Energy Event. 3 March. Available at: https://www.youtube.com/watch?v=oQ8GIp82UnU (accessed 9 Aug 2016).

Sturgeon, N. (2014b) *Last parliament speech before referendum*. Speech delivered at Scottish Parliament. 21 August. Available at: http://www.scotreferendum.com/2014/08/last-parliament-speech-before-referendum/ (accessed 9 Aug 2016).

Sunday Herald (2008) Murphy in 'arc of insolvency' attack on SNP. 12 October. Available at: http://www.heraldscotland.com/murphy-in-acr-of-insolvency-attack-on-snp-1.891802 (accessed 9 Aug 2016).

Supreme Court of Canada (1998) *Reference re Secession of Quebec*, file 25506. Ottawa: Supreme Court of Canada. Available at: http://scc-csc.lexum.com/scc-csc/scc-csc/en/item/1643/index.do (accessed 9 Aug 2016).

Swanson, I. (2014) Scottish Independence: Darling flounders in debate. *Edinburgh Evening News*. Available at: http://www.edinburghnews.scotsman.com/news/scottish-independence-darling-flounders-in-debate-1-3520547 (accessed 15 Nov 2015).

Thatcher, M. (1993) *The Downing Street Years*. London: HarperCollins.

Third Force News (2014) *Alistair Darling tells charities we're better together*. Available at: http://thirdforcenews.org.uk/tfn-news/alistair-darling-tells-charities-were-better-together#WQaHP854Gf7ECtR1.99 (accessed 9 Aug 2016).

Thoburn v Sunderland City Council [2002] EWHC 195 (Admin)

Thorhallsson, B. (2006) The Size of States in the European Union: Theoretical and Conceptual Perspectives. *European Integration*. Vol. 28(1), pp. 7–31. March.

Tierney, S. (2004) *Constitutional Law and National Pluralism*. Oxford: Oxford University Press.

Tierney, S. (2012) *Constitutional Referendums: The Theory and Practice of Republican Deliberation*. Oxford: Oxford University Press.

Tierney, S. (2013a) *The Scottish Constitution After Independence*. 2 December 2013. Available at: https://ukconstitutionallaw.org/2013/12/02/stephen-tierney-the-scottish-constitution-after-independence/ (accessed 9 Aug 2016).

Tierney, S. (2013b) The Scottish Constitution After Independence. *Centre on Constitutional Change Briefing Paper*. 29 November.

Tierney, S. and Boyle, K. (2014) *An Independent Scotland: The Road to Membership of the European Union*. Centre on Constitutional Change Briefing Paper. Available at: http://www.centreonconstitutionalchange.ac.uk/publications/research-briefings/independent-scotland-road-membership-european-union (accessed 9 Aug 2016).

Tilly, C. (1990) *Coercion, Capital and European States. AD.990–1990*. Oxford: Wiley-Blackwell.

Titmuss, R. (1958) *Essays on the Welfare State*. London: Allen & Unwin.

TNS-BMRB (2014) Poll on Scottish Politics. Available at: http://www.tns-bmrb.co.uk/press-release/referendum-effect-set-increase-political-activity-trust-main-parties-low (accessed 18 Aug 2016).

The Today Programme (2014) Alex Salmond interview. BBC Radio 4. 24 February.

Tomkins, A. (2014) Scotland and the EU. *Vote No Borders Blog*. 8 August.

Vampa, D. (2014) The Sub-State Politics of Welfare in Italy: Assessing the Effect of Territorial Mobilization on the Development of Region-Specific Social Governance. *Regional & Federal Studies*. Vol. 24(4), pp. 473–91.

de Vreese, C. (ed.) (2007) *The Dynamics of Referendum Campaigns: An International Perspective*. Basingstoke: Palgrave Macmillan.

de Vreese, C. and Semetko, H. (2004) *Political Campaigning in Referendums: Framing the Referendum Issue*. London: Routledge.

Walker, N. (2014) Hijacking the Debate. *Scottish Constitutional Futures Forum*. Available at: http://www.scottishconstitutionalfutures.org/OpinionandAnalysis/ViewBlogPost/tabid/1767/articleType/ArticleView/articleId/3068/Neil-Walker-Hijacking-the-Debate.aspx (accessed 9 Aug 2016).

Walker, N. (2015) Beyond Secession? Law in the Framing of the National Polity, in Tierney, S. (ed.) *Nationalism and Globalization*. Oxford: Hart.

Walker, W. (2014) International reactions to the Scottish referendum. *International Affairs*. Vol. 90(4), pp. 743–59.

Watt, N. (2014a) UK parties 'ganging up' to bully Scots into rejecting independence, says SNP. *The Guardian*. 12 February.

Watt, N. (2014b) Independent Scotland 'may keep pound' to ensure stability. *The Guardian*. 29 March.

Weber, M. (1919) 'Politics as a Vocation'. Lecture given at Munich, January.

Weiler, J. (2014). Scotland and the EU: a comment, UK Constitutional Law Association. Available at: http://ukconstitutionallaw.org/2014/09/10/debate-j-h-h-weiler-scotland-and-the-eu-a-comment/ (accessed 18 Aug 2016).

What Scotland Thinks (2014) *How should Scotland be governed?* Available at: http://whatscotlandthinks.org/questions/how-should-scotland-be-governed-five-response-categories-collapsed-to-three#table (accessed 9 Aug 2016).

Wincott, D. (2003) Slippery Concepts, Shifting Context: (National) States and Welfare in the Veit-Wilson/Atherton Debate. *Social Policy & Administration*. Vol. 37, pp. 305–15.

Wincott, D. (2006) Social policy and social citizenship: Britain's welfare states. *Publius: The Journal of Federalism*. Vol. 36(1), pp. 169–88.

Yes Scotland (2014) *A Yes means real gains for Scotland's people—but it's our NHS that will see the biggest cost if it's a No*. Snapshot accessed from official campaign website, www.yesscotland.net on 31 July.

YouGov (2015) YouGov Profiles: Nicola Sturgeon is Scotland's most popular person. Available at: https://yougov.co.uk/news/2015/11/01/nicola-sturgeon-scotlands-most-popular-person/ (accessed 9 Aug 2016).

Index

Tables and figures are indicated by an italic *t* and *f* following the page number.